BABY FOOD
IN AN INSTANT POT®

BABY FOOD
IN AN INSTANT POT®

125 Quick, Simple and Nutritious Recipes for Babies, Toddlers & Families

OFFICIAL
Instant Pot
BOOK

JENNIFER HOUSE, MSc, RD & MARILYN HAUGEN

Robert
ROSE

DISCLAIMER

The recipes in this book have been carefully tested by our kitchen and our tasters. To the best of our knowledge, they are safe and nutritious for ordinary use and users. For those people with food or other allergies, or who have special food requirements or health issues, please read the suggested contents of each recipe carefully and determine whether or not they may create a problem for you. All recipes are used at the risk of the consumer.

We cannot be responsible for any hazards, loss or damage that may occur as a result of any recipe use.

For those with special needs, allergies, requirements or health problems, in the event of any doubt, please contact your medical adviser prior to the use of any recipe.

At the time of publication, all URLs referenced links to existing websites. Robert Rose Inc. is not responsible for maintaining, and does not endorse the content of, any website or content not created by Robert Rose Inc.

DESIGN and PRODUCTION: Kevin Cockburn/PageWave Graphics Inc.
EDITOR: Kathleen Fraser
INDEXER: Gillian Watts

PHOTOGRAPHY: © Getty Images.

Published by Robert Rose Inc.
120 Eglinton Avenue East, Suite 800, Toronto, Ontario, Canada M4P 1E2
Tel: (416) 322-6552 Fax: (416) 322-6936
www.robertrose.ca

Printed and bound in South Korea

1 2 3 4 5 6 7 8 9 FC 27 26 25 24 23 22 21 20

CONTENTS

═══

INTRODUCTION

Congratulations on reaching another milestone of your baby's life — starting solid food! This is a fun time for both you and your little one. You'll enjoy watching as your baby explores new tastes and takes their place at the table. Starting solids is also an important time to establish your baby's palate, boost their nutrition in a time of rapid growth and create a positive eating environment, so they will enjoy family meals for years to come!

This can also be a confusing time, with lots of misinformation and outdated "rules" floating around. As a registered dietitian and mom of three, I am here to help! And Marilyn is here to provide some delicious and easy meals for your baby and whole family. The Instant Pot is the perfect tool to give busy parents a hand in the kitchen.

In this book we cover when to start solids, what nutrients your baby needs, how to prevent choking, how to avoid picky eating, how to deal with allergies, what to feed vegetarian babies and more. Plus, we answer a ton of questions parents often have when their child is starting solids, and offer a few sample meal plans as well as more than 120 baby- and family-friendly recipes. Let's get started!

JEN'S STORY

I'm happy and honored to be your guide on your starting-solids journey. My name is Jennifer House, and I'm a registered dietitian and nutritionist from Canada. I have a BSc and an MSc in nutrition and am a member of the Dietitians of Canada and the College of Dietitians of Alberta. I operate a private nutrition practice called First Step Nutrition (firststepnutrition.com), specializing in young families. I speak to moms about starting solids regularly — it's one of my favorite topics!

But besides my professional experience, I also have plenty of practical experience as the mom of three. I first started my eldest son on solids 12 years ago. His first food was fortified infant cereal.

Four years later, I was ready to start solids with my daughter, Norah. I had never heard of baby-led weaning. The first food I offered her was a homemade puréed bison. She did not like that bison — or anything I offered by spoon, for that matter. Yet she would sit with the family at the dining table, and you could tell that she was just dying to eat what we were eating. And she loved it! So Norah was my forced introduction into baby-led weaning.

By the time my third child was ready to start solids, he easily accepted both purées and finger foods. He generally loved eating what the rest of the family was eating, and he enjoyed all foods.

MARILYN'S STORY

Hi. My name is Marilyn and I am very excited to be invited to partner with Jennifer House on this cookbook. I am a bestselling cookbook author, food blogger and business owner. I have been fortunate to have authored several bestselling cookbooks with more than 200,000 copies in print, including *5-Ingredient Instant Pot Cookbook*, *175 Best Instant Pot Recipes* and *150 Best Spiralizer Recipes*. And this is the fourth cookbook I have written for a multicooker such as the Instant Pot.

I hold an MBA and a BBA from American universities with specializations in finance and accounting. Before starting my "second act," I was a finance director with a major international U.S. company and, before that, with an international food and commodity corporations. My work and personal experiences traveling the world gave me an appreciation for many cuisines and an even greater appreciation for home-cooked meals. I turned my focus to raising my daughter, spending time with family and pursuing my passion for cooking. I truly feel strongly about the importance of home-cooked meals and spending time with family around the dinner table.

For more of my recipes and cooking ideas, visit me at MavenCookery.com, where I share straightforward, comfort food dishes that are easy to make.

9

PART 1

—

FEEDING YOUR BABY

WHEN TO START SOLIDS

Most country's national health departments currently recommend feeding babies only breast milk until they reach 6 months of age. At 6 months, a baby's gut, immune system and kidneys are developed enough to start introducing solid foods.

In 2002, the World Health Organization began recommending that babies start solid foods at 6 months of age. Before that, the guideline was to introduce solids between 4 and 6 months. But as with all developmental milestones, every baby is unique. Not all babies are ready for food exactly on their half-year birthday. Some may be ready to eat slightly before or slightly after 6 months. How do you know if your baby is ready for solids? What are the risks of starting too early or too late?

SIGNS OF READINESS FOR STARTING SOLIDS

At 6 months of age your baby is most likely to be developmentally ready and eager to move on to table food. But there are some other signs to watch for, besides age, to ensure your baby is ready to begin solids.

YOUR BABY SEEMS EXCITED TO EAT AND GRABS AT YOUR FOOD. I remember my babies just vibrating with anticipation to eat food at about 5½ months. While little ones are interested in *everything* you do, a baby who is almost ready to start enjoying family food may seem especially fascinated by the contents of your plate and try to snatch it.

Did You Know?
ADJUSTED AGE FOR PREEMIES

For premature babies, use their "adjusted age" to determine when to begin solids. This means you will be offering solids 6 months after their due date, not 6 months after their birth date. Also be sure to talk to your doctor about iron supplements. Preemies may need a little boost in supplemental iron, as they didn't get the full 40 weeks in the womb to build up their own iron stores.

YOUR BABY CAN SIT UP WELL IN HIS HIGH CHAIR. Your baby needs to have solid head and neck control, as well as good arm and trunk strength before starting solids. Why? He needs to be able to lean forward to spit food out, if needed to prevent choking. Also, if you are introducing finger foods right from the start, as is recommended in Canada and the United Kingdom, your baby must be able to reach for food and bring it to his mouth independently.

There is some debate among experts about whether a baby needs to be able to

sit on his own, or if the ability to sit with support is enough before starting solids and self-feeding. Most instructors who teach baby-led weaning (all self-feeding, no purées — more on this later!) encourage you to start solids only when your baby can sit on his own without assistance. But is this really necessary? Many babies, including two of my own, didn't sit without support until long after they turned 6 months. And I wouldn't have felt comfortable waiting until they were older, knowing that they needed the nutrition from table foods starting around 6 months.

The occupational therapist I work with agrees that it is fine to start solids before your child can sit on his own, but only as long as your baby can sit well with support. This means that he can sit up in his high chair without leaning backward and can reach for food and bring it to his mouth without using his hands to support and balance himself.

Did You Know?

HOW TO SUPPORT YOUR BABY IN A HIGH CHAIR

If your baby meets all other signs of readiness but they can't fully sit without support, they can still start solids. Just make sure they are properly supported in their high chair. You can place rolled-up towels on either side of your baby to support their trunk. The high-chair tray should come between your baby's nipples and belly button, and their feet should be supported with a foot rest.

YOUR BABY HAS LOST THE EXTRUSION REFLEX. This is a reflex that babies are born with to help them suck and drink milk.

The extrusion reflex causes anything that touches a baby's tongue to be automatically pushed back out instead of kept in the mouth to move around and chew. This extrusion reflex is usually relaxed enough by 6 months to allow your baby to keep solids in their mouth, but it can be an issue if food is offered at a younger age. If your baby still displays the extrusion reflex when you start solids at 6 months, it likely won't last for long. Just let her explore and continue to experiment with food.

HOW TO PREP FOR SOLIDS BEFORE 6 MONTHS

There's plenty you can do before your baby is ready for solids to help her prepare. Once your baby is ready to sit in a high chair with support, bring her to the table for family meals in her new seat. Hand her a hard munchable (see box on page 14) to chew on while you eat. This way, she feels like she is taking part in the family meal and can practice her skills. If your baby doesn't have teeth yet, she will not be able to bite off a piece of that hard munchable and swallow it, but she will be able to experience its texture and possibly some of its flavor. This repetition will help decrease your little one's sensitive gag reflex, which will be an advantage when it comes time to actually eat.

You can also wear your baby on your back in a baby carrier when you're cooking dinner. Let her sit in your lap while you eat, if she doesn't have a high chair or isn't ready to sit in it. This allows your little one to start experiencing some of the exciting smells of family food.

At around 5 months of age, your baby will start putting everything she can get ahold of into her mouth. This is called mouthing, and it's actually a great

13

NOT JUST FOR FUN

You may have heard the saying "Food before 1 is just for fun." While solids in the first year are supplementary to milk, and much of the learning process is pure food play — it's still not 100% true! Your baby needs to be exposed to a variety of foods and textures starting at 6 months to avoid the potential risks associated with starting too late. These include low iron, increased allergies and difficulty managing textures.

way for her to learn and get ready to eat food. Mouthing will help her figure out how to move her tongue, lips and jaw in different ways than the sucking motion she's used to. It also helps develop the muscles of her mouth to increase strength and coordination, decrease the extrusion reflex and practice a munching-chewing movement pattern. Providing stick-shaped toys that your baby can mouth (long enough and not too wide, so that she can grasp and move them around) will help decrease her gag reflex so that it's not as sensitive when she starts eating. If your child isn't starting to mouth on her own by 5 months, you can assist her by putting her hand on a mouthing toy, placing your hand over hers and guiding it to her mouth.

Did You Know?

HARD MUNCHABLES

These baby-friendly foods include raw jicama, celery, Parmesan rind, rib bone and carrot. If you're not comfortable offering food items as hard munchables, you could offer baby spoons to chew on. Make sure the spoon is long enough for your baby to grasp and that it reaches into the back of her mouth. If it's plastic, it must be hard enough that she can't bite off a chunk with her gums.

Did You Know?

MEDICAL REASONS FOR STARTING SOLIDS EARLY

There are a few medical reasons why some doctors recommend starting solids before 6 months. One of these is to avoid reflux, when stomach acids enter the esophagus and cause a burning feeling. Or, if your baby is at high risk of allergy, some doctors may encourage introducing the allergen early to possibly prevent the allergy. As the research hasn't conclusively proven the benefit of this, other doctors will encourage exclusive breastfeeding until 6 months. If your baby has reflux or may be at high risk of allergy, ask your doctor if you should begin solids early.

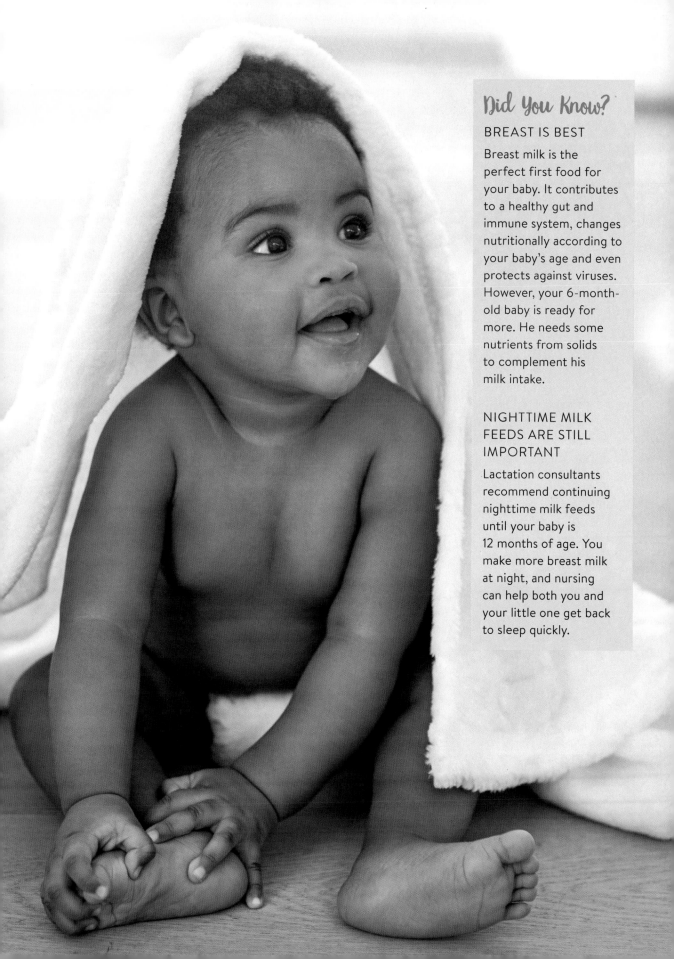

Did You Know?

BREAST IS BEST

Breast milk is the perfect first food for your baby. It contributes to a healthy gut and immune system, changes nutritionally according to your baby's age and even protects against viruses. However, your 6-month-old baby is ready for more. He needs some nutrients from solids to complement his milk intake.

NIGHTTIME MILK FEEDS ARE STILL IMPORTANT

Lactation consultants recommend continuing nighttime milk feeds until your baby is 12 months of age. You make more breast milk at night, and nursing can help both you and your little one get back to sleep quickly.

NUTRIENTS FOR YOUR BABY

Now that you know when to start your baby on solid foods, let's consider what foods you should be offering. There are a few especially important nutrients that your baby needs to start getting from food at around 6 months. On top of the extra energy they will gain through calories, your baby needs iron from foods. One of the risks when starting solids is low iron intake, as parents don't always offer iron-rich foods. But with a little planning you can avoid this. Let's take a look at why getting enough calories and certain nutrients is so important, how much your baby needs and how to meet these needs.

Did You Know?

FOOD PLAY = LEARNING

The first few months of your baby's experience with solid food will include a lot of learning through play. He may mostly seem to mush, squish and spit out food — when it does get to his mouth! This is a part of the learning process and trying out different tastes and textures. But it can result in him eating not very much. Keep in mind that you certainly can't — and don't want to — force or pressure your baby to eat.

WHY IS IRON SO IMPORTANT?
—

Your newborn baby has enough iron to support her growth for the first 6 months or so of her life. This is built up during her time in your womb. A few things will affect your baby's iron stores: the length of her gestation (premature babies have smaller iron stores), mom's iron levels during pregnancy (the higher, the better for baby) and whether delayed cord clamping was practiced at her birth (see box).

(see box)

Did You Know?

DELAYED CORD CLAMPING

When a baby is born, about one-third of the baby's total blood volume is still in the placenta. After the birth, the placenta no longer needs this blood to support the baby in the womb. But the baby does need the blood — it's full of stem cells, immune cells and red blood cells. Traditionally, many doctors clamp a baby's umbilical cord within 30 seconds after birth, but that stops the transfer of blood to the baby too early. With delayed cord clamping, the umbilical cord stays attached to the placenta, without clamping, for the 3 to 7 minutes it takes to stop pulsing. This allows your baby to receive this rich source of important cells and iron.

Babies and children need iron for their brains and bodies to develop normally, and for their immune systems to keep them healthy. Iron helps the body make hemoglobin, which carries oxygen through the blood to all cells of the body. When you don't have enough iron, red blood cells become small and pale, and a condition called anemia develops. When you're anemic, your red blood cells can't carry enough oxygen to your body's organs and muscles. Anemia in babies and children can lead neurological problems, such as poor attention span, trouble concentrating and social withdrawal. And unfortunately this can last for decades — even after the anemia is resolved.

Iron deficiency is certainly not uncommon. One Canadian study (Zlotkin et al., 1996) looked at middle-class infants ranging from 8 months to 15 months of age in four different cities and found that an average of 33.9% had iron deficiency and 4.3% had anemia.

HOW MUCH IRON DOES MY BABY NEED?

Your baby needs to consume very little iron (about 0.27 milligrams per day) until he reaches about 6 months of age, thanks to the iron stores built up in his blood before birth. Between 7 and 12 months of age, his requirement jumps all the way up to 11 milligrams of iron per day — more than an adult male needs! In the United States and Canada, this number is the recommended daily allowance (RDA) value, which is defined as the "level sufficient to meet the nutrient requirements of 97% to 98% of healthy people within each age group." This number takes into account the small amount of iron people typically absorb from plant-based foods, and compensates for a low intake of vitamin C, which helps increase iron absorption. So if you are offering your baby meat and foods rich in vitamin C, he will absorb iron at higher rate than is assumed by the scientists who set this RDA value.

What about iron from breast milk? Your baby's main source of nutrition in the first year is still milk. Breast milk is the perfect first food for your baby, supplying everything he needs to grow and be healthy for the first 6 months of life. It is still the mainstay of your baby's diet for the remaining months of that first year, and continues to be important for as long as you breastfeed.

17

SIGNS OF IRON DEFICIENCY IN BABIES

If your baby was a preemie or you had low iron stores during pregnancy, you want to be especially on guard for these symptoms. There are a number of signs of iron deficiency you can watch for:

- Poor immune system (frequent illness)
- Fatigue
- Decreased physical activity
- Paleness
- Slow weight gain
- Little or no appetite (which creates a cycle that further contributes to slow weight gain)

If your baby shows any of these signs, take her to the doctor and request a blood test to check her iron level. The American Academy of Pediatrics actually recommends that all 12-month-olds have a blood test to check their iron levels. If the test reports a low level, you can give her an iron supplement that will help prevent anemia. Food alone does not contain enough iron to bring up iron stores.

FOOD SOURCES OF IRON

There are two types of iron present in food. Understanding the difference between them will help you feed your little one plenty of this vital mineral.

RECOMMENDED IRON INTAKES

AGE	RECOMMENDED DAILY ALLOWANCE
0 to 6 months	0.27 mg per day*
7 to 12 months	11 mg per day
1 to 3 years	7 mg per day

* This value is classified as an adequate intake (AI) instead of a recommended daily allowance (RDA). AIs are based on the approximate intake of the nutrient by that group. Breastfed babies from ages 0 to 6 months take in about 0.27mg of iron per day.

SOURCE: INSTITUTE OF MEDICINE, 2001

COMBINE IRON PLUS VITAMIN C

Consuming an iron source with a vitamin C source boosts iron absorption. Vitamin C is an especially good partner to sources of non-heme iron, which is not naturally well absorbed. Vitamin C is found in fruits and veggies such as citrus, berries, broccoli and bell peppers. Luckily, sources of iron are often naturally delicious paired with sources of vitamin C. Try some of these nutritious combinations to start.

DISH	IRON SOURCE(S)	VITAMIN C SOURCE(S)
Pasta with meat sauce	Enriched pasta and beef	Tomatoes
Tofu stir-fry	Tofu	Bell peppers and broccoli
Fruit and veggie smoothie	Spinach and hemp hearts	Mango
Cereal with fruit	Fortified cereal	Berries

Heme iron, found in meat and fish, is the more absorbable form; people usually absorb it three times better than iron from non-meat sources. Some food sources of heme iron include bison, beef, liver, clams, sardines, chicken and turkey.

Non-heme iron, found mostly in plant-based foods, is the less absorbable form; people usually absorb it at an average rate of about 5%. Some food sources of non-heme iron are legumes and beans such as chickpeas and lentils, fortified infant cereal, blackstrap molasses, wheat germ, tofu, and dried fruit such as raisins and apricots.

FIVE TIPS FOR OFFERING BABY ENOUGH IRON

1. **OFFER A SOURCE OF IRON AT EACH MEAL.** This could include eggs, puréed meats, chicken thighs or drumsticks, meatloaf, shredded beef or pork roast cooked in the slow cooker or Instant Pot, black beans or hummus.

2. **INCLUDE A SOURCE OF VITAMIN C AT EACH MEAL.** A vitamin C–containing fruit or veggie served as part of a meal will increase iron absorption. For example, top iron-fortified pancakes with fruit purée, serve lentils with stewed tomatoes, or add tofu to a fruit smoothie.

3. **ADD SOME IRON-FORTIFIED INFANT CEREAL.** Iron-fortified infant cereal is an easy way to offer your baby iron. Besides simply serving this as cereal, one creative way to serve it is to add it to finger food recipes by substituting half of the flour in baking with fortified infant cereal. You can also sprinkle it onto any meal to boost the iron. Once your baby has developed a pincer grasp, you can offer finger-friendly fortified cereal from the toddler aisle, soaked in milk.

4. **MAKE SNACKS COUNT.** These mini-meals are another opportunity to include iron-rich foods. Try puréed meat as a spread or dip with toast or crackers. It's like pâté for babies!

5. **COOK WITH CAST IRON.** Cast-iron pots safely add extra iron to the dishes cooked in them. If you don't have one, you can add a product called a Lucky Iron Fish to your regular pots and pans and achieve the same result.

19

FOOD SOURCES OF IRON

Here are some common iron-containing foods. If you're eyeballing baby-sized portions, 1 ounce (30 grams) is about the same size as one-third of a deck of cards or one-third the size of the palm of your hand. Many of these foods can be served puréed, mashed or whole, depending on the age and development of your little one.

FOOD	SERVING SIZE	IRON
Clams, canned, drained	1 oz (30 g)	8.0 mg*
Iron-fortified infant cereal, prepared	¼ cup (60 mL)	3.7 mg
Tofu, cubed	¼ cup (60 mL)	3.3 mg
Soybeans (edamame), shelled, cooked	¼ cup (60 mL)	2.2 mg
Beef liver, cooked	1 oz (30 g)	1.9 mg*
Dried apricots	¼ cup (60 mL)	1.9 mg
Iron-fortified toddler cereal	¼ cup (60 mL)	1.8 mg
Lentils, cooked	¼ cup (60 mL)	1.7 mg
Spinach, cooked	¼ cup (60 mL)	1.7 mg
Hemp hearts	1 tbsp (15 mL)	1.4 mg
Chickpeas, cooked	¼ cup (60 mL)	1.2 mg
Prunes	¼ cup (60 mL)	1.2 mg
Bison, cooked	1 oz (30 g)	1.1 mg*
Kidney beans, cooked	¼ cup (60 mL)	1.0 mg
Shrimp, cooked	1 oz (30 g)	0.9 mg*
Beef, cooked	1 oz (30 g)	0.8 mg*
Sardines	1 oz (30 g)	0.8 mg*
Raisins	¼ cup (60 mL)	0.8 mg
Turkey, dark meat	1 oz (30 g)	0.7 mg*
Wheat germ	1 tbsp (15 mL)	0.7 mg
Egg, whole, cooked	1 large	0.7 mg
Lamb, cooked	1 oz (30 g)	0.6 mg*
Quinoa, cooked	¼ cup (60 mL)	0.6 mg
Pasta, enriched, cooked	¼ cup (60 mL)	0.5 mg
Tuna, light	1 oz (30 g)	0.4 mg*
Oatmeal, instant, cooked	¼ cup (60 mL)	0.4 mg
Chicken breast, cooked	1 oz (30 g)	0.3 mg*
Pork, cooked	1 oz (30 g)	0.3 mg*
Salmon, cooked	1 oz (30 g)	0.3 mg*

* A source of heme iron, absorbed two to three times better than non-heme iron (see page 19).

OTHER IMPORTANT NUTRIENTS
———

While iron is essential to start offering your baby around 6 months, there are other important nutrients that they need from food. Beyond enough calories, fat is important for brain development and vitamin D and omega-3s will support immunity and growth. Below I'll share where to find these nutrients as well as the best "superfoods" to feed your baby!

GETTING ENOUGH CALORIES AND FAT
Your baby's rate of growth and development is still very fast in the second half of their first year, at the time when they are starting solids. This is why babies this age need to be offered calorie-dense foods, to support this rapid growth.

So how do you make sure you offer plenty of high-calorie foods to your baby? Serve a variety of foods from the start, including meat, dairy products and grains — and not just fruits and vegetables. Fat is the macronutrient that contains the most calories per gram, so offering higher-fat foods will ensure that your baby consumes high-calorie foods. Babies need a higher-fat diet than adults anyway, for growth and brain development. Much of your baby's fat intake will come from breast milk, but it's still wise to offer high-fat food choices at every meal. For example, spread butter, peanut butter or mashed avocado on toast fingers instead of serving them plain. Some other tasty high-fat food choices are full-fat cheese, full-fat plain yogurt, nut and seed butters, meat, fish and eggs.

VITAMIN D
A common question I get is "When can I stop giving my baby vitamin D supplements?" The short answer is never! At least for those of us in Canada and other northern regions, we can't make enough vitamin D from skin contact with the sun between October through March. And even in warmer areas — and Canadian summers — we are encouraged to slather on sunscreen, which blocks vitamin D creation. So supplements are important for baby and for you!

It continues to be important that your baby gets 10 micrograms, or 400 international units, of vitamin D. This micronutrient works along with calcium to strengthen bones, and may play a part in the prevention of certain cancers as well as autoimmune disorders, such as diabetes and multiple sclerosis.

OMEGA-3 FATS
For a child under 1 year of age, the adequate intake value for omega-3 polyunsaturated fats is 0.5 grams (500 mg) per day. Omega-3s are essential fats, meaning our bodies can't make them, so we need to get them through food or supplements.

A specific type of omega-3 called docosahexaenoic acid (DHA), found in

ARE FRUIT AND VEGGIES THE BEST STARTER FOOD?
Multiple surveys and studies show that most parents offer fruits or veggies as starter foods. So what's wrong with introducing *only* fruits and vegetables? They are certainly healthy foods, full of vitamins and minerals, and should make up part of your baby's diet. However, they don't contain enough calories or iron to make up *all* of your baby's diet. Make sure to offer them with a source of iron.

algae and fish, is especially important for your baby's brain, eyes and nervous system development. Behavior, learning and focus may be improved if your baby gets adequate omega-3s throughout your pregnancy and in the first 2 years of life. Newer research is suggesting it also may help prevent asthma and preterm labor. As a nursing mom, you can pass DHA through your breast milk to your baby, so it's important that you eat fatty fish, such as salmon, twice a week or take a fish oil supplement. Once you start your baby on solids, you can also offer him low-mercury fish (see box) multiple times per week. Note that while walnuts, flax seeds and canola oil do contain omega-3 fat, it's in a different form that's not as useful to your baby as DHA.

Did You Know?

SAFE SEAFOOD CHOICES

Good low-mercury fish choices that contain omega-3 fats include salmon, shrimp, tilapia, cod, trout, haddock, halibut, bass, sole and canned light (not white) tuna. These can be puréed or mashed to start, but they also make a nice soft finger food as soon as your baby can pick it up!

SUPERFOODS

While there's no "superfood" that can provide your baby all of the nutrients they need, there are some foods that are especially nutrient dense. These foods are great to include regularly in your baby's diet from the start:

LEAFY GREENS. The darker the vegetable, the more nutrients it usually contains. Leafy greens like spinach and kale pack

a punch of folic acid, vitamin A and potassium. How to serve them to baby? You could try kale chips, spinach in smoothies or some recipes in this book, such as Pear and Spinach Purée (page 89) or Spinach, Pear and Mango Purée (page 102).

EGGS. Eggs pack a punch of "gold star" protein. Did you know that the quality of all other proteins is compared to eggs? The yolk also contains iron, healthy fats and choline, a difficult-to-find nutrient. Try the Broccoli, Roasted Pepper and Garlic Egg bites recipe (page 160).

HEMP HEARTS AND CHIA SEEDS. Hemp hearts are high in omega-3 fats, fiber and iron! Sprinkle them on your baby's cereal or yogurt or blend them into smoothies. Or try the recipes for Pears, Mangos, Spinach and Chia (page 119) and Summer Squash, Pears, Carrots and Chia (page 99).

SALMON. Salmon is one of the best sources of omega-3 fats. Look for wild salmon and no added salt if it's in the can. Your baby will love our Creamed Salmon and Peas with Toast recipe (page 133) and Salmon with Sweet Mustard Sauce (page 180).

BERRIES. Berries are high in antioxidants and vitamin C, which will help your baby absorb iron. They are also a good source of fiber, to keep your baby's bowels regular.

FULL-FAT PLAIN YOGURT. Yogurt is a good source of probiotics, to keep your baby's gut healthy. It's also a good source of calcium and fat for your little one.

BISON. Red meat such as bison — and beef — is great for babies, because it's high in nutrients they are often low in, such as iron, zinc and vitamin B_{12}. If you want to try bison, swap out ground bison for the ground beef in any of the recipes in this cookbook.

FOODS TO AVOID

Technically, your baby can have anything to eat after 6 months of age, except honey (see below). But there are some foods that you may eat yourself that aren't the best choices for your baby. Here are a few of them.

HIGH-SALT FOODS. Many restaurant meals and packaged foods are too high in sodium. From 7 to 12 months of age, your baby should get a maximum of 400 milligrams of sodium per day. When you're cooking at home, add most of the salt to the adults' servings after you've removed your baby's portion. If you're eating a saltier prepared food with sauce, such as chili or curry, rinse it under running water in a colander to get rid of extra sauce and therefore salt.

HIGH-SUGAR FOODS. Very small amounts of added sugar are okay. (See FAQ, page 54.) But it's best get your baby used to eating plain versions of sweet foods, so they don't get used to and prefer the supersweet food.

Yogurt is a good example: choose plain full-fat rather than sweetened, and then add your own fruit. Note also that maple syrup and agave nectar are no better than regular sugar.

HONEY AND PRODUCTS CONTAINING HONEY. Avoid these, even if they are cooked. There's a small risk that they could cause botulism, a potentially fatal foodborne illness to which your baby is especially susceptible. A few hundred cases of infant botulism in the United States every year are caused by ingestion of honey or contact with contaminated soil.

COW'S MILK AS A MAIN DRINK. Avoid providing cow's milk as your baby's main source of milk until he is between 9 and 12 months of age — and at 9 months only if he is eating lots of solid foods. Some countries recommend waiting until 12 months. Cow's milk is not as nutritious as breast milk or formula. If you continue to breastfeed, your baby won't need cow's milk.

RAW DAIRY AND FISH. Skipping these will help prevent foodborne illness. Your baby is more susceptible to bad bacteria in food than adults are.

LOW-FAT FOODS. Items in this category, such as fat-free yogurt or light cheese, aren't a good choice for little ones. Babies need lots of fat to grow.

ARTIFICIAL SWEETENERS AND COLORINGS. Sweeteners provide no nutritional value, and colorings have been linked to behavior issues in children.

NUTRIENT-POOR FOOD. This category includes most packaged and fast foods, even those targeted at babies and toddlers. Your baby doesn't need the toddler frozen meals

23

you can buy at the store. Each bite he eats should be nutrient dense.

While you don't have to be so meticulous as to never offer your baby any of these foods (other than honey), you can generally accomplish this by preparing most of your food at home. The recipes in this book are balanced for babies and the whole family, and include lots of tasty, nutritious foods to help you achieve this!

IS RAW MILK OKAY FOR MY BABY?

Unpasteurized or "raw" milk is touted as beneficial, because it contains healthy bacteria not killed by pasteurization. However, it also contains unhealthy bacteria that would get killed off by pasteurization. And infants are at higher risk of getting sick from these bacteria. Illness symptoms can include diarrhea and vomiting, even kidney failure, paralysis and death. From 1998 to 2011, there were 148 outbreaks including two deaths from consuming raw milk product reported to the Centers for Disease Control and Prevention (CDC, 2016). The majority affected were children. It's not worth the risk.

BABY-LED WEANING, PURÉES OR BOTH?

You have likely heard the term "baby-led weaning" and are wondering if it's the best method of starting solids. Or should you stick with the conventional route of purées, progressing to more textured foods, and adding in finger foods later? Every baby is different, and all methods of starting solids can be safe and healthy.

"Baby-led weaning" means to start your baby on real table food from the start, skipping the mush. Being the author of *The Parents' Guide to Baby-Led Weaning,* and running an online course and Facebook group for baby-led weaning, I'm well versed in it. And a fan, if it's done well!

Some benefits of starting finger foods right at 6 months include improving your baby's chewing and finger dexterity. And of course your baby has full control over how much they eat (no "here comes the airplane!" with a loaded spoon), which will help him grow up with a health relationship with food. And it helps babies keep the important innate ability to listen to their appetites. Many parents find baby-led weaning less stressful and just easier. Especially if this is not your first baby and you have other eager mouths to feed!

You can, however, achieve the benefits of baby-led weaning by offering finger foods along with purées as well. In fact, this is the method of starting solids that Health Canada recommends (Government of Canada, 2012) — both purées and finger foods from the start. One of the benefits of offering purées is that they can be easier for baby to eat. However, don't feel as if you need to "top up" baby with purées or get a certain amount of food in them. When you're offering purées, it's important to be very responsive to baby's signs of hunger and fullness, and to respect their appetite, which can go wildly up and down!

Many recipes in this book, including the beginning recipes, can be offered as a purée or finger food, so you can choose. Just know that there is no right or wrong way. You can be flexible. It's more important for feeding to be truly led by baby than to be an official "baby-led weaner." No matter how you start solids, don't force your baby to eat more or less than the amount he wants, or to eat certain sizes or textures of food before he can handle them. Follow your baby's lead and keep mealtimes pleasant, stress free and a fun experience for everyone!

SAFETY AND PREVENTING CHOKING

It's normal to be fearful of your baby choking when they are starting solid foods. Thankfully, a lot of this fear can be alleviated with education about what choking actually involves, especially as compared to gagging. Learning about safe textures and shapes of food to offer your baby, and learning infant first aid are also critical when it comes to preventing choking.

IS YOUR BABY MORE LIKELY TO CHOKE ON FINGER FOODS?

It's a common myth that babies fed finger foods are going to choke. In fact, some current research points toward babies being at increased risk of choking the less often they are offered finger foods (Brown, 2018).

There have been two recent studies analyzing the risk of choking when using baby-led weaning (BLW) to start solids. As a reminder, this is a method of starting solids where the baby self-feeds finger foods from the start and the parent does not offer them purées.

One study came out of a randomized control trial in New Zealand called "BLISS" (Baby Led Introduction to Starting Solids). It was published in the journal *Pediatrics* and titled "A Baby-Led Approach to Eating Solids and Risk of Choking" (Fangupo et al., 2016). The study included 206 families. The parents answered questionnaires when their baby was 6, 7, 8, 9 and 12 months old. Questions included frequency of choking and gagging. Those who reported choking were asked some follow-up questions about what the child was fed and how the choking was resolved.

A total of 35% of babies choked at least once between the ages of 6 and 8 months. There was no difference between the two groups in how often babies choked in any of the time periods. Those who started with BLW gagged more often at 6 months, but less by 8 months. The babies in the purée group were gagging more by 8 months than those in the BLW group (because, as the authors stated, these babies were now learning to eat finger foods too).

Of the three incidences of choking in which health care help was required, two babies choked on milk and one choked on food that was placed in their mouth by a caregiver (which is not recommended with BLW). This goes to show that it's possible to choke on anything.

The other study was published in 2018 by Amy Brown, titled "No difference in self-reported frequency of choking between infants introduced to solid foods using a baby-led weaning or traditional spoon-feeding approach."

Dr. Brown surveyed 1,151 moms with infants between 4 and 12 months old. The moms reported how solids were introduced (strict BLW, loose BLW or traditional weaning) and the percentage of mealtimes that included spoon-feeding purées to baby. Moms reported if their baby had ever choked and, if so, how many times and on what type of food (smooth purée, lumpy purée or finger food).

The results found that 13.6% of infants (or 155 babies out of the group of 1,151) had choked. No significant association was found between the style of starting solids and choking, or the frequency of spoon or purée feeding and choking.

Yet one interesting finding is that for infants who did choke, those following a traditional weaning approach experienced significantly more choking episodes on finger foods and lumpy purées than infants following either a strict or loose baby-led approach. This is likely because the spoon-fed babies had less practice with finger foods (Brown, 2018).

I find this a good reason to introduce finger foods from the start, whether you use purées or not. Health Canada and the National Health Services (in the United Kingdom) also recommend this.

Did You Know?

SLICE APPLES TO PREVENT CHOKING

Apples are the number one food that causes choking in baby-led weaners. It's important not to offer your baby a whole raw apple, but to peel and slice it thinly, and steam it. Once your baby has a pincer grasp and can pick up smaller pieces, you can grate raw apple for them.

GAGGING VERSUS CHOKING

What is gagging? It's a natural reflex that closes off the back of your baby's throat and pushes the tongue (and food on the tongue) to the front of the mouth to chew more. Gagging is a normal part of the process of learning how to eat solids. Your baby is likely to gag a lot when learning how much food she can manage at once. And possibly when she tastes food she doesn't like! Some babies even vomit from gagging, and that can be normal. When your baby gags, her body will be making a retching motion, her eyes may water and her tongue will push out of her mouth.

The good news is that gagging is very common and not dangerous at all. In fact, it's a protective mechanism to prevent against choking. When a baby is starting solids at 6 months of age, the gag reflex is far forward on his tongue compared to an adult's, but it moves back as your baby ages. By 8 to 9 months, babies gag much, much less than at 6 months. While some babies have a more sensitive gag reflex than others, it will decrease as your baby gets older and the reflex moves farther back in his mouth.

Choking is far less common than gagging, and occurs when a piece of food partially or completely blocks the airway and your baby can't breathe. If your baby is choking, you may hear a small whisper or gasping to communicate distress and an attempt to get in air, and your baby's lips will start turning blue.

Most often people make little to no noise when choking (as opposed to the retching, gagging noises). This is why it is so important to watch your baby while they eat. Sit facing them and eat at the same time. Don't sit them on your lap while they are eating and don't go off and do dishes or cook while your baby remains at the table on their own.

27

DON'T OVERREACT!

If your baby gags, don't overreact. This may scare your baby and decrease their interest in eating. If you notice your baby gagging, you can calmly encourage them to spit out the food. They are doing a good job.

SAFE SIZES OF FINGER FOOD

——

When your baby is starting out with self-feeding, she will need a piece of food large enough to grasp with her palm. It's not until 8 or 9 months or so that she will develop the use of her forefinger and thumb in a pincer grasp to pick up smaller pieces of food. A common recommendation is to offer baby food in stick or finger shape when starting out. But here's why I don't think this is the best shape: your baby's windpipe is about as wide as the width of a straw. If your baby bites off a chunk of the stick- or finger-shaped food and it gets past her gag reflex, then it is a shape that could become a choking hazard.

So what is a safer shape to offer to your baby? Slice the food thinly, like a potato chip! This works for foods like sweet potato, peeled apple, beet, parsnip or a large carrot, for example. (Then steam the raw slices in the Instant Pot, microwave or a pot on the stove for a few minutes until tender.) For foods that can't be sliced thinly, it's especially important to make sure they are a soft texture.

Avoid rounded foods like grape tomatoes, hot dogs, or anything that your baby could take a coin or round-shaped bite out of. Apples are a good example, and surveys show they are the most common food that self-feeders choke on. If you offer your baby a full apple, he can take a bite that results in a little chunk of apple, which, if it passes his gag reflex, could block his windpipe and cause choking. If the apple is sliced in thin wedges, it is very unlikely to cause choking. Once your baby has developed the pincer grasp, around 9 months, you can use a cheese grater to grate apples and other hard fruits and veggies such as pears and carrots. Or slice them in small pieces that your baby can safely swallow without chewing.

SAFE TEXTURE OF FOOD

——

Texture is also important to consider when offering foods to your baby. Soft foods can more easily be coughed back up into the mouth, even if your baby does choke on them. They are safer compared to harder foods, which more easily get stuck in the windpipe and need some extra help. If you can squish the food between your tongue and the roof of your mouth, then it's soft enough for your beginning self-feeder. Foods like ripe avocados and bananas automatically pass the squish test. While your baby's gums are quite strong even without teeth, of course it's still easier for your baby to mash soft foods between their gums and swallow than it is to eat tough or fibrous foods. The other good news is that when babies mash and chew, the food breakdown starts in their mouth, and they will absorb more nutrients from the food than if they swallow the food whole and it just passes through their intestinal tract into their poop!

At 6 months, your baby has a simple up-and-down munching motion, which doesn't easily break down fibrous or hard foods. By 12 months, your baby will have developed the pincer grasp and more advanced chewing skills, which will allow them to manage harder foods more easily. As your baby gets the hang of chewing and swallowing soft finger foods, you can start to offer some different textures. And once your baby can pick up small pieces, it's safest to cut her food up into bite-sized pieces and you won't have to offer potato chip–sized foods anymore.

After your baby has progressed from larger potato chip–sized foods to finely chopped foods, for how much longer do you have to grate those apples and finely chop

your baby's dinner? While classic choking hazards such as full hot dogs, full pieces of popcorn and hard round candies should be avoided until age 4, other foods will depend on your baby's skill level and practice. Generally, between ages 1 and 2 your baby will have plenty of teeth and be able to chew and swallow her food with ease. If you feel she's ready for food of the same size and texture that you eat, then see how she does with it! I find that I still slice up tough fruits and veggies for all my kids, as they are easier and more appealing for them.

IS YOUR BABY A "SHOVELLER?"

What are you to do if your baby shovels so much food into his mouth that he can't chew it, and gags? This is a common and temporary phase. Offer your baby a few pieces of food at a time, or one piece at a time, to slow him down.

HOW TO SERVE POTENTIAL CHOKING HAZARDS SAFELY

The following foods are too hard or round to be safe for your baby. Avoid lettuce, celery, whole raw carrots, whole raw apple, potato chips, rice crackers, whole nuts, whole dried fruits, whole cherries, grapes, large blueberries, cherry tomatoes, hot dogs, popcorn, whole nuts and seeds, and thick nut butters. Here are some ideas on how serve these foods in a safer way.

FOOD	HOW TO SERVE SAFELY
Sausages	Slice lengthwise or in quarters.
Nuts and larger seeds (like pumpkin seeds)	Serve finely chopped nuts or in nut butter form.
Nut butter	Spread thinly on a slice of toast.
Whole grapes, cherries, grape tomatoes, cherry tomatoes, large blueberries	Slice lengthwise in quarters. Can squish soft large blueberries with your finger.
Popcorn	Avoid until age 4, or break into small pieces, ensuring no hard kernels
Banana	Slice in long strips and roll in infant cereal or ground flax seeds if it's hard to grasp. Another popular method is to cut off part of the banana's peel but leave some as a "handle" that's easier to grasp. As bananas are so soft, this can be safe too.
Cheese	Grated or thin slices.
Chunks of meat	Pressure-cook or slow-cook and shred meat. Or offer ground meat or larger tender chunks baby can grab onto, like a rib or chicken leg (remove gristle).
Beans	Black beans are fine by the time your baby has a pincer grasp. Chickpeas: Peel skin and break in half. Kidney beans: Smoosh flat with your finger. Or serve any bean as a bean spread.
Hard raw vegetables	Slice into thin potato chip size with a knife or mandolin, so your baby can grasp, and steam to soften. Once baby has pincer grasp, grate with a cheese grater or cut into small pieces that are thinner than a straw opening.
Apples	Peel, steam and cut into thin potato chip–shaped slices. Grate with a cheese grater once baby has pincer grasp.
Lettuce	Avoid until age 4. Can serve leafy greens like kale, which can be baked as kale chips, or serve spinach in smoothies or chopped and cooked.

FOOD	HOW TO SERVE SAFELY
Citrus fruit such as mandarin oranges	Peel off the thin membranes or serve in a mesh feeder bag
Corn kernels	Serve cooked and very soft, like in a casserole.
Potato chips, corn chips, hard crackers	Too hard; avoid until age 4.
Dried fruit such as raisins or dried apricots	Chop finely.
Celery and pineapple	Are too fibrous, so avoid until age 4. Or serve pineapple in a mesh feeder bag.
Hard round candies	Avoid until age 4.
Bread	Serve toasted, or it's too gummy.

HOW TO RESPOND IF YOUR BABY CHOKES

If you are sure that your baby is choking and isn't just gagging, what do you do? Your initial instinct may be to slap your baby on the back or dig the food out of his mouth. Unfortunately, both actions may force the food further down in his throat. If you can hear that your baby is getting in air — perhaps wheezing or coughing — then let him try to cough the food up on his own. If there's no evident air movement, pull him out of his chair, start cardiopulmonary resuscitation (CPR) and call 911. (Get someone else to call, if you're not alone).

Did You Know?

BE PREPARED WITH INFANT FIRST AID

It's important for everyone to have infant first aid skills, including CPR. If it's not possible to attend a class, perhaps you can find an online course or at minimum watch videos of infant CPR online. Although you can avoid those foods that present a higher risk for choking, a recent study found that only 23% of the foods that were reported as causing choking were on the study's list of high-risk foods (Fangupo et al., 2016). Because it is impossible to prevent all food-related choking, regardless of feeding method and foods offered, you need to be prepared to act in an emergency.

31

REMEMBER THESE TIPS TO PREVENT CHOKING

Actual choking is not nearly as common as gagging, but it does happen to some babies, whether you are feeding purées or finger foods. And food is not the only choking hazard. Keep small objects out of your baby's reach, such as coins, marbles and buttons. The good thing is that many choking episodes can be prevented. Here are some tips to make sure you are doing as much as you can to offer safe foods to your baby:

- **Don't sit baby on your lap,** because you always need to be able to see your baby when they are eating.

- **Make sure your baby is sitting upright** and not running or crawling around. No eating in the car!

- **Use a proper high chair and sit with them** and enjoy your meal. Don't turn away to do dishes or prepare foods, as choking is often silent.

- **Make sure your baby is safely positioned**, well supported and seated upright in their high chair (see pages 12–13).

- **Reconsider using the buckles on your baby's high chair.** If your baby isn't at the climbing stage, and can sit safely in their high chair without the buckles, it will ensure that you can get them out quickly if they need some assistance to clear food from their throat.

- **Don't have toys to play with or the TV turned on while eating.** Your baby should concentrate on eating, without distractions.

- **Never put a piece of solid finger food into your baby's mouth.** If your baby does not have that chance to control it with their tongue and chew it, the food may immediately fall to the back of the throat. Give your baby control and let him feed himself finger foods.

- **Take an infant CPR class so you are prepared if needed.**

- **Offer food that is safe in size and texture.**

HOW OFTEN AND HOW MUCH TO FEED BABY

You're prepared to offer food high in sources of iron and calories, in safe sizes and textures. Your next question is, how often and how much food should you feed your baby?

When beginning to start your baby on solids, around 6 months, you can offer solid foods twice per day. Breakfast is a great time to start, as most babies are hungriest then (unless they have been breastfeeding all night). Lunch is a great time for a second meal. You will then have the rest of the day to watch your baby for any signs of allergy or intolerance, and for them to work the food through their system. This is a better option than making your baby's first meals at dinner, shortly before bedtime, and putting them to bed potentially with a tummy full of gas!

At 9 months of age, you can add in a third meal. Hold off on snacks until they reach 12 months, so they don't displace too much milk. It's important that milk remains your baby's main source of nutrition until about age 1. They will gradually decrease their milk intake as they eats more solids; you can follow their lead. By the end of that first year, about half of your baby's energy needs will come from table foods and half from milk.

HOW OFTEN TO FEED BABY

At 6 months: offer 2 meals per day

At 9 months: offer 3 meals per day

At 12 months: offer 3 meals + 2 snacks

As for how much to feed your baby, that is up to them! At the scheduled meal times, you can offer your baby food until they are showing you signs of fullness. To set your

IS YOUR BABY HUNGRY?

It's usually quite clear when your baby is hungry and interested in eating — and equally clear when they are done with a meal. Here are some common indicators to watch for.

SIGNS OF HUNGER	SIGNS OF FULLNESS
Leaning forward with an open mouth (when spoon-feeding). Reaching toward or pointing at food (when finger feeding)	Crying and fussing
Smiling at food and acting happy when food is presented	Throwing food
Acting alert and focused on food	Eating more and more slowly
Gesturing for more or for certain foods (this is especially helpful if you do baby sign language with your child)	Yawning or falling asleep
Licking lips and drooling	Squirming to get out of high chair

TRY FINGER FOODS. If your little one hasn't taken to purées, see if he will happily accept a finger food instead. He may want to eat what you're eating!

TRY PURÉES. If you have been offering only finger foods, in the hopes of practicing baby-led weaning, continue to offer finger foods. But you can also try purées and see if your baby is more interested. Be truly "baby led!"

MAKE FINGER FOODS EASY TO PICK UP. Offer food in a size your baby can handle, and easy to grasp when starting out. Make sure it has a soft texture so it's easy for him to bite off pieces and chew.

CHECK YOUR FEEDING STYLE. If you pressure or force your child to eat, they will actually eat less! Let them be the judge of how much to eat, and keep mealtimes fun and stress free.

KEEP YOUR COOL. Don't pressure your baby to eat, or lose heart. Just keep on offering food and she'll get it eventually.

GO SLOWLY. Offer one food at a time. Your baby might get overwhelmed if she has too many choices, or very large portions in front of her.

baby up with a healthy relationship with food, it's important to follow their signs of hunger and fullness, especially if you are in control with spoon-feeding.

You can expect your baby's appetite for solids to go up and down on a daily and weekly basis. Some weeks, baby may be popping a new tooth and it's painful to eat solids. Babies tend to make up for the decrease in solid food with an increase in milk, and that's okay. Your baby knows their appetite best, and you never have to pressure them to eat more, or take food away if they are still interested in eating more.

TIPS FOR BABIES WHO ARE SLOW TO START

It's not unusual for babies to take a few weeks or even months to figure out how to eat. It may take a while for her to build up enough interest in eating to actually do it. If you have a baby who's not too keen to put food in her mouth, here are some ideas that may help.

LET HER PLAY WITH HER FOOD. One day she will squish it, the next she may touch it to her tongue, and the next maybe she will chew it and spit it out. Every step is progress and a part of the process.

RE-OFFER REFUSED FOODS 15 TIMES.
Your baby may need to see a particular food many times before he considers it safe enough to try.

DON'T COMPARE. Babies are all different. Some eat a little; some eat a lot. It doesn't pay to compare your baby's habits against those of your friends' children.

CHECK HER IRON LEVEL. If your baby isn't eating much by 9 months, it's a good idea to ask your doctor for an iron test. Low iron levels can cause reduced appetite and growth, so it's a bad cycle to get into — and an easy one to fix with supplements.

CHECK YOUR EXPECTATIONS. Children have small tummies, and often we think they need to eat far more than they really do. Judge what your child eats on a week-by-week basis, rather than meal by meal or even daily.

OFFER PURÉES WITH A FAMILIAR TOY.
Offer a taste of puréed food from a familiar and well-loved mouthing toy. It may be more enticing to your child than on a spoon.

TIME MILK FEEDS. If your baby seems angry or frustrated at mealtimes, maybe he is too hungry when you start. Try breastfeeding 30 to 60 minutes before bringing your baby to the table to try solids, so he has a bit of an appetite but isn't too ravenous.

Did You Know?

ASK AN EXPERT

If your baby is slow to accept solids and seems to have trouble chewing, make an appointment with a speech language pathologist or occupational therapist who specializes in feeding. Other reasons you may want to consider a feeding specialist referral: if your baby pockets food in her cheek, eats only specific textures, coughs or gags all the time, has a history of frequent colds, has a tongue or lip tie, or has an oral aversion (in other words, she doesn't put anything in her mouth, including toys).

35

PREVENTING AND TREATING PICKY EATING

The most important thing you can do to both prevent and treat picky eating is follow the "Division of Responsibility in Feeding." Ellyn Satter, an international authority on feeding children, created this concept, which is published on her website, www.ellynsatterinstitute.org.

Satter's division of responsibility identifies your roles as a parent in feeding, and your child's roles in eating. The parent chooses when, where and what the baby is offered to eat. The baby chooses if and how much he will eat. By following your respective roles, your baby will grow up to have a healthy relationship with food. He will be less likely to be a picky or emotional eater, have an eating disorder or be overweight.

THE PARENTS' ROLES

WHEN

Babies up to about 1 year of age are fed milk on demand. But meals, when they begin, occur on a more regular schedule. Constant snacking prevents your child from building up an appetite for her meals — she will end up consuming less overall, as well. Following your little one around with food, trying to get her to take "just one bite" (a technique often used by parents of "small" babies) backfires, because she will never actually be hungry for meals. Aim for specific mealtimes, with a beginning and end. When your baby shows you signs she's finished, that is the end of offering her food until the next meal or snack.

WHERE

Your baby should sit in his high chair at the table and eat with the whole family. This is safest to prevent choking. Plus, family mealtimes offer a ton of benefits when your child grows into an adolescent, from better grades to decreased risk of drug and alcohol use. Family meals are not just about the food — the connection and conversation you share are just as important. They're a beneficial habit to start from the beginning.

WHAT

You choose safe and nutritious foods to offer your baby. If she doesn't want it, that's her decision — respect it and don't be offended. Most likely she's just not hungry. Don't bring out a backup food you know your baby will eat ("She didn't eat dinner, but I know she'll eat this banana!") Your little one will quickly learn that she doesn't have to try new foods because she can always wait and get her favorite. That's the perfect recipe for nurturing a picky eater. Don't become a short-order cook. Make a single family meal that's appropriate for everyone and leave it at that.

Did You Know?

OFFER ONE FAMILIAR FOOD PER MEAL

If your child resists trying new foods, you can have one "safe food" on the table: one that your little one would normally choose to eat if she's hungry and has eaten in the past. It can be as simple as bread with butter. This gives your child the chance to have something to eat if she's hungry but too stressed out to try a new food. However, it's just served as part of the meal, and not offered as backup when the rest of the meal is refused.

THE BABY OR CHILD'S ROLE

IF AND HOW MUCH

Parents often try to take over the child's role because they think it's their responsibility. It's *not* your job to "get" your baby to eat. It's your job to offer the food, and your little one's job to decide if he will eat it. If he's hungry, he will. Children are great at listening to their appetites, and parents should encourage them to maintain this skill as long as possible. And that can only happen if you fully trust your child to eat the amount he needs.

If your baby decides to eat nothing during a meal — or even throughout a whole day — that's fine. We may not understand how babies can subsist on what seems like nothing more than air, but they do. If your baby is still growing along his growth curve, missing a meal or two isn't a problem. Only in very rare cases are babies not in tune with their appetites.

Many parents pressure their children to eat using praise, rewards, bribes or punishments. Thankfully, once they know it's not their role, parents can relieve themselves of the burden of forcing the issue. Pressing children to eat backfires anyway, and they end up eating less. And not only that — bribes and other forms of coercion can encourage emotional or binge eating, an excessive sweet tooth or an intense dislike of the foods they are forced to consume. Mealtimes become battlegrounds, full of stress and tears, instead of a peaceful place where the family can connect.

How you deal with food around your child can affect him for the rest of his life. Start now, from the beginning of your child's relationship with solid food, to build good habits and feel confident that your child will eat the amount he needs. Your baby is the best judge of his own appetite.

TRACKING GROWTH

Tracking your baby's growth on the World Health Organization growth charts can be a good indicator of whether they are getting enough calories. Remember that the 50th percentile is not the "goal" weight of your baby. Half of babies are naturally above the 50th percentile, and half are below it. As long as they are following along *their own* curve, they are growing well.

Regardless of whether you have followed the Division of Responsibility, some babies and children are just inclined to be more fearful of food. It's common around the age of 18 months to 2 years for a previously not-too-choosy baby to become more selective with her food preferences. Some of this appears to be genetic.

Here are some more tips for handling picky eaters as they grow.

1. **REPEATEDLY OFFER PREVIOUSLY REFUSED FOODS.** Do this at regular meal and snack times — without applying pressure to your child to eat them. Eventually your child will get comfortable with seeing the food and she might deem it safe enough to touch. Or lick. Or chew and spit out. These are all positive steps in trying new foods for some kids! Never force the issue, because it can cause a lifetime hatred of specific foods.

2. **GET YOUR CHILD INVOLVED IN PREPARING FOOD.** Grow a garden or even a windowsill pot of vegetables. Visit a farmer's market with your child and talk to a farmer about how carrots grow. Together, pick out a new vegetable to try at the grocery store. Ask your child to wash the lettuce. Getting kids involved in the process of raising, selecting and preparing food gives them some pride and ownership of the food. And that will make them eager to taste it.

3. **TRY DIFFERENT COOKING METHODS.** Kale can be baked into yummy chips, which are more fun. Try sweet potatoes baked, mashed or in french fry form. Lots of veggies can be cut in fry or chip form and cooked; try beets, parsnips, carrots and potatoes. Some children prefer raw veggies and others like them cooked until mushy.

4. **OFFER FOOD WHEN YOUR CHILD IS HUNGRIEST.** Try offering foods when your child is hungriest, for example, as an appetizer at the beginning of a meal. They may be more willing to give it a try.

5. **GIVE VEGETABLES FUNNY NAMES.** Kids will eat more "super-sight carrots" than plain carrots. It's just more fun.

6. **TRY DIPS OR SAUCES.** Hummus or yogurt dip provides extra nutrients as well as appealing flavors to go with veggies and fruits. Cheese sauce on cooked veggies enhances their flavor.

7. **BE A GOOD ROLE MODEL.** I have a lot of clients who say, "My husband won't eat veggies." Then why would his child want them? Expand your palate — a little someone is watching you.

8. **BE PATIENT.** This is the most important advice. Picky eating is a phase that most children go through. It's a part of learning how to become independent and say no. Most picky eaters will start to improve by age 5, so hang in there.

Did You Know?

FRUIT IS NUTRITIOUS TOO

Kids often turn their noses up at vegetables. They are mostly bitter, and quite tough and hard to chew when raw. Fruit is usually better accepted, as children naturally prefer sweet food. Their very first food, breast milk, is sweet, after all! Continue to offer vegetables, but know that fruit contains similar nutrients. Vitamin C can be found in bell peppers and broccoli, but also strawberries. Folate is found in spinach, but also oranges!

AVOID RAISING AN EMOTIONAL EATER

Don't use food to soothe your child when she is crying or keep her busy when she is bored. This trains her to be an emotional eater instead of a person who eats to satisfy hunger.

FOOD ALLERGIES

When babies are starting solid foods, food allergies are another common concern. The good news is that allergies are less prevalent than most people think; about 8% of us have food allergies, some of which we outgrow. You probably want to know if you need to delay any foods, how to offer them for the first time, and what allergic symptoms look like. In this section, we review everything you need to know about allergies for your baby.

ALLERGY INTRODUCTION GUIDELINES

Back in 2000, health organizations recommended avoiding introducing high-risk allergens to babies for the first 1 to 3 years of life. The theory was that infants and toddlers didn't have guts or immune systems that were well-enough developed to tolerate allergenic proteins. Very soon after, research started coming out supporting just the opposite theory: that delaying introducing allergens may actually be harmful and introducing them early is best. Amazingly, we have seen that this updated hypothesis is true; in the 10 years after the guidelines recommended delaying allergen introduction, the incidence of allergies doubled!

In 2008, the American Academy of Pediatrics updated its position, recommending that babies avoid allergens only up to 6 months of age. Experts had learned that introducing these substances early could help promote tolerance and reduce allergy rates.

> ### Did You Know?
> #### HIGH-RISK ALLERGENIC FOODS
> The most common foods that cause allergies are milk, eggs, fish and shellfish, tree nuts (such as almonds, cashews and walnuts), peanuts, wheat and soy.

PEANUT ALLERGY GUIDELINES

In early 2017, the National Institute of Allergy and Infectious Diseases (NIAID) in the United States issued new clinical guidelines specifically related to peanut allergies. These were endorsed by the Canadian Society of Allergy and Clinical Immunology, as well. The guidelines suggest that, for most babies at low risk of allergy, peanuts should be introduced soon after starting solids, when your baby is developmentally ready. Babies with mild to moderate eczema should also start peanuts at around 6 months of age.

For babies with an egg allergy, severe eczema or both, it is recommended to have

> ### WHAT IS A FOOD ALLERGY?
> In an allergic reaction, your body's immune system mistakes a protein in food as a foreign invader and launches an attack, which releases histamines. The results are allergic symptoms, including rashes, vomiting and an itchy or constricted throat.

For all babies, including those at high risk for an allergy, introducing peanuts at 6 months of age fits within the new guidelines and is appropriate according to the most current research findings.

a peanut allergy test done before offering peanuts for the first time. Babies whose test results show a higher risk of reaction to peanuts should see an allergy specialist before feeding their baby peanuts.

Like me, you might have read the new NIAID guidelines and thought "Introducing peanuts to the most at-risk babies at 4 to 6 months? Why so early?" It's important to know that, while the LEAP study (see Research Spotlight, right) supported introducing peanuts early, and the babies studied started the study between 4 and 11 months, the average age at which the babies started the study was 7.8 months — 4 months was on the low end. The babies studied in Israel, where there are very few peanut allergies, started peanuts at around 7 months of age, not 4 months.

Besides that, current recommendations from the World Health Organization (and all government health organizations in developed nations) support exclusive breastfeeding up to 6 months of age, at which time babies can be introduced to solids along with continued breastfeeding. Exclusive breastfeeding is also protective against allergies. So then why the "as early as 4 to 6 months" statement for high-risk babies in the new guidelines? Perhaps future research will support introduction of allergens before 6 months in high-risk infants. For now, discuss with your doctor (or allergist, if you have one), whether early introduction of solids may be beneficial if you have a high-risk baby.

RESEARCH SPOTLIGHT: SUPPORT FOR THE NEW PEANUT GUIDELINES

One study that supported the new 2017 guidelines for introducing peanuts was the Learning Early About Peanut Allergy (LEAP) study in the United Kingdom (Du Toit et al., 2015). The researchers noticed that Jewish children living in the United Kingdom (where recommendations were to avoid peanuts for the first few years) had 10 times the prevalence of peanut allergy compared with Jewish children growing up in Israel. In Israel, peanuts become a regular part of a baby's diet at around 7 months. Testing the hypothesis that introducing peanuts early might actually be beneficial, the LEAP researchers studied 640 babies at high risk for peanut allergy. Half of the babies were given peanuts for the first time at 5 years of age, and the other half were given peanuts regularly starting at between 4 and 11 months of age. At the end of the study, 17% of the children who had experienced delayed peanut introduction had a peanut allergy, compared with only 3% of the children who started eating peanuts within the first year of life. These results helped solidify the knowledge that it's better to introduce high-risk allergens early to promote tolerance.

HOW TO INTRODUCE PEANUTS

The easiest way to introduce peanuts to your baby is to dilute a natural peanut butter (with no added ingredients) with

41

BABIES AT HIGH RISK FOR ALLERGIES

Babies who have a known food allergy are at higher risk for other allergies. Babies who have a sibling or parent with a food allergy or those with severe eczema also have higher risk of allergic reactions.

a bit of warm water and spoon-feed it. Or you can mix a bit of peanut butter into a fruit purée or infant cereal. For self-feeders, spread a thin layer of peanut butter on a strip of toast, banana or a pancake. Thick layers of nut butter can be a choking hazard.

For your baby's first attempt, give him a small amount to eat. Once he's consumed some, remove the peanut-containing food. Wait 10 minutes, all the time offering him other food and watching for signs of an allergic reaction, such as a rash, vomiting or difficulty breathing. *Call 911 if any of these reactions happen.*

If you are really nervous about feeding peanut butter to your baby, you can rub a bit on his cheek. Wait about 15 minutes and then rub a bit on his lip. Wait another 15 minutes and watch to see if a rash develops. If it does, don't give your baby any more peanuts and ask your doctor for an allergy test. If there is no skin reaction, feed your baby small and increasing amounts of peanut butter.

After a successful introduction, continue to offer peanut butter a few times per week. You can also try adding finely chopped peanuts to muffins or putting a spoonful of peanut butter powder in smoothies. Or try puffed peanut butter finger snacks, which you can find online or in stores.

YOU DON'T HAVE TO WAIT 3 DAYS

You may have been told to wait 3 to 5 days before giving your baby each new food so you can see if she shows any signs of allergic

reaction to the previous one. Thankfully this is an outdated recommendation, and you don't need to do this!

If your baby is at high risk for allergies (see above), you may want to wait 2 days after introducing a high-risk food before introducing another. For example, if you introduce eggs to your baby, wait 2 days before trying out dairy, fish, shellfish, wheat, tree nuts, peanuts or soy. In between attempts, you are free to start any other low-risk food.

If your baby has a variety of new foods at one meal and then appears to be having an allergic reaction, act like a detective and try each of the ingredients individually on other days to find the culprit. Sometimes other things cause similar symptoms — it's possible your baby is teething (and therefore extra crabby) or has a virus (causing vomiting after eating) and no allergies at all.

Did You Know?

WHAT ABOUT DAIRY?

Wait until your little one is 9 to 12 months old to give her cow's milk as a replacement for breast milk or formula. It is not as nutritious as either. From an allergy perspective, full-fat yogurt, cheese and milk in cereal, smoothies or cooking are fine for your baby to try as soon as she starts solids.

ALLERGIC REACTIONS

Sometimes your baby will appear to have a reaction to food. These episodes are usually mild. In fact, they may not be allergic reactions at all — your little one may just be tired or popping a tooth. Often skin can be more sensitive to acidic food such as tomato sauce or strawberries; this can cause a rash but it is not an allergy.

If you are sure your baby has had a mild reaction, there's a good chance he will outgrow his allergy. Retry the food again every 3 months.

Many babies who have a milk or egg allergy will outgrow it by the time they are 5 years old. Unfortunately, shellfish, tree nut and peanut allergies are less likely to be outgrown, so your child may need to avoid these for life if these allergies are confirmed.

If your baby has a severe reaction (see table, below), avoid the offending food completely and consult an allergist for confirmation.

WHAT IS ANAPHYLAXIS?

Serious allergy cases can cause anaphylaxis, a life-threatening allergic reaction. When this occurs, your baby's immune system overreacts to a protein in her trigger food. Her blood pressure can drop, breathing becomes difficult and her airway can close. While most allergic symptoms are mild, if you think your baby is having a severe reaction, it's an emergency. Call 911 and administer an EpiPen if you have one. After the episode is resolved, you need to make an appointment with an allergist to confirm the cause, and then strictly avoid the allergenic food — permanently.

SIGNS OF AN ALLERGIC REACTION

These are the signals to watch for when your baby is trying new foods. Most symptoms will be mild, but it's good to be aware of the symptoms of severe anaphylaxis, discussed above.

LOCATION	SYMPTOMS
Skin	Redness, bumps, swelling or rashes; these often occur around the mouth, where food has come into contact with the skin, but can spread to the body
Gastrointestinal system	Vomiting, diarrhea or pain (which often results in extra fussiness)
Respiratory system	Runny nose, watery eyes, sneezing, difficulty breathing
Cardiovascular system	Drop in blood pressure and fainting

FEEDING YOUR VEGETARIAN BABY

There are many valid reasons why people choose to become vegetarian, such as environmental sustainability, concern for animal welfare and health. If you are a vegetarian, you will have to decide whether you want to raise your baby vegetarian, too. Some vegetarian parents offer their children animal products and let the children decide whether to become vegetarian when they are older. Others raise their babies vegetarian from the start.

The wider the variety of foods you can offer your baby, the easier it is to meet his nutritional needs. But the good news is that a well-planned vegetarian, or even vegan, diet can support healthy growth and development at any stage of life. However, there are some nutrients — including omega-3 fats, iron, zinc, calcium and vitamin B_{12} — that you must pay particular attention to. We'll cover them later in this chapter.

Did You Know?

SAY NO TO RAW DIETS

Raw vegetarian diets consist only of uncooked food, such as fruit, veggies, sprouted grains and nuts. These diets are too high in fiber and too low in important nutrients to meet your baby's needs for growth and development. If raw dairy is included, your baby will also be at higher risk of foodborne illness. Raw diets are simply not a healthy choice for babies.

IMPORTANT NUTRIENTS FOR YOUR VEGETARIAN BABY
—

The type of vegetarian you and your baby are also determines which nutrients are especially important to get from food and supplements. Some important nutrients to keep an eye on include omega-3 fats, iron, zinc, calcium and vitamin B_{12}.

PROTEIN
Contrary to popular myth, it's not difficult to meet protein needs on a vegetarian diet. The amount of protein a baby needs varies

TYPES OF VEGETARIAN DIETS

There are a number of different types of vegetarianism. Each omits certain animal foods. There is a lot of gray area in terms of strictness, so these are just broad definitions.

TYPE OF VEGETARIAN	FOODS ALLOWED AND OMITTED
Lacto	Consumes dairy products, but no eggs or other animal products
Ovo	Consumes eggs, but no dairy or other animal products
Lacto-ovo	Consumes eggs and dairy products, but no other animal products
Pesco	Consumes fish, but no other animal products
Vegan	Consumes no animal products at all; the strictest vegans omit honey, as well, and don't wear wool or leather

a bit depending on his weight, but 7- to 12-month-olds need, on average, about 11 grams of protein per day. What does this look like? Let's say your 8-month-old drinks 2 to 3 cups (500 to 750 mL) of breast milk or formula every day; that alone will provide about 7 to 10 grams of protein per day. Lacto-ovo vegetarians can easily provide extra protein by offering eggs, cheese and yogurt. Sources that are suitable for vegans (and vegetarians, of course) include tofu and other soy products; legumes, such as beans and lentils; and nut and seed butters.

If you give your child a variety of different plant-based proteins, he will get the full range of essential amino acids over the course of the day or week. Don't worry about combining different proteins at each meal to achieve "balanced" amino acids or protein. Vegans do need to be a bit more vigilant to offer a protein source at each meal, because some plant-based proteins are not as highly digestible as animal-based ones. A study by Mangels and Messina (2001) reported that vegans ages 1 to 2 need 30% to 35% more protein per day than their non-vegan peers.

Did You Know?

MILK ALTERNATIVES

If you are not able to breastfeed your vegan baby, fortified soy milk infant formula is recommended until age 2. After age 2, fortified almond, hemp or coconut milk is fine, but these milk alternatives are not high enough in fat or protein for young babies, up to 24 months old. Some countries' feeding guidelines suggest that soy milk rather than soy formula is fine after 1 year of age, but a dietitian can help you determine if your baby's diet is adequate enough to switch from breast milk or formula to a fortified milk alternative.

OMEGA-3 FATTY ACIDS

The omega-3 fatty acid docosahexaenoic acid (DHA) is important for normal brain and eye development. The main dietary source of DHA is fatty fish. There are also plant sources of omega-3s, but they contain alpha-linolenic acid (ALA). Flax seeds, chia seeds, hemp seeds, walnuts and canola oil are all sources of ALA. However, very little ALA is converted into brain- and eye-building DHA.

The good news is that there is a vegetarian source of DHA: algae. In fact, fish are high in DHA because they consume algae! I recommend that vegetarians and vegans who don't consume fish take an algae supplement. This is especially important during pregnancy and breastfeeding, as some will transfer from mother to baby and help with brain and eye development. Once your vegetarian or vegan baby has started solids, you can consider a liquid plant-based algae supplement for her, too.

45

IRON AND ZINC

You've already learned that your baby needs plenty of iron in his diet to ensure healthy brain and body growth (see pages 16–20). Plants contain only non-heme iron, which isn't absorbed as well as the heme iron in meat. Plus, the absorption level of non-heme iron depends partially on the presence of inhibitors (like phytates) and enhancers (like vitamin C) in the diet. That's why it's especially important for vegetarians and vegans to pair a source of iron and a source of vitamin C at each meal.

There are plenty of suitable iron sources for babies who don't eat meat or fish, such as eggs (for ovo vegetarians), tofu, edamame, beans, lentils and hemp hearts. You can also serve iron-fortified foods, such as meat analogs or fortified infant or toddler cereals.

The American Academy of Pediatrics recommends that breastfed babies take a dietary iron supplement starting at 4 months of age. This may be especially beneficial for babies who don't eat meat. While this isn't a worldwide recommendation, you may want to ask your doctor if she thinks iron supplements would be beneficial for your vegetarian or vegan baby.

Zinc is also necessary for normal growth and immunity against viruses. The main food source of zinc is meat, but there are plenty of vegetarian sources, including soy, legumes, whole grains, seeds and nuts. Lacto-ovo vegetarians can also get zinc from dairy products and eggs.

CALCIUM

Calcium is one important nutrient necessary to help teeth and bones grow and stay strong. The recommended intake for calcium is 260 milligrams per day for 7- to 12-month-olds, but it jumps to 700 milligrams per day for 1- to 3-year-olds.

For lacto vegetarians, meeting calcium needs is no problem, but it can be a bit trickier for vegans. Vegetables that don't contain calcium binders, which reduce absorption, can contribute to the daily intake. These include kale, turnip greens and bok choy — about 50% of the calcium present in these vegetables can be used by the body. By comparison, about 30% of the calcium in dairy products is absorbed. However, many other vegetables contain lots of phytates and oxalates, both of which inhibit calcium absorption. These include spinach, beet greens and Swiss chard — only about 5% of the calcium in these gets absorbed. While it may seem as if they are good sources of this important mineral, just a fraction of the calcium they contain is available to the body.

Tofu with added calcium is another good plant-based source of calcium, as are fortified plant milks — these boast about 30% calcium absorption rates. But plant milks don't contain enough fat and protein, so they often aren't recommended for children until age 2. You may also be able to find fortified soy or coconut yogurt. White beans, almonds, sesame seed paste (tahini) and figs have about a 20% calcium absorption rate and can also serve as vegetarian calcium sources.

Did You Know?

TRY SOME TOFU

Tofu set with calcium chloride sulfate is a source of iron and calcium. Try offering plain strips of fried extra-firm tofu, or blend soft tofu into a smoothie for your little one to drink.

VITAMIN B$_{12}$

Vitamin B$_{12}$ is an especially important nutrient for vegetarians and vegans, because it's found naturally only in animal foods. Vegans who don't consume vitamin B$_{12}$–fortified foods or take a supplement will become deficient. Early deficiency can cause slow growth in infants and lead to anemia and nervous system damage. Lacto-ovo vegetarians need to be thinking about this, too — even if they consume 1 cup (250 mL) of milk and one egg per day, they won't hit their recommended daily intake.

Vitamin B$_{12}$–fortified foods include meat substitutes, soy milk, breakfast cereal, some yeast extracts and nutritional yeast. Always check the label to make sure the product is indeed fortified.

An adult vegetarian needs to consume dairy, eggs or fortified foods three times a day to meet their daily requirement — or take a 10-microgram B$_{12}$ supplement every day. If you're vegan and breastfeeding your baby, it's vital you take a supplement to ensure that your breast milk will pass a sufficient amount of this vitamin to your baby. Toddlers can take chewable or spray B$_{12}$ vitamins; aim for about 5 to 10 micrograms per day and talk to your doctor to confirm that you're giving enough. Excess vitamin B$_{12}$ not required by the body generally isn't harmful and leaves the body in the urine.

Did You Know?

NUTRITIONAL YEAST

Sprinkle vitamin B$_{12}$–fortified nutritional yeast on toast or steamed veggies, add it to a smoothie, use it as a base for dips, or stir a bit into sauces and soups. It tastes a bit like Parmesan cheese, so it's great on pasta or in vegan "cheese" sauces.

FOOD SAFETY

Children under 2 years old are at increased risk of foodborne illness. They have less stomach acid than adults and a weaker immune system. Therefore, it's important to make sure all of their food is well cooked. No sashimi, steak tartare or raw milk for baby!

You will find yourself freezing, thawing and reheating food often for your baby. They eat such small amounts and it's far more time-efficient if you don't have to cook every meal from scratch and can pull something from the freezer. Safely storing and reheating food for your baby will prevent bacteria from growing in their food. And note that you should always throw out extra food that was served to your baby but not eaten. Bacteria from the spoon that has been in their mouth can transfer to the rest of the food and multiply. This is why it's good to start with small portions, so you don't waste a lot of food!

FREEZING TIPS

If you're making baby purées, use small portion-sized containers to freeze in. I like using ice cube trays, with a lid, if you can find one. (Marilyn also recommends using a silicone egg bites pan that comes with a lid. It is great for storing baby food and cooking small "bites" in the Instant Pot.) Make sure you label what the food is, and the date it was made. Otherwise purées look similar and you won't know what it is. My nephew once accidentally ended up getting fed what my sister thought was sweet potato purée. Turns out it was orange juice concentrate! You can bet my nephew gobbled that sweet stuff right up.

THAWING TIPS

You can defrost frozen food in the fridge, or reheat it right from frozen. Don't defrost frozen food on the counter or in standing water. Bacteria can multiply rapidly at room temperature.

REHEATING TIPS

When serving your baby reheated food, make sure the internal temperature of their food goes up to 60° C/140° F when reheating. This will kill most bacteria, if it's present. Make sure you stir the food well, especially if reheated in the microwave. Otherwise it may have "hot spots" that can burn your baby.

Cooking some foods in water, as when boiling vegetables, can cause some of the water-soluble vitamins (like vitamin C) to leach into the water. Vitamin C can also degrade when heated for a long time. Pressure cooking in the Instant Pot and microwaving to reheat are both ways to cook food in a very little amount of water in the shortest time. So these are among the best methods for retaining nutrients in your food when cooking and reheating leftovers. Of course, you can also reheat the food in a pot on the stove, if you prefer.

There are a few precautions to take when reheating in a microwave, though.

- Most plastics should not be microwaved. Reheat in glass or other microwave-safe containers.
- The inside of microwaved food can get burning hot even when the outside remains cool. Make sure you stir the food well and test the temperature before feeding it to your baby.

48

STORAGE TIMES FOR EXTRAS

FRIDGE: 1 to 3 days: 1 day for food containing meat, 3 days if it's a vegetarian dish.

FREEZER: 2 to 3 months. While the food may not be "bad" after this time, the quality will start to deteriorate as freezer burn kicks in.

FAQS WHEN STARTING SOLIDS

Now you're prepared with all of the starting solids how-tos! This section will get you ready to actually bring baby to the table and start feeding. I'll answer your most common questions when it comes to starting solids.

Can my baby have spices?

Yes! As long as they don't contain lots of added salt, herbs and spices are fine to add to your baby's food. Spices such as garlic, ginger, cinnamon, oregano or basil are great. Babies don't need bland food, and it's possible that if you introduce them to lots of tastes and textures early on, you may prevent some picky eating later!

> ## Did You Know?
> ### PLACEMATS
> If you're using a high chair that pulls right up to the table, you may want some kind of placemat or bowl that suctions to the table to keep the mess contained.

How do I deal with constipation?

It's important to note that constipation is not determined by the length of time between your baby's bowel movements. If your baby has hard dry stools that are difficult and painful to pass, then he is constipated.

Constipation is very common when starting solids. It may take a few months for your baby's intestines to adapt and figure how to move food through efficiently. Here are some tips to help:

1. Increasing fluid is often the best way to promote bowel movements. Give your baby a cup of water to sip with each meal and snack. If he refuses to drink from a cup or a bottle, you can even try a medicine dropper.

2. If water doesn't work, you can offer $1/4$ to $1/2$ cup (60 to 125 mL) of apple, prune or pear juice per day. These types of juices contain a type of sugar called sorbitol, which draws water into the bowels to help make the poop easier to pass.

3. You can also offer puréed prunes, a great natural laxative!

4. Ground flax is another good natural laxative. Add it into your baby's cereal, yogurt or baking. Roll your baby's avocado and banana slices in ground flax seeds for self-feeders. Or test out the Carrots, Apricots and Flax Seeds (page 110) from this book.

5. Probiotics also help some babies. Talk to your doctor or pharmacist about adding probiotic powder or drops to your baby's food.

6. You may find certain foods make constipation worse. Fortified infant cereals, bananas and cheese seem to be common culprits according to caregivers. Try taking these out of your baby's diet for a few days to see if it helps.

When can I offer milk and milk alternatives?

Cow's milk is fine in cereal or baking for your baby after starting solids. Cheese and full-fat yogurt get the go-ahead after 6 months, too. However, cow's milk is not recommended (in Canada) as your baby's main milk source milk until 9 to 12 months of age. Some other countries recommend waiting until 12 months to offer cow's milk as a beverage. This is because milk doesn't contain the nutrients, like iron, that breast milk and formula contain. If your baby is eating plenty of solids and getting lots of iron from their food, they can start drinking cow's milk at 9 months at the earliest. If they aren't taking in much food, wait until at least a year to switch. At 1 year, offer 2 cups (500 mL) to a maximum of 3 cups (750 mL).

If you're breastfeeding and continue to do so, your baby doesn't need any other milk. Your milk adapts and changes with your baby's age, and is always more nutritious for her than the milk of another mammal!

As for milk alternatives such as soy, almond or coconut beverages, they are not recommended as your baby's main source of drinking milk until age 2. This is the recommendation in Canada; some countries say they are appropriate after age 1. Again, this depends on your baby's diet, as these milks are low in fat and protein. Consult with a dietitian to determine if your baby's diet contains enough nutrients to change from breast milk or formula to a fortified milk alternative.

How much water does my baby need?
From 6 to 12 months, babies do not need a lot of extra water beyond what is supplied in their milk. You don't want water to take the place of their milk or food intake. About 2 to 4 oz (60 to 120 mL) of water a day can be offered to your baby at meals, to get your baby used to drinking from a cup. However, if it's hot out or your baby is constipated, you can offer more, up to a maximum of 8 oz (240 mL) per day, to make sure they are hydrated.

Is food before 1 just for fun?
One positive of the popular saying "food before 1 is just for fun" is that when

parents consider food as optional, it takes the pressure off if your child decides she's not interested in solids! Much of eating in that first year will be experimenting with different textures and tastes. And we can't — and don't want to — force our baby to eat.

It's also true that milk does make up the most important part of your baby's diet until they reach 1 year. But food is an important supplement to milk, starting around 6 months of age. Why? There are many reasons for solid food, including extra calories to support your baby's rapid growth, to help develop motor skills and increased acceptance of new foods and flavors earlier on. There's also new research to support that introducing higher allergenic foods around 6 months may protect against allergies.

But the *main* reason why solids are recommended at 6 months is for iron, which supports growth and brain function. At about 6 months of age, your baby's iron stores from before birth stores start to run out. The recommended daily intake for iron increases from 0.27 mg at from birth to 6 months (the amount baby gets from breast milk) to 11 mg per day at 7 to 12 months old. And about 30% of 1-year-olds are iron deficient, so it's common. If iron deficiency progresses to anemia, there can be irreversible consequences such as learning difficulties and social withdrawal.

To make sure your baby gets iron, offer one of these options at each meal:

1. Red meat, chicken or seafood, all of which contain a type of iron that's easiest for our bodies to use

2. Eggs, beans and legumes

3. Fortified infant cereal. For self-feeders, you can bake this into foods like pancakes by substituting the cereal for half of the flour.

When can I offer my baby utensils?

Right from the start you can offer your baby a "dipping" tool for self-feeding purées. They will learn to dip this tool into infant cereal, oatmeal, yogurt or purées and get it to their mouth. When starting solids, let your baby try a baby toothbrush with soft plastic bristles or a baby spoon with ridges.

Between 9 and 12 months, most babies can start to experiment with utensils to feed themselves. A plastic fork will be the step after a "dipper," as the stabbing motion is easier for your baby than scooping. And by 12 months your baby will likely be able to self-feed with a soft plastic spoon, too. Although that doesn't mean they won't prefer their hands!

My baby is 4 months old — can I start solids?

Milk is all your baby needs until they are developmentally ready to start solids, at around 6 months. There are other developmental milestones to watch for, too (see pages 12–13). Some babies will be ready a bit before 6 months, and some after. Especially if your baby was born early, you will need to use their adjusted age (6 months from their due date rather than birth date). Until that point, while you wait, it's a good idea to sit your baby at the table during meals, and you can offer them a plastic spoon or "hard munchable" food that can't break off to practice with. This could include a stick of celery, carrot (if your baby has no teeth) or rib bone.

Occasionally solids can help babies with acid reflux before 6 months, but this would be at the recommendation of your doctor.

Can I feed both puréed and finger foods?

This is often called "mixed" or "combo" feeding. Although really, it is just traditional feeding, and what Health Canada recommends. So yes, it's okay to do mixed feeding! If you start with purées, it's also important to offer finger foods from the start so your baby has practice with them. Your baby won't be at increased risk of choking, or confused, despite unfounded warnings of this by some hard-line baby-led weaners!

When can I offer egg? Peanuts? Dairy?

Shortly after starting solids is a good time to offer allergenic foods like peanuts, dairy and eggs. While you don't want these foods to be your baby's first food (first foods should be rich in iron), experts now recommend that you introduce allergens early, rather than delay them. Introducing allergens early can help your baby build up a tolerance, and may help prevent an allergy.

To introduce peanut butter, offer your baby a thin spread on a slice of toast, or mix a teaspoon into their infant cereal or purée. Whole eggs can also be offered any time after 6 months. For a beginning eater, you can fry the egg and slice it into pieces your baby can grasp. As for dairy, you're also able to introduce full-fat yogurt or cheese right away. Wait on cow's milk as your baby's main source of milk until closer to a year. This isn't because of allergies, but for nutrition.

Check out pages 41–43 for more information on allergies.

What time of day should I offer that first meal and how often do I offer solids?

Early in the day is a great time to start solids. This will give you time to notice if your baby experiences any kind of allergic reaction, and time for them to get any extra gas or bubbles out of their tummy after eating.

You can offer solids after a milk feeding, but give it a bit of time, at least 30 to 60 minutes, so your baby isn't stuffed full of milk when you offer him food. That said, you don't want him to be starving either, or he will just get frustrated that he can't feed himself quickly enough.

And how many times a day should you offer your baby solids when starting? You can start with two meals a day, and move up to three meals at 9 months. At 12 months of age, your baby will be eating three meals and a few snacks per day. A snack or two may consist of milk, depending on your baby's nap schedule, which is always changing!

My baby just plays and throws his food. What can I do?

Most babies seem to do this around 9 to 10 months of age. It's a part of learning what happens to the food when it gets dropped! Here are a few tips to help manage it:

- If you have a clean floor and the food is not snatched up by the dog, you can put it back on your baby's tray.
- Give them a gentle reminder that "food stays on the table." We don't want to give them too much attention for this habit, or it will likely encourage it!

- Don't feed your baby a lot of food at once, to prevent waste. Because once you've fed baby from a portion of food, you don't want to serve it again because of potential bacteria growth.
- Maybe your baby is not hungry. Throwing food is often a sign they are done eating.
- Some babies do better using a tray with a lip, so they can't just "sweep" all their food on the floor. Or you can try their chair without a tray, pulled right up to the table, and with bowls or plates that have a suction cup to stick them to the table.

How do I know if my baby is eating enough food?

If your baby is growing consistently along his curve, then he is getting enough calories, whether it be through milk or food. There are other nutrients, however, that are important to get from food, such as iron and zinc.

It does take many babies a few weeks to get used to handling food and eating it. Some take a while to even get interested in trying. Try both purées and finger foods; they may prefer one or the other.

If your baby isn't interested after a month or two of offering solids, you may want to get her iron levels tested for a baseline. But under no circumstances should you pressure or force your baby to eat food. Check out pages 37–39 for some ideas that might encourage a baby to become interested in eating.

How much salt can my baby have?

Early exposure to salt can set preferences for life. And your baby's kidneys are not developed well enough to filter high salt intakes efficiently. In Canada and the United States, health authorities have not set an upper limit for sodium for salt

53

for babies under 1 year of age, but they recommend that children 1 to 3 years old consume less than 1500 mg of sodium per day. As a reference, adults should stay under 2300 mg per day, which is 1 teaspoon of salt.

Some other countries have more stringent recommendations. In Australia, a limit of 1000 mg per day is recommended for 1- to -3-year-olds. And in the United Kingdom, the guideline is less than 400 mg of sodium per day for 6- to 12-month-olds and 800 mg for ages 1 to 3 years.

To keep sodium intakes low:

- When you make a home-cooked meal, remove your baby's portion before adding salt.
- Use herbs to add flavor without the sodium.

- Look for low-sodium or sodium-free canned fish, beans, tomato sauce and other sauces.
- Avoid packaged and restaurant foods, which are almost always too high in salt.
- Read the food labels to determine how many milligrams of sodium each serving of the food contains. Keep in mind that your baby is not likely consuming a full adult-sized serving listed on the package.

How much sugar can my baby have?
The World Health Organization suggests it's best to keep added sugar to less than 5% of calorie intake. "Added" sugar does not include the sugar found naturally in fruit or unsweetened dairy, but does include the sugar added to a flavored yogurt or baking, for example.

What does 5% of calories look like for a baby in terms of sugar intake? This requires a bit of math! Many babies around 9 to 12 months consume about 300 calories a day from food. Of those 300 calories, 5% is 15 calories allowed from sugar. Since sugar contains 4 calories per gram, this is about 4 g of added sugar a day. Four grams of sugar is about 1 teaspoon (5 mL) maximum daily for your baby.

What if my baby gags a lot and even vomits after gagging?

Some babies have a more sensitive gag reflex than others. The good news is that this is a preventative against choking. At 6 months, the gag reflex will be triggered easily, since it is located forward on the tongue, nearer to the front of your baby's mouth. By the time your baby is 9 months old, it will have moved toward the back of the tongue, resulting in less gagging.

If your baby vomits after gagging, don't be alarmed! This can be common, too. If it doesn't seem to deter your baby from eating, it's no big deal (other than the annoying cleanup). However, if your baby starts to become fearful of eating because it always causes vomiting, you may need to take a bit of a break from finger foods and stick with purées for a few days.

Can my baby have gluten, and when should it be introduced?

Gluten is a protein found in wheat, rye and barley. About 1% of people have an autoimmune disorder called celiac disease, in which gluten harms their intestines. In babies who have a higher risk of having celiac disease (a parent who has celiac disease), delaying introduction of gluten may lead to later development of celiac disease, but it doesn't lower the risk of actually developing celiac disease.

The European Society for Pediatric Gastroenterology, Hepatology, and Nutrition recommends that large amounts of gluten be avoided in the first few months after starting solids, although the best amount hasn't been determined (Szajewska et al., 2016). It is easy to do this, with a varied diet focusing on iron, if you add dairy, fruits, vegetables and grains that do not contain gluten such as rice, quinoa and oats. While some regular gluten-containing breads and pasta are fine for all babies and adults, it's beneficial, even from a nutrient perspective, to try some new grain alternatives, such as pasta made from lentils or black beans!

Does my baby need supplements?

The recommendations for offering babies dietary supplements vary by country. The UK Health Department recommends that children ages 6 months to 5 years should be given a supplement of vitamins A, C and D.

In Canada, vitamin D supplements are recommended for babies from birth. In the winter in northern countries, you can continue to give vitamin D supplements every year. Even adults should be taking them!

Vegan children also need vitamin B_{12}, at a minimum. Consult a dietitian who can help plan a diet and, if needed, supplement plan for your vegan or vegetarian baby.

55

PART 2

INSTANT POT MEALS AND RECIPES

SAMPLE MEAL PLANS

To help you plan ahead, we've included 3 days of starter meal examples for babies at different ages. These assume you are starting off with two meals per day and working up to three meals for your baby at 9 months. After a year of age or so, you can add in snacks at scheduled times between meals. Offer at least two foods for a snack, as in cheese and crackers, yogurt with berries, toast with peanut butter, veggies and hummus dip, or muffin and fruit.

Breast milk or formula can still be demand-fed until around a year. After that, whole cow's milk can be included with meals (to a maximum of 2 to 3 cups per day). The cow's milk isn't needed if you continue to nurse.

Note that every meal for the first year contains a source of iron, whether it is meat, beans, fortified infant cereal or eggs. I haven't listed amounts; that's up to your baby to decide.

AGES 6 TO 8 MONTHS

	DAY 1	DAY 2	DAY 3
BREAKFAST	First Apples* Fortified infant cereal	Pears, Strawberries and Barley* Strips of banana rolled in fortified infant cereal	Strips of fried egg Peaches and Plums*
LUNCH OR DINNER	Spicy Lentil Purée*	Black Beans, Corn and Sweet Potato*	Sweet Potato and Chicken*

* These recipes appear in the Purées and Mashes recipe section.

AGES 9 TO 12 MONTHS

	DAY 1	DAY 2	DAY 3
BREAKFAST	Green Egg and Ham Scramble*	Quinoa, Peaches and Yogurt* sprinkled with fortified infant cereal	Toast strips with almond butter Peach slices rolled in infant cereal
LUNCH	White Bean and Ditalini Pasta*	Egg salad sandwich Sliced cucumbers	Tuna Macaroni and Cheese*
DINNER	Creamed Salmon and Peas with Toast*	Shredded Beef and Tender Carrots*	Old-Fashioned Chicken Noodle Soup* Steamed broccoli

* These recipes appear in the Finger Foods recipe section.

FAMILY MEALS

	DAY 1	DAY 2	DAY 3
BREAKFAST	Spinach, Mushroom and Bell Pepper Quiche*	Broccoli, Roasted Pepper and Garlic Egg Bites*	Toast with peanut butter and banana slices Berries
LUNCH	Turkey Meatball Bites* Cucumber slices	Grilled cheese sandwich Carrot slices	Chicken Paella* Bread with butter
DINNER	Herbed Salmon with Asparagus* Rice	Chicken and White Bean Chili* Buns with butter	Creamy Beef Stroganoff* Bell pepper slices
SNACK IDEAS	Maple Cinnamon Rice Pudding*	Crackers with cheese Sliced veggies	Boiled egg Apple slices

* These recipes appear in the Family Meals recipe section.

USING YOUR INSTANT POT

If you are looking for an easier way to get scrumptious meals on your table, the Instant Pot is for you. The beauty of this appliance, whether you choose its pressure-cooking or slow-cooking functions, is that you can prepare a meal with little hands-on time, and the Instant Pot will deliver consistently delicious results. It's perfect for busy families who want to get a nutritious meal on the table with little effort and minimal cleanup. Plus, few nutrients are lost when cooking under pressure.

Use your Instant Pot to make homemade stocks (see page 210–212). Make a side dish, such as steamed vegetables, to accompany a main dish prepared by other methods. On hot days, use your Instant Pot instead of heating up the house with your oven.

So how could it possibly get any better? Well, it can! The recipes in this cookbook are organized to help you take your little ones from purées and mashes to finger foods and on to sharing in the family meals. Want more purée recipes? Most of the "finger food" and "family meal" recipes can be blended or mashed. Want more finger food recipes? One great thing about the Instant Pot is that almost everything that comes out of it is soft and tender. Most of the "purée" recipes can be eaten as soft finger foods too — just omit the purée step in the instructions.

The ingredients we use are designed to give your young ones the best nutritional start. To make it even easier for you, the ingredients are readily available in the grocery store. You probably already have a lot of them on hand, in your fridge, freezer or pantry already!

GETTING STARTED WITH YOUR INSTANT POT

When you first start using your Instant Pot, do not be intimidated by all the cooking program keys, the operation keys and the LCD display. The core uses for today's Instant Pot are pressure cooking, sautéing, slow cooking and making yogurt. The remaining program keys you see also use the pressure-cooking function but are preprogrammed to High or Low pressure and the recommended cooking time. You can use these programs, if you prefer, and adjust the time to what is stated in the recipe.

There are several Instant Pot models available, and different models have different cooking programs. Refer to the user manual that came with your appliance for a more detailed explanation of its programs. In recent models, there are seven core functions:

CORE INSTANT POT FUNCTIONS
- Pressure cooking (with keys including Pressure Cook or Manual Pressure, Soup/Broth, Meat/Stew, Bean/Chili, Rice, Multigrain, Porridge, Steam, Cake and Egg)
- Slow cooking
- Sautéing
- Yogurt-making (including subprograms for making yogurt or pasteurizing milk)
- Sterilizing
- Keeping food warm
- Delaying the start of cooking (when using this function, make sure the ingredients you are using are safe to stand at room temperature until cooking begins)

PRESSURE COOKING

In some Instant Pot models, the pressure cooking function is labeled Pressure Cook; in others, it is labeled Manual (for manual pressure) instead.

You must have a minimum of 1 cup (250 mL) liquid in the pot. Check the user manual for your specific model for the amount of liquid needed to bring your pot to pressure. Many of the recipes call for 1 cup (250 mL) water to be added to the pot; if your model requires more liquid, increase the amount of water as necessary. In other recipes, there is sufficient liquid from other ingredients to meet at least the minimum requirements without the addition of water.

The cooker must be no more than two-thirds full for any recipe, and no more than half full for ingredients, such as beans and grains, that may foam or expand during cooking. After cooking thicker and stickier foods, such as beans or grains, or foods high in fat, take extra care when opening the lid, as these foods may bubble and spurt out.

Some Instant Pot models have High and Low Pressure options, some use only High Pressure, and others include Custom options. Follow the recipe instructions for choosing the pressure level. If the recipe uses Low Pressure and your model does not have that setting, you can cut the cooking time in half and use High Pressure, checking the food for doneness as per the instructions in the recipe. You may need to experiment a bit with cooking times, and the results may not be as intended.

The actual cooking time does not start until after working pressure is reached, which can take about 10 to 20 minutes, depending on the volume and temperature of ingredients in the pot.

RELEASING PRESSURE

The type of pressure release used in a recipe can increase the overall cooking time. While pressure cooking is a faster cooking method, the time the appliance takes to come to pressure and to release pressure should be accounted for when you are planning your meals.

The recipes will tell you exactly how to release your pressure, but here are some types of releases and their description that you will be using.

QUICK RELEASE. When the cooking time is done, press Cancel and turn the steam release handle to Venting. This immediately releases all of the pressure in the pot and stops the cooking process. When the float valve drops down, you will be able to open the lid. Keep your hands and face away from the hole on the top of the steam release handle so you don't get scalded by the escaping steam. You may want to use an oven mitt when turning the handle. Never cover the steam release handle with a towel or any other item that catches the releasing steam.

TIMED RELEASE (10-MINUTE RELEASE). When the cooking time is done, press Cancel and let the pot stand, covered, for 10 minutes or the amount of time designated in the recipe. After the allotted time, turn the steam release handle to Venting, wait for the float valve to drop down, then remove the lid. This release method is often used for dishes that benefit from additional minutes in the cooker's steam.

NATURAL RELEASE. When the cooking time is done, press Cancel and let the pot stand, covered, until the float valve drops down. Turn the steam release handle to Venting, as a precaution, and remove the lid. This release method can take about 15 to 25 minutes, depending on the volume of ingredients and the pressure level. It is used for dishes that foam and could cause clogging of the exhaust valve or spewing of ingredients out through the exhaust valve. It is also used for certain dishes that benefit from the additional standing time. This release method may be called NPR (natural pressure release) in other cookbooks and in recipes online.

STEAMING

Many of the recipes in this book use the Pressure Cook or Manual function to steam food, either directly on a steam rack or in a steamer basket, or in a heatproof dish, bowl or pan placed on a steam rack.

Be very careful when removing steamed items from the Instant Pot after the cooking time is done. For foods placed directly on the rack (such as eggs, peppers, potatoes, etc.), or for foods in small containers, such as silicone baking cups, custard cups or ramekins, small silicone oven mitts or silicone-coated tongs will help you remove them without burning yourself.

Shallow dishes and pans can be easily removed from the pot using the handles of the steam rack to lift the rack straight up out of the pot, with the dish or pan on top, and transfer it to the countertop. Make sure you still protect your hands with silicone oven mitts!

For deeper bowls and dishes that would be difficult to remove using the steam rack handles, use a silicone lift or sling to help you get them out of the pot easily. Silicone lifts are readily available online.

CREATING FOIL OR PARCHMENT PACKETS FOR STEAMING FOOD

In several of the recipes, the food is steamed inside of foil or parchment packets (*en papillote*) placed on the steam rack. Here's how to make the tent-style and flat packets described in the recipes:

TENT-STYLE PACKETS
1. Place the ingredients in the center of the foil or parchment paper as directed in the recipe.
2. Bring the long ends of the foil or paper up to meet over the ingredients. Fold down the foil or paper until the top of the packet is tightly sealed but there is enough of a gap between the food and the top of the packet to allow air and steam to circulate.
3. Fold or crimp up the open ends of the foil or paper until the folds are tight against the ingredients and the packet is tightly sealed.

FLAT PACKETS
1. Place the ingredients in the center of the foil or parchment paper as directed in the recipe.
2. Bring the long ends of the foil or paper up to meet over the ingredients. Fold down the foil or paper until it is tight against the ingredients.
3. Fold up the open ends of the foil or paper until the folds are tight against the ingredients and the packet is tightly sealed.

The lid must always be closed and locked and the steam release handle turned to Sealing when you are using a pressure-cooking function.

SLOW COOKING

Unless you are directed by a recipe to leave the lid off, the lid should be closed and locked, and the steam release handle turned to Venting, when you are using the slow cooking function.

- Fill the cooker half to three-quarters full to avoid over- or undercooking.
- Avoid removing the lid during the cooking time. Doing so releases valuable heat, which can alter the amount of cooking time your dish gets at the correct temperature. If looking at your slow-cooking dish is something you feel you must do, use the Instant Pot glass lid instead of the pressure cooking lid.
- All Instant Pot models have three temperature settings — Less, Normal and More — for slow cooking, and some have a Custom option as well. Follow the recipe instructions for the ideal setting.
- Never use frozen meats when slow cooking, as your dish may never reach a safe temperature.

SAUTÉING

The lid must always be kept off when you're sautéing or browning food. Do not even partially cover the pot with the lid, as you might do on the stovetop when simmering sauces, as pressure can build in the pot and be very dangerous.

- Always press Cancel when you are done sautéing, before moving on to other steps, such as pressure cooking or slow cooking.

- The Sauté function has three temperature settings — Less, Normal and More — in all Instant Pot models, and some have a Custom option. Follow the instructions in the recipe for the best setting.
- The Sauté function can also be used to simmer, boil or reheat recipes. The instructions will tell you when you will use this. Always keep the cover off.
- For best results, wait to start sautéing or browning until the display says Hot.

ALL FUNCTIONS

- Ingredients should be added in the order listed and as directed in the instructions.
- All ingredients must be added to the inner cooking pot, never directly into the cooker housing.
- Keep the steam release valve free of any obstructions. After use, make sure to clean the valve and screens.
- Keep your Instant Pot clear of any cupboards, to prevent damage from the steam release.
- Whenever you are opening the lid after cooking, tilt the lid away from you so you don't get scalded by escaping steam.
- Make sure the sealing ring inside the lid is correctly placed so that the pot has a tight seal. After many uses, you may want to replace the ring if it has lost some of its form or has picked up odors. Replace the sealing ring only with authorized Instant Pot rings.
- At altitudes above 3,000 feet (914 meters), recipes will require a change in cooking time or temperature, or both. Contact Instant Pot or refer to the manual that came with your Instant Pot to learn the adjustments needed for your altitude.

63

RECOMMENDED ACCESSORIES

Aside from your Instant Pot and some standard kitchen utensils, there are a few other kitchen gadgets that you will need (or will find handy) when preparing the recipes in this book.

- Large chef's knife
- Sieve or strainer
- Steamer basket
- Tall steam rack
- Electric mixer, either a stand mixer or a handheld mixer
- Food processor
- Immersion blender or stand blender
- Silicone egg bites molds or baby food serving storage rounds
- Ovenproof bakeware: a variety of small ramekins, casserole and soufflé dishes, a springform pan and Bundt or kugelhopf pan, and small or jumbo silicone baking cups
- Canning jars with lids (8 oz/250 mL)
- Instant-read thermometer
- Silicone sling
- Small silicone oven mitts
- Silicone-coated tongs.
- Kitchen gloves

QUICK TIPS FOR BEST RESULTS

- Use the manual included with your Instant Pot for a complete description of the control panel and all of the cooking programs, operation keys and indicators. The manufacturer is the expert on how to use its equipment for best results and safety.
- Measure ingredients carefully for optimal results.
- Follow the recipe steps exactly and in the order listed.
- Clean the cooker's inner pot, lid and housing according to the manufacturer's directions after each use.
- Clean the anti-block shield on the inside of the lid, the exhaust valve, the condensation collector and the sealing ring regularly to keep your cooker functioning properly.

Safety Note: As with any cooking appliance, parts of the Instant Pot will become very hot. Be careful when handling the inner pot and any bakeware or steaming inserts used for cooking, and always be very cautious when releasing the steam from the vent and when opening the lid.

INSTANT POT BONUSES

An Instant Pot offers many benefits to the home cook, but when it comes to ingredients, two bonuses in particular stand out:

1. You can often use tougher, and therefore less expensive, cuts of meat, and they will become fork-tender in your Instant Pot.
2. You can prepare beans, rice and stocks from scratch, without any processed ingredients.

Purées and Mashes

FIRST APPLES

MAKES 1 CUP (250 ML)

Puréed apples are an ideal first food for your baby because of their sweetness and relative mild flavor. This recipe can easily be doubled and individual servings frozen in ice cube trays or other small containers.

Steamer basket

Countertop blender

2 sweet apples (such as Gala, Golden and Red Delicious, or Honeycrisp), peeled, cored and coarsely chopped

2 tbsp (30 mL) pure unsweetened apple juice (approx.) (optional)

1. Add 1 cup (250 mL) water to the inner pot and place the steamer basket in the pot. Arrange apples in the basket.

2. Close and lock the lid and turn the steam release handle to Sealing. Set your Instant Pot to pressure cook on High for 2 minutes.

3. When the cooking time is done, press Cancel and turn the steam release handle to Venting. When the float valve drops down, remove the lid. The apples should be fork-tender. (If more cooking time is needed, continue pressure cooking on High for 0 minutes.) Reserve liquid in pot.

4. Transfer apples to a countertop blender. Add 2 tbsp (30 mL) reserved liquid. Cover and purée until smooth. Add additional reserved liquid or apple juice (if using), 2 tbsp (30 mL) at a time, until desired consistency.

5. Spoon a small amount into serving bowl. Test temperature before serving. Transfer remainder to ice cube trays.

TIPS

If doubling this recipe, transfer the apples, in batches, to the blender, filling the blender no more than halfway.

Apple purée can be refrigerated up to 3 days or frozen in airtight containers for up to 2 months.

NUTRITION TIPS

The vitamin C in apples will help your baby's body to absorb iron. So serve these apples with a side of fortified infant cereal or scrambled eggs as an iron-rich food.

The apple juice in this recipe is optional. However, constipation is common when starting solids, and a bit of juice can help!

If purées are too runny after freezing and thawing, add some dry infant cereal or mashed banana to thicken them up. If they are too thick, stir in a bit of pumped breast milk, formula or water.

FIRST CARROTS

MAKES 1 CUP (250 ML)

Fresh, sweet carrots with their bright orange color livens up just about any meal. This puréed version should put a little sunshine in your baby's tummy too.

Steamer basket

Countertop blender

7 medium carrots (about 1 bunch), peeled and cut into evenly sized chunks

1. Add 1 cup (250 mL) water to the inner pot and place the steamer basket in the pot (see tip). Arrange carrots in the basket.

2. Close and lock the lid and turn the steam release handle to Sealing. Set your Instant Pot to pressure cook on High for 8 minutes.

3. When the cooking time is done, press Cancel and turn the steam release handle to Venting. When the float valve drops down, remove the lid. The carrots should be tender. (If more cooking time is needed, continue pressure cooking on High for 0 minutes.) Reserve liquid in pot.

4. Transfer carrots to a countertop blender. Add 2 tbsp (30 mL) reserved liquid. Cover and purée until smooth. Add additional reserved liquid, 2 tbsp (30 mL) at a time, until desired consistency.

5. Spoon a small amount into serving bowl. Test temperature before serving. Transfer remainder to ice cube trays.

Variation

Once your baby has a pincer grasp, you can grate raw carrots with a cheese grater to serve!

TIPS

Choose medium carrots that are thin, with no white roots. Large, thick carrots can have a woody taste in the middle. Carrots that are growing white roots have been stored longer.

If your steamer basket doesn't have legs, place a steam rack in the pot first and place the steamer basket on the rack.

This recipe can easily be doubled and individual servings frozen in ice cube trays.

Pressure cooking on High for 0 minutes allows the steam and pressure to build up inside adding a slight more time to cooking without overcooking.

NUTRITION TIP

Have leftover carrot purée in the freezer once your baby has moved on to more complicated textures? Vegetable purées like this one make a great addition to pasta sauce, stew or soups!

FIRST SWEET PEAS

MAKES 1½ CUPS (375 ML)

Sweet peas are a great first food for your little one because of their bright green color and mild, sweet taste. They are also a great source of fiber, vitamins and minerals.

Steamer basket

Countertop blender

3 cups (750 mL) frozen sweet peas (about two 10 oz/300 g packages)

1. Add 1 cup (250 mL) water to the inner pot and place the steamer basket in the pot (see tip). Arrange peas in the basket.

2. Close and lock the lid and turn the steam release handle to Sealing. Set your Instant Pot to pressure cook on High for 3 minutes.

3. When the cooking time is done, press Cancel and turn the steam release handle to Venting. When the float valve drops down, remove the lid. The peas should be tender. (If more cooking time is needed, continue pressure cooking on High for 0 minutes.) Reserve liquid in pot.

4. Transfer peas to a countertop blender. Add 2 tbsp (30 mL) reserved liquid. Cover and purée until smooth. Add additional reserved liquid, 1 tbsp (15 mL) at a time, until desired consistency.

5. Spoon a small amount into serving bowl. Test temperature before serving. Transfer remainder to ice cube trays.

Variation

Omit step 4. Using a fork or potato masher, mash peas until desired consistency.

TIPS

You can use fresh peas in place of frozen. You will need about 2 lbs (1 kg) peas in the pod. Choose bright green peas that are in peak season for the best results.

If your steamer basket doesn't have legs, place a steam rack in the pot first and place the steamer basket on the rack.

Pea purée can be refrigerated for up to 3 days and frozen up to 2 months.

NUTRITION TIP

It's common to serve baby only veggies and fruits when starting out. They're easy and nutritious! But they don't contain enough calories and iron to be your baby's only food. Offer these peas with beans, meat or eggs to make it a balanced meal.

SWEET POTATO PURÉE

MAKES 1¾ CUPS (425 ML)

Sweet potatoes always seem to find a spot at the table, whether for a first baby food or a holiday feast. This sweet nutritious purée is wonderful alone or mix it with enriched cereal per our serving suggestion.

Steam rack

Countertop blender

3 medium sweet potatoes (about 1 lb/500 g), scrubbed and rinsed

1. Add 1 cup (250 mL) water to the inner pot and place the steam rack in the pot. Arrange sweet potatoes on the rack.

2. Close and lock the lid and turn the steam release handle to Sealing. Set your Instant Pot to pressure cook on High for 14 minutes.

3. When the cooking time is done, press Cancel and turn the steam release handle to Venting. When the float valve drops down, remove the lid. The sweet potatoes should be tender. (If more cooking time is needed, continue pressure cooking on High for 2 minutes.) Reserve liquid in pot.

4. Transfer sweet potatoes to a work surface and cut in half. Let stand until cool enough to handle. Using a metal spoon, scoop the flesh into a countertop blender. Discard skins. Cover and purée until smooth. Add reserved liquid, 1 tbsp (15 mL) at a time, if needed until desired consistency.

5. Spoon a small amount into serving bowl. Test temperature before serving. Transfer remainder to ice cube trays.

SERVING SUGGESTION

Combine 1 tbsp (15 mL) enriched baby cereal with formula or breast milk according to package directions. Stir mixture into ¼ cup (60 mL) purée.

TIPS

You can used frozen cubed sweet potatoes in place of whole. You will need 2 cups (500 g) frozen cubes. Reduce the cooking time to 6 minutes.

Sweet potato purée can be refrigerated for up to 3 days or frozen in airtight containers for up to 2 months.

NUTRITION TIP

Orange vegetables like sweet potato contain beta-carotene, which is partially converted to vitamin A in our bodies. Vitamin A is an antioxidant and important for eye health.

ACORN SQUASH PURÉE

MAKES 1½ CUPS (375 ML)

Acorn squash is the "little squash that could," with its abundance of vitamins and nutrients all packed into its orange-yellow flesh. From babies to adults, you can't go wrong adding this gourd to your diet.

Steam rack

Countertop blender

1 acorn squash (about 1 lb/500 g), seeded and cut into 6 wedges

1. Add 1 cup (250 mL) water to the inner pot and place the steam rack in the pot. Arrange wedges on the rack.

2. Close and lock the lid and turn the steam release handle to Sealing. Set your Instant Pot to pressure cook on High for 6 minutes.

3. When the cooking time is done, press Cancel and turn the steam release handle to Venting. When the float valve drops down, remove the lid. The squash and rind should be tender. (If more cooking time is needed, continue pressure cooking on High for 1 minute.) Reserve liquid in pot.

4. Transfer squash to a work surface. Let stand until cool enough to handle. Using a metal spoon, scoop the flesh into a countertop blender. Discard rind. Cover and purée until smooth. Add reserved liquid, 1 tbsp (15 mL) at a time, if needed until desired consistency.

5. Spoon a small amount into serving bowl. Test temperature before serving. Transfer remainder to ice cube trays.

TIPS

Choose squash that are firm and mostly dark green. The stem should be firmly attached with no soft spots around the base.

This recipe can easily be doubled and individual servings frozen in ice cube trays.

If doubling this recipe, transfer the squash in batches to the blender, filling the blender no more than halfway.

Acorn squash purée can be refrigerated up to 3 days or frozen in airtight containers for up to 2 months.

NUTRITION TIP

Acorn squash is a colorful vegetable that's high in vitamin C, an important nutrient to keep your baby's immune system strong and healthy.

SWEET POTATO PEACH PURÉE

MAKES 1½ CUPS (375 ML)

Sweet potatoes and peaches are a great first combination. Separately they are popular with babies and combined, the sweetness and bright colors make this one inviting dish.

Steamer basket

Countertop blender

3 medium sweet potatoes (about 1 lb/500 g), cleaned and scrubbed

2 peaches, flesh scored with an x

1. Add 1 cup (250 mL) water to the inner pot and place the steamer basket in the pot (see tip). Arrange sweet potatoes in the basket.

2. Close and lock the lid and turn the steam release handle to Sealing. Set your Instant Pot to pressure cook on High for 13 minutes.

3. When the cooking time is done, press Cancel and turn the steam release handle to Venting. When the float valve drops down, remove the lid. The sweet potato flesh should be tender. (If more cooking time is needed, continue pressure cooking on High for 2 minutes.) Discard liquid in pot.

4. Scoop out flesh from the sweet potatoes and discard skin. Transfer flesh to a countertop blender. Set aside.

5. Add 1 cup (250 mL) water to the inner pot and place the steamer basket in the pot. Arrange peaches in the basket.

6. Close and lock the lid and turn the steam release handle to Sealing. Set your Instant Pot to pressure cook on High for 3 minutes.

7. When the cooking time is done, press Cancel and turn the steam release handle to Venting. When the float valve drops down, remove the lid. Reserve liquid in pot.

8. Plunge peaches into cold water. When easy to handle, remove skin and discard. Pit peaches, carefully cutting out any course pieces, and cut into chunks. Transfer to the blender with the sweet potatoes. Add 2 tbsp (30 mL) reserved liquid. Cover and purée until smooth. Add additional reserved liquid, 2 tbsp (30 mL) at a time, until desired consistency.

9. Spoon a small amount into serving bowl. Test temperature before serving. Transfer remainder to ice cube trays.

NUTRITION TIP

Orange vegetables like sweet potato are very high in vitamin A. Vitamin A is important for immunity as well as healthy eyesight and bone growth in your baby.

APPLE AND PEAR BLEND

MAKES 2 CUPS (500 ML)

After your baby has become accustomed to single-fruit purées, you can begin to add more variety such as this apple and pear blend. Follow our suggestion for adding a little superfood to this combination.

Steam rack

Countertop blender

2 sweet apples (such as Gala, Golden and Red Delicious, or Honeycrisp)

2 firm pears

1. Add 1 cup (250 mL) water to the inner pot and place the steam rack in the pot. Arrange apples and pears on the rack.

2. Close and lock the lid and turn the steam release handle to Sealing. Set your Instant Pot to pressure cook on High for 4 minutes.

3. When the cooking time is done, press Cancel and turn the steam release handle to Venting. When the float valve drops down, remove the lid. The apples and pears should be tender and pierce easily with a fork. (If more cooking time is needed, continue pressure cooking on High for 0 minute.) Reserve liquid in pot.

4. Transfer apples and pears to a work surface. Let stand until cool enough to handle. Peel and core fruits; scraping flesh into the blender. Cover and purée until smooth. Add reserved liquid, 1 tbsp (15 mL) at a time, if needed until desired consistency.

5. Spoon a small amount into serving bowl. Test temperature before serving. Transfer remainder to ice cube trays.

SERVING SUGGESTION

Add 2 tsp (10 mL) chia seeds to the blender in step 4 and purée with the fruits for a super-powered pudding-like blend.

NUTRITION TIP

Both apples and pears are high in sorbitol, a type of sugar that helps draw water into the bowels. They can help if your baby is backed up, a common occurrence after starting solids.

APPLES AND APRICOTS

MAKES 1½ CUPS (375 ML)

This apple and apricot purée is naturally sweet, smooth and delicious. The optional nutmeg is a great way to introduce your baby to different tastes and seasoning. Give it an added boost of enriched baby cereal and the vitamins from the fruit will assist with iron absorption from the cereal.

Steam rack

Countertop blender

1 sweet apple (such as Gala, Golden and Red Delicious, or Honeycrisp), peeled and cored

2 apricots, peeled, halved and pitted

Nutmeg (optional)

1. Add 1 cup (250 mL) water to the inner pot and place the steam rack in the pot. Arrange apples and apricots on the rack.

2. Close and lock the lid and turn the steam release handle to Sealing. Set your Instant Pot to pressure cook on High for 3 minutes.

3. When the cooking time is done, press Cancel and turn the steam release handle to Venting. When the float valve drops down, remove the lid. The apples and apricots should be tender and pierce easily with a fork. (If more cooking time is needed, continue pressure cooking on High for 0 minute.) Reserve liquid in pot.

4. Transfer apples and apricots into the blender. Cover and purée until smooth. Add reserved liquid, 1 tbsp (15 mL) at a time, if needed until desired consistency.

5. Spoon a small amount into serving bowl. Stir in a pinch of nutmeg (if using). Test temperature before serving. Transfer remainder to ice cube trays.

SERVING SUGGESTION

Combine 1 tbsp (15 mL) enriched baby cereal with formula or breast milk according to package directions. Stir mixture into ¼ cup (60 mL) purée.

Variation

LITTLE DIPPERS APRICOTS AND APPLES: Before starting step 4, reserve one quarter of a cooked apple. Using a mandoline, cut apple into thin slices and set aside. Continue with step 4. Serve apple slices with purée for little dippers.

NUTRITION TIP

The variations for this recipe can be translated to most other purées. Adding in the infant cereal powder boosts essential iron. And serving purée as a "dip" for a finger food can help your baby practice and improve their dexterity!

BANANA PEACH RASPBERRY

MAKES 1½ CUPS (375 ML)

This powerhouse blend of delicately sweet and nutritious fruits and berries will be a hit with your little one. The banana adds a smoothie-like texture to this meal.

Steam rack

Countertop blender

2 peaches, peeled, halved and pitted

1 banana, peeled and cut in half

¼ cup (60 mL) raspberries

1. Add 1 cup (250 mL) water to the inner pot and place the steam rack in the pot. Arrange peaches on the rack.

2. Close and lock the lid and turn the steam release handle to Sealing. Set your Instant Pot to pressure cook on High for 3 minutes.

3. When the cooking time is done, press Cancel and turn the steam release handle to Venting. When the float valve drops down, remove the lid. The peaches should be tender. (If more cooking time is needed, continue pressure cooking on High for 0 minute.) Reserve liquid in pot.

4. Transfer peaches into the blender. Add banana and raspberries. Cover and purée until smooth. Add reserved liquid, 1 tbsp (15 mL) at a time, if needed until desired consistency.

5. Spoon a small amount into serving bowl. Test temperature before serving. Transfer remainder to ice cube trays.

TIPS

Replace the raspberries with the same quantity of blueberries or cored and sliced strawberries.

Purée can be refrigerated in airtight containers for up to 3 days and frozen for up to 2 months.

NUTRITION TIP

This delicious recipe would also make a great topping for pancakes, waffles or oatmeal. Or stir it into some plain yogurt for baby — and yourself!

PEACH OATMEAL BANANA

MAKES 2 CUPS (500 ML)

This delicious dish combines the sweetness of peaches, the smooth texture of banana and fiber-loaded oatmeal for a tasty and nutritious meal.

Steamer basket

Countertop blender

2 peaches, flesh scored with an x

1 banana, peeled and halved

¼ cup (60 mL) baby oatmeal cereal

Formula or breast milk (about 1 cup/250 mL)

1. Add 1 cup (250 mL) water to the inner pot and place the steamer basket in the pot. Arrange peaches in the basket.

2. Close and lock the lid and turn the steam release handle to Sealing. Set your Instant Pot to pressure cook on High for 3 minutes.

3. When the cooking time is done, press Cancel and turn the steam release handle to Venting. When the float valve drops down, remove the lid. Reserve liquid in pot.

4. Plunge peaches into cold water. When easy to handle, remove skin and discard. Pit peaches, carefully cutting out any coarse pieces, and cut into chunks. Transfer to the blender with the banana. Add 1 tbsp (15 mL) reserved liquid. Cover and purée until smooth. Add additional reserved liquid, 1 tbsp (30 mL) at a time, until desired consistency.

5. In a medium bowl add cereal. Stir in formula, according to package directions and until desired consistency. Stir in peach banana purée.

6. Spoon a small amount into serving bowl. Test temperature before serving. Transfer remainder to ice cube trays.

TIPS

After baby is used to this combination, add a pinch of cinnamon or nutmeg to individual servings.

Purée can be refrigerated in airtight containers for up to 3 days and frozen for up to 2 months.

NUTRITION TIP

By adding pumped breast milk or formula to this recipe, you are adding in more nutrition compared to mixing with just plain water. The final recipe will also have a slightly familiar taste to your baby!

TROPICAL FRUIT OATMEAL

MAKES ABOUT 2½ CUPS (625 ML)

Oatmeal provides a great start to the morning. When warm and filling oatmeal is combined with coconut and mango, you can almost envision yourself in the tropics.

4-cup (1 L) heatproof bowl

Steam rack

3 tbsp (45 mL) unsweetened coconut flakes

⅔ cup (150 mL) large-flake (old-fashioned) rolled oats

Pinch salt

1⅓ cup (150 mL) unsweetened coconut milk

½ cup (2 mL) butter

⅔ cup (150 mL) mango chunks

Granulated or coconut sugar (optional)

1. Set your Instant Pot to sauté on More. Add the coconut and cook, stirring, 2 minutes or until lightly toasted. Transfer to a small plate and set aside. Press Cancel.

2. In the heatproof bowl, combine oats, salt, coconut milk and butter.

3. Add 2 cups (500 mL) water to the inner pot and place the steam rack in the pot. Place the bowl on the rack.

4. Close and lock the lid and turn the steam release handle to Sealing. Set your Instant Pot to pressure cook on High for 7 minutes.

5. When the cooking time is done, press Cancel and let stand, covered, until the float valve drops down, then remove the lid. The oatmeal should be creamy. (If more cooking time is needed, continue pressure cooking on High for 1 minute, then quickly release the pressure.)

6. Using the handles of the rack, carefully remove the rack and bowl. Stir oats and serve immediately. For babies and toddlers, test temperature before serving.

Variations

Use fresh, frozen or canned pineapple chunks in place of the mango. If using frozen, thaw before using. If canned, use pineapple in its own juice, not canned in syrup.

TIP

You can use fresh or frozen mango chunks. If using frozen, thaw before using.

NUTRITION TIP

The mangos in this recipe are a delicious source of vitamin C and fiber. With the fat from coconut milk and whole grains from oats, this recipe is a well-balanced and delicious way to start your day!

APPLES AND BLUEBERRIES

MAKES 1½ CUPS (375 ML)

Since baby has become accustomed to puréed apples, this is a wonderful way to introduce a new combination. Superfood blueberries add a bright purple hue to this dish.

Steamer basket

Countertop blender

2 sweet apples (such as Gala, Golden and Red Delicious, or Honeycrisp), peeled, cored and coarsely chopped

1 cup (250 mL) blueberries

1. Add 1 cup (250 mL) water to the inner pot and place the steamer basket in the pot (see tip). Arrange apples in the basket.

2. Close and lock the lid and turn the steam release handle to Sealing. Set your Instant Pot to pressure cook on High for 2 minutes.

3. When the cooking time is done, press Cancel and turn the steam release handle to Venting. When the float valve drops down, remove the lid. The apples should be fork-tender. (If more cooking time is needed, continue pressure cooking on High for 0 minutes.) Reserve liquid in pot.

4. Transfer apples to a countertop blender. Add blueberries and 1 tbsp (15 mL) reserved liquid. Cover and purée until smooth. Add additional reserved liquid, 1 tbsp (15 mL) at a time, until desired consistency.

5. Spoon a small amount into serving bowl. Test temperature before serving. Transfer remainder to ice cube trays.

Variation

In step 4, transfer small chunks of apples to a plate. Add enriched baby cereal to apples, rolling to coat. Serve coated apples alongside the purée.

TIPS

Apples should be fully ripened.

If your steamer basket doesn't have legs, place a steam rack in the pot first and place the steamer basket on the rack.

Apple blueberry purée can be refrigerated up to 3 days or frozen in airtight containers for up to 2 months.

Pressure cooking on High for 0 minutes allows the steam and pressure to build up inside adding a slight more time to cooking without overcooking.

NUTRITION TIP

Blueberries are very high in antioxidants, such as anthocyanins. These antioxidants give berries their deep color and are linked to increased brain function!

APPLE PUMPKIN CARROTS

MAKES 3 CUPS (750 ML)

This bright orange medley of apples, pumpkin and carrots is loaded with all the nutrients and flavor that orange fruits and veggies provide. The pie pumpkin makes enough that there will be leftover pumpkin purée for other recipes.

Steam rack

Steamer basket

Food processor

Strainer

1 small (3 lbs/1.5 kg) pie pumpkin, seeded and cut into 6 wedges (see tips)

2 sweet apples (such as Gala, Golden and Red Delicious, or Honeycrisp), peeled, cored and coarsely chopped

3 medium carrots, peeled and cut into evenly sized chunks

1. Add 1 cup (250 mL) water to the inner pot and place the steam rack in the pot. Arrange pumpkin wedges on the rack. Place steam basket on top of the pumpkin. Place carrots in the basket.

2. Close and lock the lid and turn the steam release handle to Sealing. Set your Instant Pot to pressure cook on High for 9 minutes.

3. When the cooking time is done, press Cancel and turn the steam release handle to Venting. When the float valve drops down, remove the lid. The pumpkin and carrots should be tender. (If more cooking time is needed, continue pressure cooking on High for 1 minute.) Reserve liquid in pot.

4. Remove basket with the carrots and set aside.

5. Remove pumpkin wedges and let stand until cool enough to handle. Scoop pumpkin into food processor and process until smooth. Spoon pumpkin mixture into a strainer set over a bowl. Let drain and reserve liquid.

6. Meanwhile, transfer apples to the steamer basket and place in the pot.

7. Close and lock the lid and turn the steam release handle to Sealing. Set your Instant Pot to pressure cook on High for 2 minutes.

8. When the cooking time is done, press Cancel and turn the steam release handle to Venting. When the float valve drops down, remove the lid.

9. Transfer apples, carrots and 1 cup (250 mL) pumpkin purée to the food processor. Add 1 tbsp (15 mL) reserved pumpkin juice and process until desired consistency.

10. Transfer remaining pumpkin purée into measured storage containers (see tip).

11. Spoon a small amount of the apple, pumpkin, carrot medley into serving bowl. Test temperature before serving. Transfer remainder to ice cube trays.

PEACHES AND PLUMS

MAKES 2 CUPS (500 ML)

This fruity and colorful duo of peaches and plums is combined with enriched rice cereal for a balanced and healthy blend.

Steamer basket

Countertop blender

2 peaches, flesh scored with an x

2 plums, flesh scored with an x

¼ cup (60 mL) baby brown rice cereal

Formula or breast milk (about 1 cup/250 mL)

1. Add 1 cup (250 mL) water to the inner pot and place the steamer basket in the pot. Arrange peaches and plums in the basket.

2. Close and lock the lid and turn the steam release handle to Sealing. Set your Instant Pot to pressure cook on High for 3 minutes.

3. When the cooking time is done, press Cancel and turn the steam release handle to Venting. When the float valve drops down, remove the lid. Reserve liquid in pot.

4. Plunge peaches and plums into cold water. When easy to handle, remove skin and discard. Pit peaches and plums, carefully cutting out any coarse pieces. Transfer to the blender. Add 1 tbsp (15 mL) reserved liquid. Cover and purée until smooth. Add additional reserved liquid, 1 tbsp (30 mL) at a time, until desired consistency.

5. In a medium bowl add cereal. Stir in formula, according to package directions and until desired consistency. Stir in peach plum purée.

6. Spoon a small amount into serving bowl. Test temperature before serving. Transfer remainder to ice cube trays.

Variation

Replace plums or peaches with 2 pears that are halved and seeded.

TIPS

After baby is used to this combination, add a pinch of cinnamon or nutmeg to individual servings.

Purée can be refrigerated in airtight containers for up to 3 days.

NUTRITION TIP

Fruit purée is a great addition to naturally flavored plain yogurt. You add a bit of sweetness plus nutrition with the fruit, without the added sugar of sweetened yogurts.

PEAR, BLUEBERRY AND BANANA MEDLEY

MAKES 2 CUPS (500 ML)

Here is baby's version of a superfood smoothie. This one looks and tastes so fabulous that you may even want to make one for yourself!

Steamer basket
Countertop blender

2 pears, peeled, halved and seeded
½ cup (125 mL) blueberries
1 banana

1. Add 1 cup (250 mL) water to the inner pot and place the steamer basket in the pot. Arrange pears in the basket.

2. Close and lock the lid and turn the steam release handle to Sealing. Set your Instant Pot to pressure cook on High for 3 minutes.

3. When the cooking time is done, press Cancel and turn the steam release handle to Venting. When the float valve drops down, remove the lid. Reserve liquid in pot.

4. Transfer to the blender. Add blueberries and banana. Add 1 tbsp (15 mL) reserved liquid. Cover and purée until smooth. Add additional reserved liquid, 1 tbsp (30 mL) at a time, until desired consistency.

5. Spoon a small amount into serving bowl. Test temperature before serving. Transfer remainder to ice cube trays.

TIPS

After baby is used to this combination, add a pinch of turmeric to individual servings.

Purée can be refrigerated in airtight containers for up to 3 days or frozen for up to 2 months.

Frozen mini-sized cubes are great for a teething baby, served in a mesh feeder bag.

NUTRITION TIP

By making your baby's own purées, you can choose more exciting flavor combinations without any of the added preservatives you will find in some store-bought baby food.

APPLES AND PRUNES

MAKES 1 CUP (250 ML)

This royal purple blend of fruits is sweet and a great addition to baby's diet to help prevent or ease constipation.

Steamer basket

Countertop blender

1 sweet apple (such as Gala, Golden and Red Delicious, or Honeycrisp), peeled and cored

2 prunes, pitted

Nutmeg (optional)

1. Add 1 cup (250 mL) water to the inner pot and place the steamer basket in the pot. Arrange apples and prunes in the basket.

2. Close and lock the lid and turn the steam release handle to Sealing. Set your Instant Pot to pressure cook on High for 3 minutes.

3. When the cooking time is done, press Cancel and turn the steam release handle to Venting. When the float valve drops down, remove the lid. The apples and prunes should be tender and pierce easily with a fork. (If more cooking time is needed, continue pressure cooking on High for 0 minute.) Reserve liquid in pot.

4. Transfer apples and prunes into the blender. Cover and purée until smooth. Add reserved liquid, 1 tbsp (15 mL) at a time, if needed until desired consistency.

5. Spoon a small amount into serving bowl. Test temperature before serving. Transfer remainder to ice cube trays.

SERVING SUGGESTION
Combine 1 tbsp (15 mL) enriched baby rice cereal with formula or breast milk according to package directions. Stir mixture into $\frac{1}{4}$ cup (60 mL) purée.

TIPS

If your steamer basket doesn't have legs, place a steam rack in the pot first and place the steamer basket on the rack.

If doubling this recipe, transfer the apples and prunes, in batches, to the blender, filling the blender no more than halfway.

Apple prune purée can be refrigerated up to 3 days or frozen in airtight containers for up to 2 months.

NUTRITION TIP

If your baby struggles with constipation after starting solids, this will become a favorite recipe to feed to your baby often. Both prunes and apples are great natural laxatives! If the purée is thick, you can even spread it on toast like a jam.

PLUMS, BEETS AND AVOCADO BLEND

MAKES 1½ CUPS (375 ML)

Beets are a nutritional powerhouse and this purée is a great way to introduce your baby to this wonderful ruby delight. Combine beets with plums and avocados and you have a nutrient-rich meal.

Steam rack

Countertop blender

2 medium beets, cleaned and scrubbed

2 plums, peeled and pitted

1 avocado, halved and pitted

1. Add 1 cup (250 mL) water to the inner pot and place the steam rack in the pot. Arrange beets on the rack.

2. Close and lock the lid and turn the steam release handle to Sealing. Set your Instant Pot to pressure cook on High for 25 minutes.

3. When the cooking time is done, press Cancel and turn the steam release handle to Venting. When the float valve drops down, remove the lid. The beets should be tender with the skin loosening. (If more cooking time is needed, continue pressure cooking on High for 4 minutes.) Plunge beets into cold water. Remove skins and discard. Cut beets into wedges.

4. Transfer beets to the blender. Add plums and avocado to the beets. Cover and purée until smooth.

5. Spoon a small amount into serving bowl. Test temperature before serving. Transfer remainder to ice cube trays.

TIPS

Wear disposable kitchen gloves when handling beets to prevent them from staining your hands.

Choose plums that are firm and feel heavy for their size. Any variety of plums will work.

Purée can be refrigerated in airtight containers for up to 2 days and frozen in individual portions for up to 3 months.

NUTRITION TIP

Did you know that avocado is technically a fruit? And it's the only fruit to contain healthy monounsaturated fat. Avocados are a great soft first finger food for baby, too. Try thin slices of avocado rolled in fortified infant cereal for a source of added iron and to make it less slippery to hold!

BARLEY AND APPLE CEREAL

MAKES ABOUT 2½ CUPS (625 ML)

Cereal and apples are among the preferred starters for your baby, as they are easy to introduce. You may have started with oatmeal or rice cereals, but give barley a try, too. Barley is loaded with important nutrients like iron and selenium.

Countertop blender

2 cups (500 mL) water (approx.)

1 cup (250 mL) dry pot barley

½ apple, peeled, cored and chopped (about 6 tbsp/90 mL)

1 tsp (5 mL) ground cinnamon (optional)

Water, breast milk or formula

1. In the inner pot, combine water and barley.

2. Close and lock the lid and turn the steam release handle to Sealing. Set your Instant Pot to pressure cook on High for 27 minutes.

3. When the cooking time is done, press Cancel and turn the steam release handle to Venting. When the float valve drops down, remove the lid. Add the apples and cinnamon (if using).

4. Close and lock the lid and turn the steam release handle to Sealing. Set your Instant Pot to pressure cook on High for 2 minutes. When the cooking time is done, press Cancel and turn the steam release handle to Venting. When the float valve drops down, remove the lid. The mixture should be tender and most of the liquid absorbed. If more cooking time is needed, set your Instant Pot to sauté on Low and cook, stirring, until the mixture is tender and most of the liquid is absorbed.

5. Transfer the cereal, in batches, to a countertop blender, filling the blender no more than halfway. Cover and purée until smooth. Add water, 2 tbsp (30 mL) at a time, stirring until desired consistency.

6. Spoon a small amount into serving bowl. Test temperature before serving. Transfer leftovers to small containers.

TIPS

Leftover barley can be stored in an airtight container in the refrigerator up to 2 days. Reheat on the stovetop, stirring in additional water as needed.

NUTRITION TIP

Whole grains such as barley are rich in fiber and nutrients not found in refined grains. This is because refined grains such as white rice, pasta or bread have the germ and the bran of the grain removed. The germ and the bran are where the fiber and nutrients such as magnesium and B vitamins are found!

PEAR AND SPINACH PURÉE

MAKES 1 CUP (250 ML)

Babies love their puréed pears, so this is a great way to introduce leafy greens into their diet.

Steamer basket
Countertop blender

1 pear, peeled, halved and cored
1 cup (250 mL) lightly packed spinach leaves

1. Add 1 cup (250 mL) water to the inner pot and place the steamer basket in the pot. Arrange pears in the basket and add spinach to the top.

2. Close and lock the lid and turn the steam release handle to Sealing. Set your Instant Pot to pressure cook on High for 2 minutes.

3. When the cooking time is done, press Cancel and turn the steam release handle to Venting. When the float valve drops down, remove the lid. The spinach should be wilted and the pears should be tender. (If more cooking time is needed for the pears, transfer the spinach to the blender and continue pressure cooking pears on High for 1 minute.) Reserve liquid.

4. Transfer spinach and pears to the blender. Cover and purée until smooth. Add reserved liquid, 1 tbsp (15 mL) at a time, stirring until desired consistency.

5. Spoon a small amount into serving bowl. Test temperature before serving. Transfer remainder to ice cube trays.

Variations

Stir in a pinch of turmeric in step 5 for an added boost of nutrients.

Before step 4, set aside a small portion of pears and cut into small chunks. Serve alongside purée for baby to eat with the blend.

TIP

Purée can be refrigerated in airtight containers for up to 2 days and frozen in individual portions for up to 3 months.

NUTRITION TIPS

The darker the color of the produce, the more nutrient dense! For example, spinach contains far more nutrients (such as folic acid) than romaine or iceberg lettuce. Purées or smoothies are a good way to add spinach into your baby's diet.

89

SWEET POTATOES, BEETS AND CUMIN

MAKES 1½ CUPS (375 ML)

This nutrient-packed meal is a good way to introduce baby to beets and new seasoning. Experimenting with these early helps baby to expand their palate.

Steam rack

Countertop blender

2 small beets, stem trimmed to 1 inch (2.5 cm) and scrubbed

1 medium sweet potato, scrubbed

Cumin

1. Add 1 cup (250 mL) water to the inner pot and place the steam rack in the pot. Arrange the beets and sweet potato on the rack.

2. Close and lock the lid and turn the steam release handle to Sealing. Set your Instant Pot to pressure cook on High for 12 minutes.

3. When the cooking time is done, press Cancel and turn the steam release handle to Venting. When the float valve drops down, remove the lid. The beets and sweet potatoes should be tender. (If more cooking time is needed, continue pressure cooking on High for 2 minutes.) Plunge beets into cold water. Remove stem and skins; discard. Cut beets into wedges. Cut sweet potato in half and scoop flesh into the blender.

4. Transfer beets to the blender with the sweet potatoes. Cover and purée until smooth.

5. Spoon a small amount into serving bowl. Stir in a pinch of cumin. Test temperature before serving. Transfer remainder to ice cube trays.

TIPS

Wear disposable kitchen gloves when handling beets to prevent them from staining your hands.

If you want to introduce vegetables without the seasoning, serve this purée one or more times without the cumin and then introduce the cumin to the mixture.

Purée can be refrigerated in airtight containers for up to 3 days and frozen in individual portions for up to 2 months.

NUTRITION TIP

Beets are a good source of folate and potassium. Just make sure baby is wearing a good bib for this meal or it might ruin their shirt!

BUTTERNUT SQUASH AND MINTY QUINOA

MAKES 3 CUPS (750 ML)

Butternut squash is a favorite among little ones. Quinoa adds texture and nutrients to this dish. Mint adds a new taste to baby's diet while adding nutritional benefits.

Steam rack

Countertop blender

1 butternut squash (about 2½ to 3 lbs/1.25 to 1.5 kg), seeded and sliced

Fresh mint leaves

2 tsp (10 mL) vegetable oil

1 cup (250 mL) quinoa, rinsed and well drained

1. Add 1 cup (250 mL) water to the inner pot and place the steam rack in the pot. Arrange squash slices on the rack.

2. Close and lock the lid and turn the steam release handle to Sealing. Set your Instant Pot to pressure cook on High for 5 minutes.

3. When the cooking time is done, press Cancel and turn the steam release handle to Venting. When the float valve drops down, remove the lid. The squash should be tender. Reserve liquid in pot.

4. When cool enough to handle, scoop flesh into blender and discard skins. Add 1 mint leaf, or to taste. Cover and purée until smooth. Add reserved liquid, 1 tbsp (15 mL) at a time, and purée until desired consistency. Set aside.

5. Discard remaining liquid and wipe out pot until dry.

6. Set your Instant Pot to sauté on Normal. When the display says Hot, add oil and heat until shimmering. Add quinoa and cook, stirring, for 2 to 3 minutes or until lightly toasted and fragrant. Press Cancel. Add 11/2 cups (375 mL) water, stirring well.

7. Close and lock the lid and turn the steam release handle to Sealing. Set your Instant Pot to pressure cook on High for 2 minutes.

8. When the cooking time is done, press Cancel and let stand, covered, for 10 minutes, then turn the steam release handle to Venting. When the float valve drops down, remove the lid. The quinoa should be tender.

9. Fluff quinoa with a fork. Spoon a small amount into serving bowl. Stir in butternut squash purée until desired consistency. Test temperature before serving.

10. Transfer remaining butternut squash and quinoa to separate storage containers.

NUTRITION TIP

Mixing quinoa into a purée is a great texture progression from smooth purées.

SUMMER VEGETABLE DINNER

MAKES 1½ CUPS (375 ML)

The abundance of fresh summer produce is the perfect time to introduce your little one to new tastes and textures. The farmer's market, home gardens and grocery stores will bring fresh-off-the vine nutrients to this dinner.

Steamer basket

Countertop blender

1 zucchini, cut into chunks

8 oz (250 g) green beans, ends trimmed

¼ cup (60 mL) chopped bell pepper (optional)

Unsweetened pure apple juice

1. Add 1 cup (250 mL) water to the inner pot and place the steamer basket in the pot (see tip). Arrange zucchini, green beans and bell pepper (if using) in the basket.

2. Close and lock the lid and turn the steam release handle to Sealing. Set your Instant Pot to pressure cook on High for 3 minutes.

3. When the cooking time is done, press Cancel and turn the steam release handle to Venting. When the float valve drops down, remove the lid. The zucchini, bean and peppers should be tender. (If more cooking time is needed, continue pressure cooking on High for 0 minutes.) Reserve liquid in pot.

4. Transfer zucchini, beans and bell pepper to the blender. Add 2 tbsp (30 mL) reserved liquid. Cover and purée until smooth. Add apple juice, 1 tbsp (15 mL) at a time, until desired consistency.

5. Spoon a small amount into serving bowl. Test temperature before serving. Transfer remainder to ice cube trays.

93

TIPS

You may want to try the zucchini and green bean mixture by itself with your baby until they are used to the flavors before introducing the bell pepper.

If your steamer basket doesn't have legs, place a steam rack in the pot first and place the steamer basket on the rack.

Purée can be refrigerated in airtight containers for up to 3 days and frozen for up to 2 months.

NUTRITION TIP

Fresh zucchini is a great starter finger food, too. Slice it thinly using a mandoline or knife and offer your baby a "potato chip" shape piece either raw or steamed. Offer a slice along with the purée, for some practice picking up food, getting it to the mouth and chewing.

SWEET POTATO AND CHICKEN

MAKES ABOUT 1½ CUPS (375 ML)

The sweetness of sweet potatoes and their early introduction into your baby's diet make for a wonderful first combination with chicken.

Countertop blender

1 tbsp (15 mL) vegetable oil

4 oz (125 g) chicken breast, cut into cubes

1 medium sweet potato, peeled and cubed

1 cup (250 mL) No-Salt-Added Chicken Stock (page 210) or ready-to-use no-salt-added chicken broth

¾ tsp (3 mL) ground ginger

1. Set your Instant Pot to sauté on Normal. When the display says Hot, add oil and heat until shimmering. Add chicken breast cubes and cook, stirring often, for 4 minutes or until browned. Stir in sweet potato, chicken stock and ginger. Press Cancel.

2. Close and lock the lid and turn the steam release handle to Sealing. Set your Instant Pot to pressure cook on High for 4 minutes.

3. When the cooking time is done, press Cancel and turn the steam release handle to Venting. When the float valve drops down, remove the lid. The chicken and sweet potatoes should be tender. (If more cooking time is needed, continue pressure cooking on High for 0 minutes.)

4. Using a slotted spoon, transfer chicken and sweet potatoes to the blender. Add 3 tbsp (45 mL) stock from the pot. Cover and purée until smooth. Continue adding stock, 1 tbsp (15 mL) at a time, until desired consistency.

5. Spoon a small amount into serving bowl. Test temperature before serving. Transfer remainder to ice cube trays.

TIPS

Before step 5, set aside a small portion of chicken and sweet potatoes and cut into small chunks. Serve alongside purée for baby to eat with the blend.

Purée can be refrigerated in airtight containers for up to 3 days and frozen for up to 2 months.

NUTRITION TIP

It's a myth that babies can't eat or digest meat right from 6 months of age when they start solids. In fact, meat is my favorite starter food for babies. It's high in absorbable iron, which is the most important nutrient for your baby to get from food at this stage.

TURKEY AND VEGETABLE DINNER

MAKES ABOUT 2 CUPS (500 ML)

Get your little one ready to enjoy holiday feasts with the flavors of turkey, potatoes and green beans.

Countertop blender

1 tbsp (15 mL) vegetable oil

4 oz (125 g) ground turkey

3 gold-skinned potatoes (such as Yukon gold), peeled and cubed

¾ cup (175 mL) halved green beans, trimmed

1 cup (250 mL) No-Salt-Added Chicken Stock (page 210) or ready-to-use low-sodium chicken broth

2 tsp (10 mL) onion flakes

1. Set your Instant Pot to sauté on Normal. When the display says Hot, add oil and heat until shimmering. Add turkey and cook, breaking up pieces and stirring, for 5 minutes or until no longer pink. Stir in potatoes, green beans, chicken stock and onion flakes. Press Cancel.

2. Close and lock the lid and turn the steam release handle to Sealing. Set your Instant Pot to pressure cook on High for 3 minutes.

3. When the cooking time is done, press Cancel and turn the steam release handle to Venting. When the float valve drops down, remove the lid. The potatoes and green beans should be tender. (If more cooking time is needed, continue pressure cooking on High for 0 minutes.)

4. Using a slotted spoon, transfer turkey, potatoes and beans to the blender. Add ¼ cup (60 mL) stock from the pot. Cover and purée until smooth. Continue adding stock, 1 tbsp (15 mL) at a time, until desired consistency.

5. Spoon a small amount into serving bowl. Test temperature before serving. Transfer remainder to ice cube trays.

95

TIPS

Before step 5, set aside a small portion of the mixture, cutting potatoes and beans into smaller chunks. Serve alongside purée for baby to eat with the blend.

For babies weaned from purées, omit blending and cut potatoes and beans into smaller chunks, or mash turkey, potatoes and beans to desired consistency.

NUTRITION TIP

Your baby loves to be included at the table in family meals. There are many benefits, even from a young age. Your baby can experience conversation, and watching you eat teaches them how to feed themselves!

TOMATO, RICE AND LENTIL FEAST

MAKES ABOUT 2 CUPS (500 ML)

In this recipe, hearty brown rice and lentils are paired with tomatoes and brightened with garlic and spice.

Countertop blender

2 tsp (10 mL) vegetable oil

1 clove garlic, minced

6 tbsp (90 mL) brown rice, rinsed

6 tbsp (90 mL) brown lentils, picked over and rinsed

1¼ cups (300 mL) No-Salt-Added Vegetable Stock (page 211) or ready-to-use no-salt-added vegetable broth

1 can (14 to 19 oz/398 to 540 mL) peeled and diced tomatoes

1 tsp (5 mL) ground cumin

1. Set your Instant Pot to sauté on Normal. When the display says Hot, add oil and heat until shimmering. Add garlic and cook, stirring, for 1 minute or until fragrant. Stir in rice, lentils, stock, tomatoes and cumin. Press Cancel.

2. Close and lock the lid and turn the steam release handle to Sealing. Set your Instant Pot to pressure cook on High for 15 minutes.

3. When the cooking time is done, press Cancel and let stand 10 minutes and then turn the steam release handle to Venting. When the float valve drops down, remove the lid. The rice, lentils and tomatoes should be tender. (If more cooking time is needed, continue pressure cooking on High for 2 minutes then quickly release pressure.)

4. Using a slotted spoon, transfer mixture to the blender. Add ¼ cup (60 mL) liquid from the pot. Cover and purée until smooth. Continue adding liquid, 1 tbsp (15 mL) at a time, until desired consistency.

5. Spoon a small amount into serving bowl. Test temperature before serving. Transfer remainder to ice cube trays.

TIPS

Before step 5, set aside a small portion of the mixture and mash with a fork. Stir mixture into the purée.

For babies weaned from purées, omit blending in step 5. Mixture can then be mashed or served as is.

NUTRITION TIP

This is a great combination, not only of tastes, but nutrients too! The vitamin C from the tomatoes will help your baby absorb the iron from the lentils.

CREAMED CAULIFLOWER SPINACH

MAKES ABOUT 2 CUPS (500 ML)

Steamed and blended cauliflower with a hint of garlic makes the ideal nutrient-rich cream sauce for the steamed spinach.

Steamer basket

Countertop blender

2 tsp (10 mL) butter

1 clove garlic, minced

2 cups (500 mL) cauliflower florets, chopped

2 cups (500 mL) No-Salt-Added Vegetable Stock (page 211) or ready-to-use no-salt-added vegetable broth

1 cup (250 mL) packed spinach leaves

3 tbsp (45 mL) formula or breast milk

1. Set your Instant Pot to sauté on Normal. When the display says Hot, add butter and heat until melted. Add garlic and cook, stirring, for 1 minute or until fragrant. Stir in stock. Press Cancel. Add the steamer basket to the pot. Arrange the cauliflower in the basket. Place the spinach on top.

2. Close and lock the lid and turn the steam release handle to Sealing. Set your Instant Pot to pressure cook on High for 2 minutes.

3. When the cooking time is done, press Cancel and turn the steam release handle to Venting. When the float valve drops down, remove the lid. The cauliflower should be tender. (If more cooking time is needed for the cauliflower, continue pressure cooking on High for 0 minutes.) Reserve liquid.

4. Transfer spinach, cauliflower and $\frac{1}{2}$ cup (125 mL) liquid to the blender. Cover and purée until smooth. Add formula, 1 tbsp (15 mL) at a time, stirring until desired consistency.

5. Spoon a small amount into serving bowl. Test temperature before serving. Transfer remainder to ice cube trays and refrigerate up to 2 days or freeze for up to 3 months.

Variation

Substitute torn Swiss chard leaves, with stems removed, for the spinach.

NUTRITION TIPS

Cauliflower is a cruciferous vegetable, along with brussel sprouts, cabbage and broccoli. While these vegetables are delicious and nutritious, they are more difficult for some of us to digest. If your baby seems to have an upset tummy after eating cruciferous vegetables, try to offer a smaller portion size. Cooked versions of these vegetables will also be easier to digest than raw.

Cow's milk can be substituted for the formula or pumped breast milk. While your baby can't have cow's milk as their main source of milk until closer to a year of age, small amounts in mixed dishes are fine from age 6 months and up.

SUMMER SQUASH, PEARS, CARROTS AND CHIA

MAKES ABOUT 2 CUPS (500 ML)

This introduction to yellow summer squash and chia seeds is balanced by the sweet and already familiar flavors of pears and carrots.

Steamer basket

Countertop blender

2 medium carrots, peeled and cut into evenly sized chunks

1 yellow squash, peeled and cut into chunks

2 pears, peeled, halved and seeded

¼ cup (60 mL) plain Greek yogurt

1 tsp (5 mL) chia seeds

1. Add 1 cup (250 mL) water to the inner pot and place the steamer basket in the pot (see tip). Arrange carrots in the basket.

2. Close and lock the lid and turn the steam release handle to Sealing. Set your Instant Pot to pressure cook on High for 6 minutes.

3. When the cooking time is done, press Cancel and turn the steam release handle to Venting. When the float valve drops down, remove the lid. Add the squash and pears to the basket.

4. Close and lock the lid and turn the steam release handle to Sealing. Set your Instant Pot to pressure cook on High for 2 minutes. The carrots, squash and pears should be tender. Reserve liquid.

5. Transfer carrots, squash and pears to the blender. Add 2 tbsp (30 mL) reserved liquid. Cover and purée until smooth. Add yogurt and chia seeds; purée until smooth, adding 1 tbsp (15 mL) reserved liquid at a time, if needed until desired consistency.

6. Spoon a small amount into serving bowl. Test temperature before serving. Transfer remainder to ice cube trays.

TIP

The mixture will thicken to a pudding-like consistency after storing. You may want to stir in liquid such as formula, breast milk or water until it reaches desired consistency.

NUTRITION TIP

Chia is a superfood for your baby! It's full of protein, omega-3 fats, calcium and fiber. The seeds are nice and soft when rehydrated and too small to be a choking hazard, so don't worry about that.

ZUCCHINI, PARSNIPS AND PEAS

MAKES ABOUT 1½ CUPS (375 ML)

Peas add the sweetness and texture your baby has tried earlier to this new combination of zucchini and parsnips. The addition of sumac boosts the antioxidant properties and adds a slightly tangy taste to these veggies.

Steamer basket
Countertop blender

1 zucchini, peeled and cut into chunks
1 parsnip, peeled and sliced
1 cup (250 mL) frozen sweet peas
1 tsp (5 mL) ground sumac (approx.)

1. Add 1 cup (250 mL) water to the inner pot and place the steamer basket in the pot (see tip). Arrange zucchini, parsnips and peas in the basket.

2. Close and lock the lid and turn the steam release handle to Sealing. Set your Instant Pot to pressure cook on High for 3 minutes.

3. When the cooking time is done, press Cancel and turn the steam release handle to Venting. The zucchini, parsnips and peas should be tender. (If more cooking time is needed, continue pressure cooking on High for 0 minutes.) Reserve liquid in pot.

4. Transfer vegetables to the blender. Add 2 tbsp (30 mL) reserved liquid and the sumac. Cover and purée until smooth. Add additional reserved liquid, 1 tbsp (15 mL) at a time, if needed until desired consistency.

5. Spoon a small amount into serving bowl. Test temperature before serving. Transfer remainder to ice cube trays.

SERVING SUGGESTION
Combine 1 tbsp (15 mL) enriched baby cereal with formula or breast milk according to package directions. Stir mixture into ¼ cup (60 mL) purée.

TIP

If your steamer basket doesn't have legs, place a steam rack in the pot first and place the steamer basket on the rack.

Purée can be refrigerated in airtight containers for up to 3 days or frozen up to 2 months.

NUTRITION TIP

Yes, babies can have spices! Other than added salt or super-hot spices, it's great to expose your baby to lots of different flavors from early on. It may help make them less picky later!

SWEET PEAS, BROWN RICE, CUMIN AND YOGURT

MAKES ABOUT 3 CUPS (750 ML)

Mixed with sweet peas, a touch of cumin and creamy yogurt, this nutrient-dense brown rice medley will help your little one explore new tastes.

Countertop blender

2 tbsp (30 mL) butter

½ cup (125 mL) chopped onion

1⅓ cups (325 mL) long- or short-grain brown rice, rinsed

1 cup (250 mL) No-Salt-Added Vegetable or Chicken Stock (pages 210–211) or ready-to-use no-salt-added vegetable or chicken broth

⅔ cup (175 mL) water

1 tsp (5 mL) ground cumin

1½ cups (375 mL) frozen sweet peas

½ cup (125 mL) plain yogurt

1. Set your Instant Pot to sauté on Normal. When the display says Hot, add butter and heat until melted. Add onion and cook, stirring, for 3 minutes or until softened. Stir in rice until coated in butter. Stir in stock, water and cumin. Press Cancel.

2. Close and lock the lid and turn the steam release handle to Sealing. Set your Instant Pot to pressure cook on High for 18 minutes.

3. When the cooking time is done, press Cancel and let stand, covered, for 10 minutes, then turn the steam release handle to Venting. When the float valve drops down, remove the lid. The rice should be tender. (If more cooking time is needed, continue pressure cooking on High for 2 minutes, then quickly release the pressure.)

4. Stir in peas. Close and lock the lid and let stand 10 minutes. Peas should be tender and heated through. (If more cooking time is need, close and lock the lid and let stand for 3 minutes.)

5. Transfer mixture to a countertop blender. Add ¼ cup (60 mL) yogurt. Cover and purée until smooth. Add remaining yogurt, 2 tbsp (30 mL) at a time, until desired consistency.

6. Spoon a small amount into serving bowl. Test temperature before serving. Transfer remainder to ice cube trays.

Variation

Omit the peas and skip step 4. Add 1 cup (250 mL) puréed Apples and Apricots (page 76) in step 5 to the blender after the first addition of yogurt.

101

NUTRITION TIP

When buying yogurt, look for plain yogurt with at least 3% M.F. (milk fat) on the label. Your baby needs high-fat foods for growth and brain development.

SPINACH, PEAR AND MANGO PURÉE

MAKES ABOUT 2½ CUPS (625 ML)

This is your little one's version of an adult-inspired smoothie. For babies and their families, too, it is a great way to add some extra greens to diets while blending it with sweet fruits. A pinch of turmeric makes this blend a true powerhouse.

Steamer basket
Countertop blender

1 pear, peeled, halved and cored

1¼ cups (300 mL) firmly packed spinach leaves

2 mangos, peeled, pitted and cut into small pieces

2 tsp (10 mL) ground turmeric

1. Add 1 cup (250 mL) water to the inner pot and place the steamer basket in the pot. Arrange pears in the basket and add spinach to the top.

2. Close and lock the lid and turn the steam release handle to Sealing. Set your Instant Pot to pressure cook on High for 2 minutes.

3. When the cooking time is done, press Cancel and turn the steam release handle to Venting. When the float valve drops down, remove the lid. The spinach should be wilted and the pears should be tender. (If more cooking time is needed for the pears, transfer the spinach to the blender and continue pressure cooking pears on High for 1 minute.) Reserve liquid.

4. Transfer spinach and pears to the blender. Add mangos and turmeric. Cover and purée until smooth. Add reserved liquid, 2 tbsp (30 mL) at a time, stirring until desired consistency.

5. Spoon a small amount into serving bowl. Test temperature before serving. Transfer remainder to ice cube trays.

Variation

Before step 4, cut a small portion of the pear off and cut into bite-size pieces. You may want to only cut enough that baby can eat in one sitting if you are first introducing finger foods. Serve alongside purée.

TIP

Purée can be refrigerated in airtight containers for up to 2 days and frozen in individual portions for up to 3 months.

NUTRITION TIP

Turmeric is a bright yellow Indian spice, thanks to curcumin. Curcumin is the pigment that gives turmeric its characteristic color and it is also a powerful antioxidant!

TIPS

Choose mangos that give slightly
when squeezed in the palm of your
hand. The color of the mango is not
an indication of ripeness.

BEETS AND SWISS CHARD

MAKES ABOUT 2 CUPS (500 ML)

Beets grew out of favor for a number of years but they are back in the spotlight thanks to their nutritional value. Introduce baby early to this powerhouse vegetable so they learn to love it. The Swiss chard adds even more nutrients and a surprise variation.

Steam rack

Countertop blender

1 lb (500 g) beets, scrubbed and stems trimmed to within 1-inch (2.5 cm)

1 tbsp (15 mL) vegetable oil

1 clove garlic, minced

½ lb (250 g) Swiss chard, stems trimmed and reserved

1 tsp (5 mL) Dijon mustard

¼ cup (60 mL) unsweetened pure apple juice

1. Add 1 cup (250 mL) water to the inner pot and place the steam rack in the pot. Arrange beets on the rack.

2. Close and lock the lid and turn the steam release handle to Sealing. Set your Instant Pot to pressure cook on High for 25 minutes.

3. When the cooking time is done, press Cancel and turn the steam release handle to Venting. When the float valve drops down, remove the lid. The beets should be tender with the skin loosening. (If more cooking time is needed, continue pressure cooking on High for 4 minutes.) Plunge beets into cold water. Remove skins and discard. Cut beets into wedges.

4. Transfer beets to the blender. Set aside.

5. Rinse out inner pot and wipe dry. Set your Instant Pot to sauté on Normal. When the display says Hot, add the oil and heat until shimmering. Add garlic and cook, stirring, for 1 minute or until fragrant. Add Swiss chard leaves and cook, stirring, until wilted. Press Cancel.

6. Using a spatula, transfer leaves, garlic and any remaining oil to the blender. Add mustard and 2 tbsp (30 mL) apple juice. Cover and purée until smooth. Add additional apple juice, 1 tbsp (15 mL) at a time, and purée until desired consistency.

7. Spoon a small amount into serving bowl. Test temperature before serving. Transfer remainder to ice cube trays.

Variation

QUICK-PICKLED SWISS CHARD STEMS: Cut stems into ¼-inch (0.5 cm) by 1-inch (2.5 cm) pieces and arrange in a covered jar. Add 1 cup (250 mL) water and ¼ cup (60 mL) granulated sugar to the clean Instant Pot. Set your Instant Pot to sauté on Normal. Cook, stirring, until sugar is dissolved. Press Cancel. Stir in ½ cup (125 mL) seasoned rice wine vinegar, 1 tbsp (15 mL) red wine vinegar and 2 tsp (10 mL) kosher salt. Pour mixture over Swiss chard stems, cover tightly and refrigerate for at least 2 day and up to 2 weeks. Gently shake jar occasionally to blend.

BROWN RICE AND GINGER CAULIFLOWER

MAKES ABOUT 2⅓ CUPS (525 ML)

Brown rice and cauliflower get internationally inspired flavors with ginger, garlic and coconut. Introduce your little one early to world flavors.

Steam rack
4-cup (1 L) heatproof dish
1 large rectangle aluminum foil
Countertop blender

1⅓ cups (325 mL) long- or short-grain brown rice, rinsed

1⅔ (400 mL) cups water

2 cups (500 mL) cauliflower florets

1 tsp (5 mL) vegetable oil

½ tsp (2 mL) garlic powder

½ tsp (2 mL) ground ginger

3 tbsp (45 mL) coconut milk (approx.)

1. Add 1 cup (250 mL) water to the inner pot and place steam rack in the pot. Add the rice, 1⅔ cups (400 mL) water and the oil to the heatproof dish. Place the dish on the rack.

2. Arrange the cauliflower down the center of the foil and drizzle with oil. Sprinkle with garlic powder and ginger; toss gently to coat. Fold into tent-style packets (see page 62), sealing edges tightly. Arrange packet on top of dish in pot.

3. Close and lock the lid and turn the steam release handle to Sealing. Set your Instant Pot to pressure cook on High for 18 minutes.

4. When the cooking time is done, press Cancel and let stand, covered, for 10 minutes, then turn the steam release handle to Venting. When the float valve drops down, remove the lid. Carefully remove and open the foil packet. The cauliflower and rice should be tender. (If more cooking time is needed for both, seal the foil packet, continue pressure cooking on High for 2 minutes, then quickly release the pressure.)

5. Transfer cauliflower, with liquids, to the blender. Add 3 tbsp (30 mL) coconut milk. Cover and pulse until desired consistency. Fluff rice with a fork.

6. Spoon a small amount of rice into serving bowl. Ladle cauliflower over rice. Test temperature before serving. Transfer remainder to ice cube trays.

Variation

Replace coconut milk with almond milk or another milk, being careful to watch for any nut allergies.

NUTRITION TIP

Cauliflower is a cruciferous vegetable, delicious and nutritious, but difficult for some of us to digest. If your baby seems to have an upset tummy after eating cruciferous vegetables, offer a smaller portion. Cooked versions are easier to digest than raw.

BLACK BEANS, CORN AND SWEET POTATO

MAKES ABOUT 2 CUPS (500 ML)

This heart Southwestern-inspired medley gets an added boost of iron from the black beans. The sweet potatoes assist in absorbing the iron.

Countertop blender

1 cup (250 mL) dried black beans

⅔ cup (150 mL) frozen cubed sweet potatoes

1 clove garlic, crushed

½ tsp (2 mL) ground cumin

¼ tsp (1 mL) ground oregano

1 tsp (5 mL) vegetable oil

¼ cup (60 mL) frozen corn kernels

2 tsp (10 mL) freshly squeezed orange juice

½ cup (125 mL) No-Salt-Added Vegetable Stock (page 211) or ready-to-use no-salt-added vegetable broth (approx.)

1. Place beans in a large bowl, add 4 cups (1 L) cold water and let soak at room temperature for 8 hours or overnight. Drain and rinse beans.

2. Add beans, sweet potatoes, garlic, cumin, oregano, oil and 2¼ cups (1 L) water to the inner pot. Close and lock the lid and turn the steam release handle to Sealing. Set your Instant Pot to pressure cook on High for 8 minutes.

3. When the cooking time is done, press Cancel and let stand, covered, for 10 minutes, then turn the steam release handle to Venting. When the float valve drops down, remove the lid. The beans and sweet potatoes should be tender. (If more cooking time is needed, continue pressure cooking on High for 1 minute, then quickly release the pressure.)

4. Stir in corn. Close and lock the lid and let stand 10 minutes. Beans should be tender and heated through. (If more cooking time is need, close and lock the lid and let stand for 2 minutes.)

5. Transfer mixture to a countertop blender. Add orange juice. Cover and purée until smooth. Add stock, 1 tbsp (15 mL) at a time, and purée until desired consistency.

6. Spoon a small amount into serving bowl. Test temperature before serving. Transfer remainder to ice cube trays.

NUTRITION TIP

Black beans are one of my favorite starter finger foods. Keep a few separate from the purée or mashed dish and put them plain on your baby's tray. They are great practice for developing a pincer grasp between the thumb and forefinger!

APPLE, CINNAMON AND BUTTERNUT SQUASH

MAKES 3 CUPS (750 ML)

Two of your little one's first fruits and vegetables are paired in this delightful, tasty cinnamon flavored mix.

Steam rack

Steamer basket

Countertop blender

1 butternut squash (about 2½ to 3 lbs/1.25 to 1.5 kg), seeded and sliced

2 sweet apples (such as Gala, Golden and Red Delicious, or Honeycrisp), peeled, cored and thinly sliced

2 tbsp (30 mL) raisins (optional)

2 tbsp (30 mL) pure unsweetened apple juice (approx.) (optional)

Ground cinnamon

1. Add 1 cup (250 mL) water to the inner pot and place the steam rack in the pot. Arrange squash slices on the rack.

2. Close and lock the lid and turn the steam release handle to Sealing. Set your Instant Pot to pressure cook on High for 5 minutes.

3. When the cooking time is done, press Cancel and turn the steam release handle to Venting. When the float valve drops down, remove the lid. The squash should be tender. (If more cooking time is needed, continue pressure cooking on High for 0 minutes.)

4. Remove squash from pot and let stand until cool enough to handle.

5. Meanwhile, add water to bring liquid in the pot to approximately 1 cup (250 mL). Add steamer basket to the pot and arrange apple slices in the basket.

6. Close and lock the lid and turn the steam release handle to Sealing. Set your Instant Pot to pressure cook on High for 2 minutes.

7. When the cooking time is done, press Cancel and turn the steam release handle to Venting. When the float valve drops down, remove the lid. The apples should be fork-tender. (If more cooking time is needed, continue pressure cooking on High for 0 minutes.) Reserve liquid in pot.

8. Set aside some apple slices as finger food for baby, if desired. Transfer remaining apples to the blender.

9. Scoop squash flesh into blender and discard skins. Add raisins (if using). Cover and purée until smooth. Add reserved liquid or apple juice, 1 tbsp (15 mL) at a time, and purée until desired consistency.

10. Spoon a small amount into serving bowl. Stir in a pinch of cinnamon. Test temperature before serving. Transfer remainder to ice cube trays.

107

PEARS, STRAWBERRIES AND BARLEY

MAKES ABOUT 2½ CUPS (625 ML)

Pears are one of the first foods for many babies, and adding strawberries adds a sweet bright taste and vitamin C . The barley cereal adds nutrients such as iron and selenium.

2 cups (500 mL) water (approx.)

1 cup (250 mL) dry pot barley

1 pear, peeled, halved and cored

Pinch ground chicory root (optional)

2 strawberries, hulled

Water, breast milk or formula

1. In the inner pot, combine water and barley.

2. Close and lock the lid and turn the steam release handle to Sealing. Set your Instant Pot to pressure cook on High for 27 minutes.

3. When cooking time is done, press Cancel and turn steam release handle to Venting. When float valve drops down, remove lid. Add pear and chicory (if using).

4. Close and lock the lid and turn the steam release handle to Sealing. Set your Instant Pot to pressure cook on High for 2 minutes. When the cooking time is done, press Cancel and turn the steam release handle to Venting. When the float valve drops down, remove the lid. The mixture should be tender and most of the liquid absorbed. If more cooking time is needed, set your Instant Pot to sauté on Low and cook, stirring, until the mixture is tender and most of the liquid is absorbed.

5. Transfer the cereal, in batches, to a countertop blender, filling the blender no more than halfway. Add the strawberries. Cover and purée until smooth. Add water, 2 tbsp (30 mL) at a time, stirring until desired consistency.

6. Spoon a small amount into serving bowl. Test temperature before serving. Transfer leftovers to small containers.

Variations

Stir in a pinch of turmeric in step 5 for an added boost of nutrients.

Before step 4, cut small chunks from a strawberry and set aside. Serve alongside purée for baby to eat with the blend.

TIP

Leftover barley can be stored in an airtight container in the refrigerator up to 2 days. Reheat on the stovetop, stirring in additional water as needed.

NUTRITION TIP

Like all whole grains, barley is full of vitamins and minerals. It also contains a type of soluble fiber called beta-glucan, which can help lower blood cholesterol and help control blood sugars. It's a great grain to add to the whole family's diet!

CARROTS, APRICOTS AND FLAX SEEDS

MAKES 1½ CUPS (375 ML)

Almost as bright as sunshine, this carrot and apricot purée is naturally sweet and vitamin rich. This is a great way to have baby try ground flax seeds (flaxseed meal).

Steamer basket

Countertop blender

4 medium carrots, peeled and sliced

2 apricots, peeled, halved and pitted

1 tbsp (15 mL) ground flax seeds (flaxseed meal)

1. Add 1 cup (250 mL) water to the inner pot and place the steamer basket in the pot. Arrange carrots and apricots in the basket.

2. Close and lock the lid and turn the steam release handle to Sealing. Set your Instant Pot to pressure cook on High for 3 minutes.

3. When the cooking time is done, press Cancel and turn the steam release handle to Venting. When the float valve drops down, remove the lid. The carrots and apricots should be tender and pierce easily with a fork. (If more cooking time is needed, continue pressure cooking on High for 1 minute.) Reserve liquid in pot.

4. Transfer carrots and apricot into the blender. Cover and purée until smooth. Add reserved liquid, 1 tbsp (15 mL) at a time, if needed, until desired consistency.

5. Spoon a small amount into serving bowl. Test temperature before serving. Transfer remainder to ice cube trays.

Variation

Before starting step 4, reserve a few carrot slices. Continue with step 4. Serve carrot slices with purée for little dippers.

SERVING SUGGESTION

Combine 1 tbsp (15 mL) enriched baby cereal with formula or breast milk according to package directions. Stir mixture into ¼ cup (60 mL) purée.

TIPS

Choose medium carrots that are thin, with no white roots. Large, thick carrots can have a woody taste in the middle. Carrots that are growing white roots have been stored longer.

NUTRITION TIP

Ground flax seeds (flaxseed meal) make a great addition to your baby's diet. Not only are they high in omega-3 fats, but they also can help cure constipation! You can sprinkle ground flax seeds on top of cereals or yogurt if your baby is suffering from constipation.

SWEET POTATO, APRICOT AND CHICKEN FEAST

MAKES ABOUT 2½ CUPS (625 ML)

Sweet veggies and apricots provide a great base for adding tender chicken breast to baby's diet.

Steamer basket

Countertop blender

1 cup (250 mL) No-Salt-Added Chicken stock (page 210) or ready-to-use no-salt-added chicken broth

12 oz (375 g) boneless, skinless chicken breasts

1 large sweet potato, peeled and cubed

2 apricots, peeled, halved and pitted

1. Add the stock and chicken breasts to the inner pot and place the steamer basket on top. Arrange sweet potatoes and apricots in the basket.

2. Close and lock the lid and turn the steam release handle to Sealing. Set your Instant Pot to pressure cook on High for 5 minutes.

3. When the cooking time is done, press Cancel. Let stand 5 minutes and turn the steam release handle to Venting. When the float valve drops down, remove the lid. Transfer the sweet potatoes and apricots to the blender. An instant-read thermometer inserted horizontally into the thickest part of the breast should register at least 165°F (74°C) and the chicken should no longer be pink inside. (If more cooking time is needed, close and lock the lid and let stand for 1 to 2 minutes.) Reserve liquid in pot.

4. Transfer chicken to a work surface and, using a fork, shred chicken. Transfer chicken and 2 tbsp (30 mL) reserved liquid to the blender. Cover and purée until smooth. Add additional reserved liquid, 1 tbsp (15 mL) at a time, if needed until desired consistency.

5. Spoon a small amount into serving bowl. Test temperature before serving. Transfer remainder to ice cube trays.

Variation

Before starting step 4, cut some pieces of chicken into small chunks and set aside. Continue with step 4. Serve chicken pieces with purée for babies that are starting solids.

NUTRITION TIP

Your baby may prefer more savory meat dishes with the addition of something naturally slightly sweet (like the apricots and sweet potatoes in this recipe). Babies naturally are drawn to sweet foods, as they provide an easy source of quick energy. And breast milk is sweet! And that's okay. Just be sure to continue offering all tastes and flavors of foods to expand your baby's palate.

TURKEY AND VEGGIES

MAKES ABOUT 3½ CUPS (875 ML)

In this recipe, lean ground turkey is blended with green beans and red potatoes for a "full-course" meal. Onion powder and paprika are added to intrigue baby's taste buds.

Countertop blender

1 tsp (5 mL) vegetable oil

1 lb (500 g) ground turkey

1 tsp (5 mL) ground onion powder

½ tsp (2 mL) ground paprika

1 lb (500 g) fresh green beans, trimmed and cut into 1-inch (2.5 cm) pieces

1 lb (500 g) small red potatoes, scrubbed and quartered

1. Set your Instant Pot to sauté on Normal. When the display says Hot, add oil and heat until shimmering. Add the turkey, onion powder and paprika; cook, stirring and breaking up into small pieces, 3 minutes or until pale gray. Press Cancel.

2. Add 1 cup water, green beans and potatoes to the inner pot, stirring.

3. Close and lock the lid and turn the steam release handle to Sealing. Set your Instant Pot to pressure cook on High for 3 minutes.

4. When the cooking time is done, press Cancel and turn the steam release handle to Venting. When the float valve drops down, remove the lid. The turkey should no longer be pink and the beans and potatoes should be fork-tender. (If more cooking time is needed, close and lock the lid and cook for 1 minute.)

5. Using a slotted spoon, transfer turkey mixture to the blender. Add 2 tbsp (45 mL) liquid from the pot. Cover and purée until smooth. Continue adding liquid, 1 tbsp (15 mL) at a time, until desired consistency.

6. Spoon a small amount into serving bowl. Test temperature before serving. Transfer remainder to ice cube trays.

Variation

Before starting step 5, set aside some green beans. Continue with step 5. Serve beans with purée for babies who are starting solids.

NUTRITION TIP

While you may wonder if your baby will like spices like onion powder and paprika, they've likely experienced the flavor of spices before. Did you know that your breast milk changes flavor according to what you eat? If you've been nursing your baby, then they've experienced different flavors even before starting solids.

TURKEY, SWEET POTATO AND CRANBERRY

MAKES ABOUT 1½ CUPS (375 ML)

Little ones can have this wonderful holiday feast at any time of the year. A treat of sweet potatoes combined with lean turkey and the slightly tart-sweet taste of cranberries will make them happy and healthy.

Countertop blender

1 tsp (5 mL) vegetable oil

4 oz (125 g) turkey tenderloins or turkey roast, cut into cubes

1 small sweet potato, peeled and cubed

2 tbsp (30 mL) dried cranberries

1 tsp (5 mL) ground thyme

1 cup (250 mL) No-Salt-Added Chicken Stock (page 210) or ready-to-use no-salt-added chicken broth

1. Set your Instant Pot to sauté on Normal. When the display says Hot, add oil and heat until shimmering. Add chicken breast cubes and cook, stirring often, for 4 minutes or until browned. Stir in sweet potato, cranberries, thyme and chicken stock. Press Cancel.

2. Close and lock the lid and turn the steam release handle to Sealing. Set your Instant Pot to pressure cook on High for 4 minutes.

3. When the cooking time is done, press Cancel and turn the steam release handle to Venting. When the float valve drops down, remove the lid. The turkey and sweet potatoes should be tender. (If more cooking time is needed, continue pressure cooking on High for 0 minutes.)

4. Using a slotted spoon, transfer turkey mixture to the blender. Add 2 tbsp (30 mL) stock from the pot. Cover and purée until smooth. Continue adding stock, 1 tbsp (15 mL) at a time, until desired consistency.

5. Spoon a small amount into serving bowl. Test temperature before serving. Transfer remainder to ice cube trays.

Variation

Before step 5, set aside a small portion of turkey cubes. Continue with step 5. Serve cubes with purée for babies who are starting solids.

NUTRITION TIP

If you are able to include some dark turkey meat, your baby will be getting more iron. Dark poultry (such as chicken thighs versus breasts) contain more iron than the white meat.

GREEN BEANS, ARUGULA AND PEARS WITH MINT

MAKES 2 CUPS (500 ML)

This recipe adds a bit of mint to introduce your baby to a new flavor and reduce the boredom of green purées while also keeping the flavor of pears which they love.

Steamer basket

Countertop blender

1 lb (500 g) green beans, trimmed and cut into 1-inch (2.5 cm) pieces

2 pears, peeled, halved and cored

1 cup (250 mL) lightly packed arugula

1 tsp (5 mL) ground cinnamon

2 tsp (10 mL) chopped fresh mint

1. Add 1 cup (250 mL) water to the inner pot and place the steamer basket in the pot. Arrange green beans and pears in the basket. Sprinkle with $1/2$ tsp (2 mL) cinnamon. Arrange arugula on the top.

2. Close and lock the lid and turn the steam release handle to Sealing. Set your Instant Pot to pressure cook on High for 2 minutes.

3. When the cooking time is done, press Cancel and turn the steam release handle to Venting. When the float valve drops down, remove the lid. The arugula should be wilted, and the pears and beans should be tender. (If more cooking time is needed for the pears or beans, transfer the arugula to the blender and continue pressure cooking on High for 1 minute.) Reserve liquid.

4. Transfer pears, beans, remaining cinnamon and mint to the blender. Cover and purée until smooth. Add 1 tbsp (15 mL) reserved liquid. Cover and purée until smooth. Continue adding liquid, 1 tbsp (15 mL) at a time, until desired consistency.

5. Spoon a small amount into serving bowl. Test temperature before serving. Transfer remainder to ice cube trays.

Variations

Stir in a pinch of turmeric in step 5 for an added boost of nutrients.

Before step 4, set aside a small portion of beans and/or pears and cut into small pieces. Continue with step 4. Serve pieces with purée for babies who are starting solids.

NUTRITION TIP

Arugula has a strong, slightly peppery taste. Your baby may make a face at first, but that doesn't mean he doesn't like the flavor — it's just new! Keep on introducing tastes, even if they've been refused before.

RED BEETS, CHICKPEAS AND CUMIN

MAKES 2 CUPS (500 ML)

Your little one's version of hummus is a brightly colored, well-balanced meal with protein, fiber and fruit along with a powerhouse of nutritional benefits.

Steam rack

Countertop blender

1 cup (250 mL) dried chickpeas (see tip)

2 small red beets, stem trimmed to 1 inch (2.5 cm) and scrubbed

3 tbsp (45 mL) tahini

1 tbsp (15 mL) lemon juice

1½ tbsp (22 mL) extra virgin olive oil

1 tsp (5 mL) ground cumin

1. In a large bowl, combine chickpeas and 4 cups (1 L) cold water. Let stand at room temperature for 8 hours or overnight. Drain and rinse.

2. Add chickpeas and 2 cups (500 mL) fresh cold water to the inner pot. Close and lock the lid and turn the steam release handle to Sealing. Set your Instant Pot to pressure cook on High for 10 minutes.

3. When the cooking time is done, press Cancel and let stand, covered, until the float valve drops down, then remove the lid. The chickpeas should be al dente. Drain and rinse chickpeas with cold water and let cool to room temperature.

4. While the chickpeas are cooling, rinse and dry the inner pot and return to the cooker. Add 1 cup (250 mL) water to the inner pot and place the steam rack in the pot. Arrange the beets on the rack.

5. Close and lock the lid and turn the steam release handle to Sealing. Set your Instant Pot to pressure cook on High for 12 minutes.

6. When the cooking time is done, press Cancel and turn the steam release handle to Venting. When the float valve drops down, remove the lid. The beets should be tender. (If more cooking time is needed, continue pressure cooking on High for 2 minutes.) Plunge beets into cold water. Remove stem and skins; discard. Cut beets into wedges and transfer to the blender.

7. Add chickpeas, tahini, lemon juice, olive oil and cumin to beets in the blender. Cover and purée until smooth.

8. Spoon a small amount into serving bowl. Test temperature before serving. Transfer remainder to ice cube trays.

TIPS

Double the amount of chickpeas and water for soaking and cooking. Set aside half of the chickpeas to use in another recipe or as an addition to adults or children's salads.

Wear disposable kitchen gloves when handling beets.

Serve as a dip for crackers, thin vegetable sticks or a spread on toast for added nutrition and flavor.

116

RED LENTIL AND FENNEL BLEND

MAKES 3 CUPS (750 ML)

Nutrient-packed lentils are married with a blend of vegetables for a hearty purée. Add the optional turmeric and paprika for more flavor and nutritional value.

Countertop blender

2 tbsp (30 mL) vegetable oil

1 fennel bulb, stems removed and bulb cored and cut into wedges

1 small onion, chopped

1 rib celery, sliced

1 clove garlic, minced

2 small carrots, peeled and sliced

1½ cups (375 mL) dried red lentils, rinsed

4 cups (1 L) No-Salt-Added Vegetable Stock, (page 211) or ready-to-use no-salt-added vegetable broth

1 tsp (5 mL) turmeric (optional)

½ tsp (2 mL) paprika (optional)

1. Set your Instant Pot to sauté on Normal. When the display says Hot, add oil and heat until shimmering. Add the fennel, onions and celery; cook, stirring often, for 5 minutes or until mixture is softened. Add garlic and cook, stirring, 1 minute or until fragrant. Stir in carrots, lentils and stock. Press Cancel.

2. Close and lock the lid and turn the steam release handle to Sealing. Set your Instant Pot to pressure cook on High for 10 minutes.

3. When the cooking time is done, press Cancel and turn the steam release handle to Venting. When the float valve drops down, remove the lid. The lentils and carrots should be tender. (If more cooking time is needed, continue pressure cooking on High for 1 minute.) Press Cancel.

4. Using a slotted spoon, transfer mixture to the blender. Add turmeric and paprika (if using). Add 3 tbsp (45 mL) stock from the pot. Cover and purée until smooth. Continue adding stock, 1 tbsp (15 mL) at a time, until desired consistency (see tip).

5. Spoon a small amount into serving bowl. Test temperature before serving. Transfer remainder to ice cube trays.

TIPS

In step 4, add additional reserved stock and purée into a soup consistency.

NUTRITION TIP

Red lentils are a great plant-based source of protein for your family. Try blending cooked red lentils into smoothies for added fiber and protein.

POACHED TOMATO BASIL TILAPIA

MAKES 6 SERVINGS

Tilapia is a very mild fish and a great way to introduce your baby to the taste and benefits of fish. The tomato and basil hint of the aroma of Mediterranean dishes.

4-cup (1 L) round heatproof dish, sprayed with nonstick cooking spray

Steam rack

2 tomatoes, peeled, thickly sliced, divided

6 oz (175 g) skinless tilapia fillets

2 cloves garlic, minced

1 tbsp (15 mL) virgin olive oil

Freshly ground black pepper

2 tbsp (30 mL) fresh basil, chopped

1½ cups (375 mL) water

1. Arrange half the tomatoes in prepared dish, overlapping as necessary. Carefully place fish in a single layer on top.

2. In a small bowl, combine garlic and oil. Brush top of fish with garlic oil. Season with pepper. Top with basil. Arrange the remaining tomatoes on top.

3. Add water to the inner pot and place the steam rack in the pot. Place the dish on the rack.

4. Close and lock the lid and turn the steam release handle to Sealing. Set your Instant Pot to pressure cook on Low for 3 minutes.

5. When the cooking time is done, press Cancel and turn the steam release handle to Venting. When the float valve drops down, remove the lid. The fish should be opaque and should flake easily when tested with a fork. (If more cooking time is needed, close and lock the lid for 1 minute.) Reserve liquid in pot.

6. Transfer the tilapia combination with liquids in the dish to a countertop blender. Cover and purée until smooth. Add reserved water, 2 tbsp (30 mL) at a time, stirring until desired consistency.

7. Spoon a small amount into serving bowl. Test temperature before serving. Transfer leftovers to small containers.

TIPS

You can substitute flounder, cod, sole or grouper for the tilapia.

Using your fingers, carefully check the tilapia fillets for tiny pin bones. Remove any bones with tweezers or needle-nose pliers.

NUTRITION TIP

This recipe contains garlic, pepper and basil to add flavor. Babies don't need totally bland foods! The more you expose them to different flavors at a young age, the more likely they will be an adventurous eater when they're older.

PEARS, MANGOS, SPINACH AND CHIA

MAKES 1½ CUPS (375 ML)

Fruits, greens and a superfood merge to bring a bounty of nutrients to your growing baby. The mango adds a slightly tropical and sweeter taste to this combination.

Steamer basket

Countertop blender

1 pear, peeled, halved and cored

1 cup (250 mL) lightly packed spinach leaves

1 mango, peeled and pitted

2 tsp (10 mL) chia seeds

1. Add 1 cup (250 mL) water to the inner pot and place the steamer basket in the pot. Arrange pears in the basket and add spinach to the top.

2. Close and lock the lid and turn the steam release handle to Sealing. Set your Instant Pot to pressure cook on High for 2 minutes.

3. When the cooking time is done, press Cancel and turn the steam release handle to Venting. When the float valve drops down, remove the lid. The spinach should be wilted and the pears should be tender. (If more cooking time is needed for the pears, transfer the spinach to the blender and continue pressure cooking pears on High for 1 minute.) Reserve liquid.

4. Transfer spinach and pears to the blender. Add mango and chia seeds. Cover and purée until smooth. Add reserved liquid, 1 tbsp (15 mL) at a time, puréeing until desired consistency.

5. Spoon a small amount into serving bowl. Test temperature before serving. Transfer remainder to ice cube trays.

Variation

Before step 4, set aside a small portion of pears and cut into small chunks. Serve with purée for babies who are starting solids.

TIP

Purée can be refrigerated in airtight containers for up to 3 days and frozen in individual portions for up to 2 months.

NUTRITION TIP

Let your baby play with their food! This recipe would provide a slimy sensory experience with the addition of chia seeds. While finger play is messy, it is one way that babies can learn about food.

BEEF, CARROTS AND POTATO MEDLEY

MAKES 2½ CUPS (625 ML)

When your little one is beginning to expand her palate, this combination of beef, sweet carrots and baby potatoes is the perfect medley to try.

Countertop blender

1 lb (500 g) beef stew meat, cut into 1½-inch (4 cm) cubes

Onion powder

2 tbsp (30 mL) vegetable oil (approx.)

1 cup (250 mL) Low-Sodium Beef Bone Broth (page 212) or ready-to-use low-sodium beef broth

2 carrots, cut into 1½-inch (4 cm) chunks

8 oz (250 g) small white potatoes, quartered

1 tbsp (15 mL) fresh thyme leaves

1. Season beef lightly with onion powder. Set your Instant Pot to sauté on Normal. When the display says Hot, add oil and heat until shimmering. Working in batches, add beef and cook, stirring, for 2 minutes or until browned on all sides, adding more oil as needed between batches. Using tongs or a slotted spoon, transfer beef to a plate as it is browned.

2. Add broth to the pot and cook, stirring and scraping up any brown bits from the bottom of the pot, for 2 minutes. Return beef and any accumulated juices to the pot and stir in carrots, potatoes and thyme. Press Cancel.

3. Close and lock the lid and turn the steam release handle to Sealing. Set your Instant Pot to pressure cook on High for 20 minutes.

4. When the cooking time is done, press Cancel and let stand, covered, for 10 minutes, then turn the steam release handle to Venting. When the float valve drops down, remove the lid. The beef and vegetables should be fork-tender. (If more cooking time is needed, continue pressure cooking on High for 5 minutes.)

5. Using a slotted spoon, transfer beef mixture to the blender. Add 3 tbsp (45 mL) liquid from the pot, cover and purée. Add additional liquid, 1 tbsp (15 mL) at a time, puréeing until desired consistency.

6. Spoon a small amount into serving bowl. Test temperature before serving. Transfer remainder to ice cube trays.

Variation

Omit the potatoes and add ¾ cup (175 mL) Easy Rice Pilaf (page 213) to the beef mixture in step 6 and purée.

NUTRITION TIP

I love recipes that contain beef for babies! It's one of the best sources of iron that you can find. And cooking beef in the Instant Pot ensures that it's nice and tender for your baby to eat safely.

FLOUNDER WITH TOMATOES AND AVOCADO

MAKES ABOUT 1¼ CUPS (300 ML)

Flounder is a great choice for introducing babies to fish. The tomatoes and basil add a nice balance of flavor to the fish and the avocado adds nutrient-rich fruit to the mix.

2-cup (500 mL) round heatproof dish, sprayed with nonstick cooking spray

Steam rack

Countertop blender

2 plum (Roma) tomatoes, skinned, thickly sliced and seeded, divided

5 oz (150 g) skinless flounder fillet

1 clove garlic, minced

1½ tsp (7 mL) virgin olive oil

2 tsp (10 mL) dried basil leaves

½ avocado, peeled and pitted

1. Arrange half the tomatoes in prepared dish, overlapping as necessary. Carefully check flounder for any small bones. Place in a single layer on top of tomatoes.

2. In a small bowl, combine garlic and oil. Brush top of fish with garlic oil. Sprinkle with basil. Arrange the remaining tomatoes on top.

3. Add 1½ cups (375 mL) water to the inner pot and place the steam rack in the pot. Place the dish on the rack.

4. Close and lock the lid and turn the steam release handle to Sealing. Set your Instant Pot to pressure cook on Low for 3 minutes.

5. When cooking time is done, press Cancel and turn steam release handle to Venting. When the float valve drops down, remove lid. The fish should be opaque and should flake easily when tested with a fork. (If more cooking time is needed, close and lock lid for 1 minute.)

6. Using a spatula, transfer fish, tomatoes and liquids from the dish to the blender. Add the avocado. Cover and purée until desired consistency.

7. Spoon a small amount into serving bowl. Test temperature before serving. Transfer remainder to ice cube trays.

Variation

The avocado can be cut into thin slices and rolled in enriched infant cereal instead of puréed for babies who are starting solids.

NUTRITION TIP

Even though fish is a higher risk allergen, it's okay to offer fish from the start. We now know that introducing allergenic foods from a young age can promote tolerance to allergy.

COD WITH CORN AND BROCCOLI

MAKES ABOUT 1¼ CUPS (300 ML)

The mild taste of cod gets a boost of sweet corn and iron-rich broccoli. A little bit of sweet bell pepper and a splash of orange juice adds a hint of spice and sweet.

One 18- by 12-inch (45 by 30 cm) sheet parchment paper

Steam rack

½ cup (125 mL) frozen sweet corn kernels

¼ cup (60 mL) chopped red bell pepper

¾ cup (175 mL) small broccoli florets

5 oz (150 g) skinless cod fillet

1 tbsp (15 mL) orange juice

1 tbsp (15 mL) virgin olive oil

1 tsp (5 mL) paprika

1 tsp (5 mL) chopped fresh parsley

1. Arrange corn and peppers in the center of the parchment paper, in a mound the size and shape of your cod fillet. Place fish on top. Arrange broccoli florets around the fish. Drizzle with orange juice and olive oil. Sprinkle with paprika and parsley. Fold parchment paper into tent-style packets (see page 62) and seal edges tightly.

2. Add 1½ cups (375 mL) water to the inner pot and place the steam rack in the pot. Place packet on the rack.

3. Close and lock the lid and turn the steam release handle to Sealing. Set your Instant Pot to pressure cook on Low for 4 minutes (see tip).

4. When the cooking time is done, press Cancel and turn the steam release handle to Venting. When the float valve drops down, remove the lid. Carefully open a packet. The fish should be opaque and flake easily when tested with a fork. (If more cooking time is needed, reseal packet and continue pressure cooking on Low for 1 minute.)

5. Empty contents of packet into the blender. Cover and purée until desired consistency.

6. Spoon a small amount into serving bowl. Test temperature before serving. Transfer remainder to ice cube trays.

TIPS

Carefully check cod for any small bones before cooking.

If your Instant Pot doesn't have a Low pressure setting, cook on High for 2 minutes.

NUTRITION TIP

Fish contains two important omega-3 fats for health: EPA and DHA. These are not found in plant sources of omega-3 fats, such as flax seeds. And they're important for your baby's brain and eye development, so try to serve fish at least twice per week.

PROTEIN-POWERED CHICKEN AND VEGGIES

MAKES ABOUT 1¾ CUPS (425 ML)

Cannellini beans add an extra boost of protein, along with the chicken, for baby's healthy development. Vitamins, minerals and fiber from the sweet potatoes and peaches add to the abundance of this recipe.

Countertop blender

1 cup (250 mL) cannellini beans, drained and rinsed

8 oz (250 g) boneless skinless chicken breast, cubed

1½ cups (375 mL) frozen sweet potato cubes

1 cup (250 mL) frozen sliced peaches

1 tsp (5 mL) ground sumac

1 tsp (5 mL) ground turmeric

½ tsp (2 mL) vegetable oil

1¼ cups (300 mL) No-Salt-Added Chicken Stock (page 210) or ready-to-use no-salt-added chicken broth

1. Add beans, chicken breast, sweet potatoes, peaches, sumac, turmeric, oil and stock to the inner pot. Close and lock the lid and turn the steam release handle to Sealing. Set your Instant Pot to pressure cook on High for 7 minutes.

2. When the cooking time is done, press Cancel and let stand, covered, for 10 minutes, then turn the steam release handle to Venting. When the float valve drops down, remove the lid. The chicken breast should no longer be pink in the middle and the beans, sweet potatoes and peaches should be tender. (If more cooking time is needed, continue pressure cooking on High for 1 minute, then quickly release the pressure.)

3. Using a slotted spoon, transfer mixture to the countertop blender. Add ¼ cup (60 mL) liquid from the pot. Cover and purée until smooth. Add additional liquid, 1 tbsp (15 mL) at a time, and purée until desired consistency.

4. Spoon a small amount into serving bowl. Test temperature before serving. Transfer remainder to ice cube trays.

NUTRITION TIP

Beans such as the cannellini beans in this recipe are an inexpensive and easy source of fiber and plant-based protein for the whole family. Most of us don't get enough fiber and it's important for digestive health and cholesterol control and even absorbs carcinogens in the bowel.

SPICY LENTIL PURÉE

MAKES ABOUT 2½ CUPS (625 ML)

When you want to introduce your little one to some spicier foods that are also packed with protein and vegetables, this recipe is a great place to start.

Countertop blender

1 tbsp (15 mL) vegetable oil

1 lb (500 g) lean ground turkey

½ cup (125 mL) chopped onion

1½ cups (375 mL) dried brown lentils, rinsed and drained

1 tsp (5 mL) chile powder

1 can (14.5 oz/411 g) no-salt-added diced tomatoes

4 cups (1 L) No-Salt-Added Vegetable Stock (page 211) or ready-to-use no-salt-added vegetable broth

1. Set your Instant Pot to sauté on Normal. When the display says Hot, add oil and heat until shimmering. Add the ground turkey and onion and cook, stirring and breaking turkey up with a spoon, for 7 minutes or until turkey is no longer pink and onion is softened. Stir in lentils, chile powder, tomatoes with juice and stock. Press Cancel.

2. Close and lock the lid and turn the steam release handle to Sealing. Set your Instant Pot to pressure cook on High for 10 minutes.

3. When the cooking time is done, press Cancel and let stand, covered, for 10 minutes, then turn the steam release handle to Venting. When the float valve drops down, remove the lid. The lentils should be tender. (If more cooking time is needed, continue pressure cooking on High for 2 minutes, then quickly release the pressure.)

4. Transfer mixture to the countertop blender. Cover and purée until smooth. Add water if needed, 1 tbsp (15 mL) at a time, and purée until desired consistency.

5. Spoon a small amount into serving bowl. Test temperature before serving. Transfer remainder to ice cube trays.

Variation

VEGETARIAN LENTIL CHILI: Omit the ground turkey and follow directions, reducing the cooking time in step 1 to 5 minutes.

SERVING SUGGESTION

Stir in a small spoonful of Greek Yogurt (variation on page 206) into the bowl just before serving.

NUTRITION TIP

The reason why the recipes call for no-salt-added stocks and broths is because early exposure to salt can create a lifelong preference for it. Also, your baby's kidneys have not developed well enough to efficiently filter out large amounts of sodium. If your whole family is eating a meal, add the salt to the adult portions at the table, after removing baby's portion.

QUINOA, SWEET PEAS AND YOGURT

MAKES ABOUT 1½ CUPS (375 ML)

This combination of quinoa, sweet peas and yogurt is loaded with protein, vitamins and minerals. The addition of mint adds a nice flavor for baby explore.

Steamer basket

Countertop blender

1 tbsp (15 mL) vegetable oil

1 cup (250 mL) quinoa, rinsed

1 cup (250 mL) fresh sweet peas

2 tsp (10 mL) chopped fresh mint

¼ cup (60 mL) Homemade Yogurt (page 206)

1. Set your Instant Pot to sauté on Normal. When the display says Hot, add oil and heat until shimmering. Add quinoa and cook, stirring, for 2 to 3 minutes or until lightly toasted. Press Cancel. Add 1½ cups (300 mL) water, stirring well. Add peas to the steamer basket and place on top of the quinoa. Sprinkle with mint.

2. Close and lock the lid and turn the steam release handle to Sealing. Set your Instant Pot to pressure cook on High for 1 minute.

3. When the cooking time is done, press Cancel and turn the steam release handle to Venting. When the float valve drops down, remove the lid. The peas and quinoa should be tender. (If more cooking time is needed, close and lock the lid and let stand for 1 minute.)

4. Transfer peas and quinoa to the blender. Add yogurt. Cover and purée until desired consistency.

5. Spoon a small amount into serving bowl. Test temperature before serving. Transfer remainder to ice cube trays.

TIP

The mixture can be stored in airtight containers in the refrigerator for up to 2 days. Do not freeze.

NUTRITION TIP

Quinoa is often called a superfood. It is higher in protein, magnesium, iron, fiber and zinc than most other grains.

Finger Foods

GREEN EGG AND HAM SCRAMBLE

MAKES 2 SERVINGS

Before long, your baby will be reading and enjoying all kinds of wonderful rhymes. Until then, give them a brain boost with these scrumptious cheesy eggs, spinach and ham.

6-oz (175 mL) ramekin, bottom and sides buttered

Steam rack

2 tbsp (30 mL) diced ham

4 baby spinach leaves, stems removed

1½ tbsp (22 mL) shredded Cheddar cheese, divided

2 large eggs

Freshly ground black pepper

1. Layer ham, spinach and 1 tbsp (15 mL) cheese in the prepared ramekin. Crack eggs side by side on top of the cheese. Sprinkle eggs with the remaining cheese.

2. Add 1 cup (250 mL) water to the inner pot and place the steam rack in the pot.

3. Close and lock the lid and turn the steam release handle to Sealing. Set your Instant Pot to pressure cook on High for 10 minutes.

4. When the timer beeps, press Cancel and turn the steam release handle to Venting. When the float valve drops down, remove the lid. Carefully remove the ramekin from the pot. Let stand 5 minutes or until cool enough to handle.

5. Spoon half of mixture into individual serving bowl. Season to taste with pepper. Test temperature before serving.

TIPS

A bowl of fresh berries makes the perfect accompaniment to this delightful dish.

When using the Quick release method to release pressure, keep your hands and face away from the hole on the top of the steam release handle so you don't get scalded by the escaping steam.

NUTRITION TIP

While I don't encourage "hiding" foods like spinach in smoothies or other dishes, this recipe is a great way to include spinach and make it fun. Your kids know it's there (hence the "green" eggs!), and if they make the decision to eat it themselves without being tricked or forced, they will be more likely to enjoy the spinach!

STEAMED CARROT COINS

MAKES 4 SERVINGS

Tender little carrot coins are great finger foods. Served by themselves or as a dipper for mashed fruits and purées, they are sure to be a hit. The optional sumac is loaded with antioxidants to turn this dish into a powerhouse.

Steamer basket

2 medium carrots, peeled and sliced crosswise into ¼-inch (0.5 cm) rounds

Powdered sumac (optional)

1 tsp (5 mL) butter, softened (optional)

1. Add 1 cup (250 mL) water to the inner pot and place the steamer basket in the pot (see tip). Arrange carrots in the basket. Season with sumac (if using).

2. Close and lock the lid and turn the steam release handle to Sealing. Set your Instant Pot to pressure cook on High for 3 minutes.

3. When the cooking time is done, press Cancel and turn the steam release handle to Venting. When the float valve drops down, remove the lid. The carrots should be tender. (If more cooking time is needed, continue pressure cooking on High for 0 minutes.)

4. Spoon ¼ of the carrots into a serving bowl. Add a dab of butter, tossing gently until melted. Test temperature before serving. Transfer remaining carrots to an airtight container and refrigerate for up to 3 days.

TIPS

Choose medium carrots that are thin, with no white roots. Large, thick carrots can have a woody taste in the middle. Carrots that are growing white roots have been stored longer.

Sumac adds a slightly lemony flavor and bright red sprinkles to these carrots without being too overpowering. Sumac also works well on other steamed or roasted vegetables.

Refrigerated carrot coins can be reheated in the microwave, adding butter if desired, or served chilled.

Carrot coins make great little dippers for mashed bananas, mashed avocados or fruit purées.

NUTRITION TIP

Carrots are very high in vitamin A. Vitamin A is a fat-soluble vitamin. So adding butter to your baby's carrots (or serving another source of fat in the meal), helps your baby absorb the vitamin A!

TOASTY TOMATO SOUP

MAKES 6 CUPS (1.5 L)

Tomato soup is the ideal comfort meal for chilly days. This creamy tomato soup is perfect for the whole family or just your little one. Serve it with grilled cheese finger sandwiches for a real treat!

Countertop blender

½ cup (125 mL) loosely packed fresh basil leaves, chopped

1 tsp (5 mL) granulated sugar

3¾ cups (925 mL) Low-Sodium Chicken Stock (page 210) or ready-to-use reduced-sodium chicken broth

2 cans (each 14½ oz/411 mL) diced tomatoes with garlic and onion, with juice

1 cup (250 mL) half-and-half (10%) cream

¼ cup (60 mL) butter, softened

Freshly ground black pepper

1. To the inner pot, add basil, sugar, stock and tomatoes with juice. Do not stir (see tip).

2. Close and lock the lid and turn the steam release handle to Sealing. Set your Instant Pot to pressure cook on High for 5 minutes.

3. When the cooking time is done, press Cancel and let stand, covered, for 5 minutes, then turn the steam release handle to Venting. When the float valve drops down, remove the lid.

4. Transfer the soup, in batches, to a countertop blender, filling the blender no more than halfway. Be very careful when transferring soup, as it is very hot. Cover and purée until smooth. Return soup the inner pot.

5. Set your Instant Pot to sauté on Less. Stir in cream and butter; cook, stirring, for 2 to 3 minutes or until heated through (do not let boil). Set your Instant Pot to keep warm. Ladle amounts for baby into a bowl. Test temperature before serving.

6. Season soup in pot with pepper. Ladle into serving bowls.

SERVING SUGGESTION

Serve with grilled cheese sandwiches. For babies, remove crusts and cut sandwiches into 5 strips.

TIPS

Do not be tempted to add the tomatoes first or to stir the ingredients. Tomatoes can scorch on the bottom of the cooker if added first.

NUTRITION TIP

Babies should have limited salt intake, as their kidneys aren't fully developed to process higher intakes (see FAQ on page 53). Adults sharing in the meal can add extra salt to their own bowl.

JUICY MINI-BURGERS

MAKES 16 MINI-BURGERS

Forget the grill or griddle — make these juicy burgers in a jiffy. See the variation for making these for the whole family.

4 sheets of foil

Steam rack

1¼ lbs (625 g) lean ground beef

1 tsp (5 mL) onion powder or garlic

1 tbsp (15 mL) Worcestershire sauce

1. In a medium bowl, using your hands, combine beef, onion powder and Worcestershire sauce. Form into sixteen ½-inch (1 cm) thick patties. Transfer 4 patties to each foil sheet and fold into flat packets (see page 62), sealing edges tightly.

2. Add 1¼ cups (300 mL) water to the inner pot and place the steam rack in the pot. Arrange packets on the rack, stacking them in alternating layers (like stacking bricks).

3. Close and lock the lid and turn the steam release handle to Sealing. Set your Instant Pot to pressure cook on High for 6 minutes.

4. When the cooking time is done, press Cancel and turn the steam release handle to Venting. When the float valve drops down, remove the lid and carefully open a packet. An instant-read thermometer inserted horizontally into the center of the patty should register at least 160°F (71°C). (If more cooking time is needed, continue pressure cooking on High for 1 minute.) Using tongs, transfer packets to a work surface and let stand for 5 minutes.

5. Carefully open packets and pour off liquid. Test temperature before serving. Remaining burgers can be stored in the refrigerator for up to 3 days.

SERVING SUGGESTIONS

Serve with ketchup, mustard or mayonnaise for dipping.

Top the patties with slices of sharp (old) Cheddar, provolone or Monterey Jack immediately after opening the packets.

Variation

In step 1, divide beef into halves. Form 8 patties from 1 half and 2 patties from the remaining half. Continue with the remaining steps. Serve the larger patties to adults or older children.

NUTRITION TIP

Beef is one of the best sources if dietary iron for your little one. Ground beef is tender enough for baby to chew and burgers are easy to hold, making this a super meal for your baby!

CREAMED SALMON AND PEAS WITH TOAST

MAKES 1 CUP (250 ML)

Salmon is loaded with nutrients and healthy oils. Paired with sweet peas and herbs and served on tiny pieces of toast, it makes a great introduction to the healthy fish.

Steamer basket

Countertop blender

1 cup (250 mL) No-Salt-Added Chicken Stock (page 210) or ready-to-use no-salt-added chicken broth

3 peppercorns

5 oz (150 g) skin-on salmon fillet

Virgin olive oil

Fresh dill

1 cup (250 g) sweet peas

1 tbsp (15 mL) butter

Slice whole grain or white bread, toasted, crusts removed and cut into bite-size strips

1. Add stock and peppercorns to the inner pot and place the steamer basket in the pot. Place salmon skin side down on one side of the basket and brush top with oil. Sprinkle with dill. Add peas to the basket to the side of the salmon and on top if needed.

2. Close and lock the lid and turn the steam release handle to Sealing. Set your Instant Pot to pressure cook on Low for 5 minutes.

3. When the cooking time is done, press Cancel and turn the steam release handle to Venting. When the float valve drops down, remove the lid. The fish should be opaque and should flake easily when tested with a fork. (If more cooking time is needed, continue pressure cooking on Low for 1 minute.)

4. Transfer salmon to a work surface and remove the skin. Add salmon and $\frac{1}{2}$ cup (125 mL) peas to blender. Set aside remaining peas.

5. Set your Instant Pot to sauté on More. Cook, stirring often, for 3 minutes or until liquid is reduced to $\frac{1}{4}$ cup (60 mL). Press Cancel. Discard peppercorns. Stir in butter until melted. Add liquids to the blender. Cover and blend until desired consistency.

6. Spoon a small amount into serving bowl. Stir in the desired amount of peas. Test temperature before serving. Transfer remainder to ice cube trays.

NUTRITION TIP

Wild and farmed salmon are both good nutrition sources. Buy wild salmon when possible, as it contains fewer chemical contaminants.

MINI MEATBALLS AND MARINARA SAUCE

MAKES 12 MEATBALLS

Frozen mini meatballs make this recipe easy. The homemade marinara sauce makes it easier for you to control the seasonings and eliminate any processed additives.

1 can (28 oz/796 mL) whole tomatoes (preferably San Marzano), with juice

¾ cup (175 mL) water

¼ cup (60 mL) virgin olive oil

6 cloves garlic, slivered

Pinch hot pepper flakes (optional)

1 sprig fresh basil

12 frozen mini meatballs (approx. half of a 2 lb/1 kg package)

1. Pour tomatoes into a large bowl. Add ¾ cup (175 mL) water to the can, swishing it to collect the remaining juices. Set aside. Using your hands, crush tomatoes until pieces are about ½ inch (1 cm).

2. Set your Instant Pot to sauté on Normal. When the display says Hot, add oil and heat until shimmering. Add garlic and cook, stirring, for 1 minute or until fragrant. Add tomatoes, tomato water and hot pepper flakes (if using), stirring well. Place basil on top and just push down into sauce; do not stir. Press Cancel.

3. Close and lock the lid and turn the steam release handle to Sealing. Set your Instant Pot to pressure cook on High for 5 minutes.

4. When the cooking time is done, press Cancel and turn the steam release handle to Venting. When the float valve drops down, remove the lid. Add the meatballs, stirring just enough to cover with sauce. Close and lock the lid and turn the steam release handle to Sealing. Set your Instant Pot to pressure cook on High for 4 minutes. When the cooking time is done, press Cancel and turn the steam release handle to Venting. When the float valve drops down, remove the lid. The meatballs should be heated through and the sauce should be thickened. (If more cooking time is needed, set your Instant Pot to sauté on Less and simmer, stirring often, for 3 to 5 minutes or until thickened to your liking.) Discard basil sprig.

Variation

Instead of store-bought frozen meatballs, use the recipe for Turkey Meatball Bites (page 190).

NUTRITION TIP

It's a great idea to have a bag of frozen mini meatballs on hand, or make up a batch of Turkey Meatball Bites (page 190). You can add them to any fruit or veggie purée to add protein and iron for a more balanced meal.

TIPS

Use the best canned tomatoes you can find. San Marzano tomatoes are known for their quality and rich flavor, but any high-quality brand will would work.

You can use fresh, in-season tomatoes in place of canned. You will need about 10 to 12 plum (Roma) tomatoes, peeled, for this recipe. To quickly peel tomatoes, score one end of each tomato and add them to a pot of boiling water for 45 seconds or until the skin begins to wrinkle. Using tongs, quickly transfer them to a bowl of ice water, then peel and chop. Transfer tomatoes, with any accumulated juices, to a 4-cup (1 L) measuring cup and add enough water to measure $3\frac{1}{2}$ cups (875 mL). Add in place of the tomatoes and tomato water in step 2. Increase the cooking time in step 3 to 7 minutes.

The sauce can be refrigerated for up to 3 days or frozen for up to 3 months. Before freezing tomato sauce, divide it into measured amounts and label each container with the amount and date.

PORK, CARROTS, SPINACH AND STARS

MAKES ABOUT 2 CUPS (500 ML)

Tiny little star pasta, known as Pastina, are sure to light up your little one's face. A vitamin-rich mixture of carrots and spinach along with lean ground pork complete this meal.

Steamer basket

Countertop blender

¾ cup (175 mL) Pastina (star-shaped pasta)

2 tsp (10 mL) virgin olive oil

4 oz (125 g) lean ground pork

¼ cup (60 mL) chopped onion

1 carrot, thinly sliced

1 cup (250 mL) No-Salt-Added Vegetable Stock (page 211) or ready-to-use no-salt-added vegetable broth

1 cup (250 mL) lightly packed baby spinach

1 plum (Roma) tomato, peeled, seeded and diced

1. Set your Instant Pot to sauté on High. Add 12 cups (3 L) water to the inner pot. When the water is boiling, add the Pastina and cook, uncovered, according to package directions. Press Cancel. Strain pasta and rinse lightly with lukewarm water. Drain and set aside.

2. Rinse and dry the inner pot and return to the cooker. Set your Instant Pot to sauté on High. Add the oil and heat until shimmering. Add the ground pork and onion and cook, stirring and breaking meat up with a spoon, for 7 minutes or until pork is no longer pink and onion is softened. Press Cancel. Stir in carrots and stock. Arrange spinach in basket and place on top of pork mixture.

3. Close and lock the lid and turn the steam release handle to Sealing. Set your Instant Pot to pressure cook on High for 3 minutes.

4. When the cooking time is done, turn the steam release handle to Venting. When the float valve drops down, remove the lid. The carrots should be tender and the spinach should be wilted. (If more cooking time is needed, close and lock the lid and let stand 1 minute.)

5. Transfer spinach to the blender. Cover and pulse until desired consistency. Return spinach to the pot, stirring well. Stir in tomatoes and pasta.

6. Ladle a small amount into serving bowl. Test temperature before serving. Transfer remainder to ice cube trays.

NUTRITION TIP

Small shaped pasta such as stars, fuscilli or macaroni make a great starter finger food. Being so soft, pasta is easy to eat for toothless babies and fun for your baby to learn self-feeding skills.

WHITE BEAN AND DITALINI PASTA

MAKES ABOUT 2¼ CUPS (560 ML)

This rustic Italian-inspired dish is a delectable way for your little one to try new cuisines and food tastes and textures. It is versatile enough for babies who prefer softer, mushier textures and for ones that are ready to try more bite-size ingredients.

Countertop blender (optional)

¾ cup (175 mL) dried cannellini beans

2 medium carrots, peeled

1 clove garlic, smashed

1 bay leaf

1 tsp (5 mL) vegetable oil

4 oz (125 g) ditalini pasta

1 cup (250 mL) pasta sauce

Freshly grated Parmesan cheese (optional)

1. In a large bowl, combine beans and 3 cups (750 mL) cold water. Let stand at room temperature for 8 hours or overnight. Drain and rinse.

2. Add beans, carrots, garlic, bay leaf, 1½ cups (375 mL) cold water and oil to the inner pot. Close and lock the lid and turn the steam release handle to Sealing. Set your Instant Pot to pressure cook on High for 8 minutes.

3. When the cooking time is done, press Cancel and let stand, covered, until the float valve drops down, then remove the lid. The beans should be al dente. (If more cooking time is needed, continue pressure cooking on High for 2 minutes, then quickly release the pressure.) Discard garlic and bay leaf. Transfer carrots to a cutting board. Cut into bite-size pieces and set aside. Drain beans and set aside. Rinse the inner pot and return to the cooker.

4. Set your Instant Pot to sauté on High. Add 12 cups (3 L) water to the inner pot. When the water is boiling, add the ditalini and cook, uncovered, according to package directions. Press Cancel. Drain pasta and return to the pot. Stir in carrots, beans and pasta sauce; mixing well.

5. Ladle a small amount into serving bowl. Test temperature before serving. Sprinkle with Parmesan, if using. Transfer remainder to storage containers.

Variation

After step 3, beans can be puréed in a blender or mashed with a fork, depending upon the consistency you desire.

TIPS

Do not be tempted to quick soak the beans or omit soaking. The overnight soaking decreases the gas that could be caused by the beans.

SOUTHERN-INSPIRED PEAS AND GREENS

MAKES ABOUT 1⅓ CUPS (325 ML)

Not only are black-eyed peas believed to bring good luck if eaten at New Year's, they are also packed with protein, fiber, vitamin and minerals for your growing baby.

Steamer basket

Countertop blender

¾ cup (175 mL) dried back-eyed peas, rinsed and drained

2 slices bacon, quartered

¼ sweet onion (such as Vidalia), diced

1 clove garlic, minced

1½ cups (375 mL) No-Salt-Added Vegetable Stock (page 211) or ready-to-use no-salt-added vegetable broth

2 cups (500 mL) loosely packed collard greens

1. In a large bowl, combine peas and 3 cups (750 mL) cold water. Let stand at room temperature for 8 hours or overnight. Drain and rinse. Set aside.

2. Set your Instant Pot to sauté on Normal. Add bacon and cook, turning once, 5 minutes until bacon is crisp-tender and fat is rendered. Transfer bacon to a paper towel–lined plate. Add onion to the pot and cook, stirring often, 4 minutes or until softened. Add in garlic and cook, stirring, 1 minute or until fragrant. Stir stock and peas. Arrange collard greens in basket and place on top of pea mixture.

3. Close and lock the lid and turn the steam release handle to Sealing. Set your Instant Pot to pressure cook on High for 4 minutes.

4. When the cooking time is done, press Cancel and let stand, covered, 10 minutes. Turn the steam release handle until the float valve drops down, then remove the lid. The peas and greens should be al dente. (If more cooking time is needed, continue pressure cooking on High for 1 minute, then quickly release the pressure.) Transfer collard greens to the blender. Add the bacon pieces and pulse until desired consistency.

5. Drain peas and transfer to a bowl. Using a fork, mash mixture until desired consistency. Stir in collard green mixture.

6. Spoon a small amount into serving bowl. Test temperature before serving. Transfer remainder to storage containers.

NUTRITION TIP

Like kale and spinach, collard greens are a nutrition powerhouse. The vibrant green color indicates that it's full of antioxidants to help your baby grow and stay healthy. Purées and smoothies are a great way to offer these leafy greens to young eaters.

PENNE PASTA WITH MEATLESS TOMATO SAUCE

MAKES ABOUT 6 CUPS (1.5 L)

Penne pasta are the perfect tubular shapes to soak up lots of yummy sauce. This dish can be puréed, mashed or served whole depending upon your little one's eating stage.

Countertop blender (optional)

6 tbsp (90 mL) virgin olive oil

4 garlic cloves, crushed

1 can (28 oz/796 mL) peeled tomatoes, with juice

1 tbsp (15 mL) finely chopped fresh basil

1 lb (500 g) dried penne pasta

Grated Parmesan cheese (optional)

1. Set your Instant Pot to sauté on Normal. When the display says Hot, add oil and heat until shimmering. Add the garlic and cook, stirring, for 1 to 2 minutes or until golden. Using your hands, gently crush tomatoes before adding to the pot. Pour in remaining juice from the can. Add basil and cook, stirring, for 5 minutes. Press Cancel.

2. Add pasta, pushing it down into sauce. Add 1¼ cups (300 mL) water to the tomato can, swishing it to collect the remaining juices, and pour on top of pasta.

3. Close and lock the lid and turn the steam release handle to Sealing. Set your Instant Pot to pressure cook on High and adjust the time to half the time recommended on the pasta package minus 1 minute. (If the cooking time is a range, use half of the higher number minus 1 minute.)

4. When the cooking time is done, press Cancel and turn the steam release handle to Venting. When the float valve drops down, remove the lid. The pasta should be al dente. (If more cooking time is needed, continue pressure cooking on High for 1 minute.) Stir pasta and sauce.

5. Spoon a small amount into serving bowl. Test temperature before serving. Sprinkle with Parmesan cheese (if using). Transfer remainder to storage containers.

NUTRITION TIP

This is an easy, basic tomato sauce. It's flexible in that you can add beans or leftover meat to the finished product to add in some extra protein.

RED PEPPER HUMMUS WITH CARROT DIPPERS

MAKES ABOUT 3 CUPS (750 ML) HUMMUS

A creamy hummus gets an uptick in flavor from roasted red peppers. The peppers add a sweet and spicy bite and color to this dip. The little carrot coins your little one has tried earlier are great paired with this hummus.

Countertop blender

¾ cup (175 mL) dried chickpeas, rinsed

¼ tsp (1 mL) salt

1 tsp (5 mL) vegetable oil

2 cloves garlic, peeled and halved

1½ cups (375 mL) roasted red peppers, drained

6 tbsp (90 mL) extra virgin olive oil

1 tbsp (15 mL) lemon juice

Steamed Carrot Coins (page 129)

1. In a large bowl, combine beans and 3 cups (750 mL) cold water. Let stand at room temperature for 8 hours or overnight. Drain and rinse.

2. Add beans, salt and 1½ cups (375 mL) cold water and oil to the inner pot. Close and lock the lid and turn the steam release handle to Sealing. Set your Instant Pot to pressure cook on High for 12 minutes.

3. When the cooking time is done, press Cancel and let stand, covered, until the float valve drops down, then remove the lid. The beans should be al dente. (If more cooking time is needed, continue pressure cooking on High for 2 minutes, then quickly release the pressure.) Drain beans, reserving ½ cup liquid.

4. Meanwhile, add the garlic to the blender and pulse until minced. Add the peppers, olive oil, lemon juice, chickpeas and 6 tbsp (90 mL) of the reserved cooking liquid. Blend, scraping down the sides with a spatula and adding more liquid as needed, until smooth. Let cool.

5. Spoon a small amount into serving bowl. Serve with carrot dippers. Transfer remaining hummus and carrots to storage containers.

TIP

The hummus can be refrigerated in airtight containers for up to 2 days for little ones or up to 3 days for adults.

NUTRITION TIP

Dips are a great way to encourage your baby to have fun with vegetables. It improves their dexterity while also adding some nutrition (and flavor!) to the vegetables.

QUINOA, PEACHES AND YOGURT

MAKES ABOUT 1¾ CUPS (425 ML)

Quinoa and yogurt power up this wonderful breakfast or snack. Sweet bit of peaches add a nice sweet addition of finger foods.

2 tsp (10 mL) vegetable oil

1 cup (250 mL) quinoa, rinsed and well drained

1½ (375 mL) cups water

¾ cup (175 mL) Homemade Yogurt (page 206)

1 ripe peach, peeled, pitted and chopped

Ground cinnamon

1. Set your Instant Pot to sauté on Normal. When the display says Hot, add oil and heat until shimmering. Add quinoa and cook, stirring, for 2 to 3 minutes or until lightly toasted and fragrant. Press Cancel. Add 1½ cups (375 mL) water, stirring well.

2. Close and lock the lid and turn the steam release handle to Sealing. Set your Instant Pot to pressure cook on High for 2 minutes.

3. When the cooking time is done, press Cancel and let stand, covered, for 10 minutes, then turn the steam release handle to Venting. When the float valve drops down, remove the lid. The quinoa should be tender. (If more cooking time is needed, continue pressure cooking on High for 0 minutes, then quickly release the pressure.)

4. Fluff quinoa with a fork and let cool. Stir in yogurt.

5. Spoon a small amount into serving bowl. Stir in a pinch of cinnamon. Serve with chopped peaches. Transfer remainder to storage containers.

TIPS

While some packages say the quinoa is already rinsed, I like to rinse it again to remove any bitter taste.

If peaches are not perfectly ripened, store them in a paper bag at room temperature for 1 day or until ripened.

NUTRITION TIP

Use plain full-fat yogurt if you don't have the homemade version available. I suggest looking for a plain yogurt that contains at least 3% Milk Fat (MF). The added fat adds a creamy, tasty texture and provides extra fat your baby needs to support growth.

SHREDDED BEEF AND TENDER CARROTS

MAKES 2½ CUPS (625 ML)

Tender beef and carrots is an easy comfort food to serve your little one. Tarragon adds a new spice with delicious results. Serve in bite-size pieces or partially blended.

Countertop blender

2 tbsp (30 mL) vegetable oil (approx.)

Ground tarragon

1 lb (500 g) beef chuck roast, cut into large chunks

1 cup (250 mL) Low-Sodium Beef Bone Broth (page 212) or ready-to-use low-sodium beef broth

5 carrots, cut into 1½-inch (4 cm) chunks

1 tbsp (15 mL) fresh thyme leaves

1. Season beef lightly with tarragon. Set Instant Pot to sauté on Normal. When display says Hot, add oil and heat until shimmering. Working in batches, add beef and cook, stirring, for 3 minutes or until browned on all sides, adding more oil as needed. Using tongs, transfer beef to a plate as it is browned.

2. Add broth to the pot and cook, stirring and scraping up any brown bits from the bottom of the pot, for 2 minutes. Return beef and any accumulated juices to the pot and stir in carrots, potatoes and thyme. Press Cancel.

3. Close and lock the lid and turn the steam release handle to Sealing. Set your Instant Pot to pressure cook on High for 20 minutes.

4. When the cooking time is done, press Cancel and let stand, covered, for 10 minutes, then turn the steam release handle to Venting. When the float valve drops down, remove the lid. The beef and vegetables should be fork-tender. (If more cooking time is needed, continue pressure cooking on High for 5 minutes.)

5. Using a slotted spoon, transfer beef mixture to a work surface. Using a fork, shred beef into small pieces. Cut carrots into bite-size pieces.

6. Spoon a small amount into serving bowl. Test temperature before serving. Transfer remainder to storage trays.

Variation

In step 6, transfer a portion of the beef and carrots to a countertop blender. Add 1 tbsp (15 mL) liquid from the pot, cover and pulse until desired consistency. Serve blended mixture with bite-size pieces of carrots and beef.

NUTRITION TIP

Shredded beef is a great way to introduce meat to your baby. It's tender and easy to grasp and chew the shreds of meat. Your baby may just suck on the shreds to begin with, and that's okay. They do get a little bit of nutrition out of the juice.

ZESTY CARROT AND CAULIFLOWER SOUP

MAKES ABOUT 4 CUPS (1 L)

Carrots, cauliflower and gingerroot are cooked and blended to make a creamy, colorful soup. Blending in coconut milk and lime juice gives this soup a tropical flare.

Countertop blender

2 tbsp (30 mL) virgin olive oil

8 oz (500 g) carrots, chopped

8 oz (500 g) cauliflower florets, chopped

1 onion, chopped

2 tsp (10 mL) grated gingerroot

4 cups (1 L) No-Salt-Added Vegetable Stock (page 211) or ready-to-use no-salt-added vegetable broth

½ cup (125 mL) coconut milk

1 tbsp (15 mL) freshly squeezed lime or lemon juice

1. Set your Instant Pot to sauté on More. When the display says Hot, add oil and heat until shimmering. Add carrots and onion; cook, stirring often, for 5 minutes or until onion is softened. Stir in cauliflower and ginger; cook, stirring, for 1 minute. Stir in stock. Press Cancel.

2. Close and lock the lid and turn the steam release handle to Sealing. Set your Instant Pot to pressure cook on High for 5 minutes.

3. When the cooking time is done, press Cancel and turn the steam release handle to Venting. When the float valve drops down, remove the lid. The carrots and cauliflower should be fork-tender. (If more cooking time is needed, continue pressure cooking on High for 1 minute.)

4. Working in batches, transfer mixture to the blender and purée until smooth. Pulse in coconut milk and lime juice.

5. Pour a small amount into a sippy cup. Test temperature before serving. Transfer remainder to storage containers.

TIPS

The mixture can be refrigerated in airtight containers for up to 2 days or frozen for up to 3 months.

Before step 4, set aside some of the carrots and cauliflower to be used as little dippers in the soup.

NUTRITION TIP

This soup is a tasty powerhouse of nutrients. Surprisingly (as it's not orange!), cauliflower is an excellent source of vitamin C. And carrots are one of the highest sources of vitamin A. Both of these vitamins are antioxidants.

CARROT AND GINGER SOUP

MAKES 4 TO 6 SERVINGS

This soup's bright orange color makes it pleasing to the eye and tempting to your palate. The marrying of carrots with slightly spicy ginger and creamy coconut milk gives it a mouthwatering depth of flavor.

Immersion blender (see tip)

2 tbsp (30 mL) virgin olive oil

1 lb (500 g) carrots, chopped

1 onion, chopped

2 tsp (10 mL) grated gingerroot

4 cups (1 L) No-Salt-Added Vegetable Stock (page 211) or ready-to-use no-salt-added vegetable broth

½ cup (125 mL) coconut milk

Salt and freshly ground black pepper

1 to 2 tbsp (15 to 30 mL) freshly squeezed lime or lemon juice

1. Set your Instant Pot to sauté on More. When the display says Hot, add oil and heat until shimmering. Add carrots and onion; cook, stirring often, for 5 minutes or until onion is softened. Stir in ginger and cook, stirring, for 1 minute. Stir in stock. Press Cancel.

2. Close and lock the lid and turn the steam release handle to Sealing. Set your Instant Pot to pressure cook on High for 5 minutes.

3. When the cooking time is done, press Cancel and turn the steam release handle to Venting. When the float valve drops down, remove the lid. The carrots should be fork-tender. (If more cooking time is needed, continue pressure cooking on High for 1 minute.)

4. Using the immersion blender, purée soup until smooth. Stir in coconut milk. Season to taste with salt, pepper and lime juice. Transfer soup to sippy cups or ladle into serving bowls (see tip). Test temperature before serving.

TIPS

In step 4, instead of using an immersion blender, you can transfer the soup, in batches, to a countertop blender. Be very careful when transferring soup, as it is very hot. Do not fill your blender more than halfway, to prevent hot soup from spewing out the top. After puréeing, return soup to the cooker. Set your Instant Pot to sauté on Less. Cook, stirring often, until heated through.

If using serving bowls, serve with crackers or breadsticks for dipping.

NUTRITION TIP

Ginger can help treat nausea and indigestion and has anti-inflammatory effects.

ROTINI PASTA WITH SUN-DRIED TOMATOES AND BASIL

MAKES ABOUT 2 CUPS (500 ML)

Rotini pasta with its corkscrew shape is a nice shape for little fingers to more easily pick up and also adds more visual interest to their meal. Chose a dried veggie pasta for added vegetables or start with a traditional wheat pasta.

4 oz (60 g) rotini pasta

1 tsp (5 mL) butter

1 tsp (5 mL) pure olive oil

1 clove garlic

2 tsp (10 mL) chopped fresh basil leaves

$1/4$ cup (60 mL) sun-dried tomatoes, drained

$1/4$ cup (60 mL) half-and-half (10%) cream

$3/4$ cup (175 mL) milk

$1/4$ cup (60 mL) No-Salt-Added Chicken Stock (page 210) or ready-to-use no-salt-added chicken broth

$1/8$ tsp (1 mL) salt

2 cups (500 mL) spinach

1. Set your Instant Pot to sauté on Normal. When the display says Hot, add oil and heat until shimmering. Add the garlic and cook, stirring, for 1 minute or until fragrant. Using your hands, gently crush tomatoes before adding to the pot. Pour in remaining juice from the can. Add basil and cook, stirring, for 5 minutes. Press Cancel.

2. Add pasta, pushing it down into sauce. Add $1\frac{1}{4}$ cups (300 mL) water to the tomato can, swishing it to collect the remaining juices, and pour on top of pasta.

3. Close and lock the lid and turn the steam release handle to Sealing. Set your Instant Pot to pressure cook on High and adjust the time to half the time recommended on the pasta package minus 1 minute. (If the cooking time is a range, use half of the higher number minus 1 minute.)

4. When the cooking time is done, press Cancel and turn the steam release handle to Venting. When the float valve drops down, remove the lid. The pasta should be al dente. (If more cooking time is needed, continue pressure cooking on High for 1 minute.) Stir pasta and sauce.

5. Spoon a small amount into serving bowl. Test temperature before serving. Sprinkle with Parmesan cheese, if using. Transfer remainder to storage containers.

NUTRITION TIP

Both butter and olive oil are good sources of fat for your baby. While different oils contain different fat profiles (butter is mostly saturated, while olive oil is mostly unsaturated), variety is good to strive for!

TORTELLINI AND CRANBERRY BEAN SALAD

MAKES 4 SERVINGS

This powerhouse salad is a tasty vegetarian dish for a warm summer's day. The pepperoncini adds a slightly spicy kick to this interesting combination of flavors.

2 cups (500 mL) dried borlotti (cranberry) beans, rinsed

Water

1 tbsp (15 mL) vegetable oil

1 package (9 oz/255 g) fresh three-cheese tortellini pasta

9 pepperoncini peppers with brine

3 tbsp (45 mL) chopped fresh parsley

⅓ cup (75 mL) extra virgin olive oil

Salt and freshly ground black pepper

6 tbsp (90 mL) shredded Parmesan cheese

1. In a large bowl, combine beans and 8 cups (2 L) cold water. Let stand at room temperature for 8 hours or overnight. Drain and rinse.

2. Add beans, oil and 4 cups (1 L) fresh cold water to the inner pot. Close and lock the lid and turn the steam release handle to Sealing. Set your Instant Pot to pressure cook on High for 8 minutes.

3. When the cooking time is done, press Cancel and let stand, covered, for 15 minutes, then turn the steam release handle to Venting. When the float valve drops down, remove the lid. The beans should be al dente. (If more cooking time is needed, continue pressure cooking on High for 1 minute, then quickly release the pressure.) Drain and rinse beans with cold water and let cool to room temperature.

4. Set your Instant Pot to sauté on More. Add water according to pasta package directions and bring to a boil. Reduce heat to Normal. Add tortellini and cook according to package directions until al dente. Drain pasta, rinse with cold water and let cool to room temperature.

5. Meanwhile, drain peppers, reserving 1½ tbsp (22 mL) brine. Slice peppers and set aside.

6. In a small bowl, whisk together parsley, oil and pepper brine. Season to taste with salt and pepper.

7. In a large bowl, combine beans, tortellini, peppers and dressing, tossing gently. Serve sprinkled with Parmesan.

TIP

You can use a 7-oz (196 g) box of dried tortellini in place of fresh. In step 4, adjust the cooking time to half the time recommended on the box.

STEAMED CAULIFLOWER AND BROCCOLI WITH AVOCADO MASH

MAKES 1½ CUPS (375 ML)

Here, cauliflower and broccoli florets get gently steamed to retain all their nutrients and offer an eye-catching colorful finger food. The avocado mash makes a great little dip for the veggies.

Steamer basket

¾ cup (175 mL) broccoli florets (about 4 oz/125 g)

¾ cup (175 mL) cauliflower florets (about 8 oz/250 g)

1 tbsp (5 mL) butter, softened

½ avocado, peeled and pitted

Freshly squeezed lemon juice

Chopped fresh cilantro (optional)

Red pepper flakes (optional)

1. In the inner pot, add 1 cup (250 mL) water and place the steamer basket in the pot. Arrange broccoli and cauliflower florets in the basket.

2. Close and lock the lid and turn the steam release handle to Sealing. Set your Instant Pot to pressure cook on High for 1 minute.

3. When the cooking time is done, press Cancel and turn the steam release handle to Venting. When the float valve drops down, remove the lid. The florets should be tender. (If more cooking time is needed, continue pressure cooking on High for 0 minutes.)

4. Transfer florets to a serving bowl. Cut florets, into bite-size pieces, if desired. Add butter, if using, tossing gently until melted. Test temperature before serving. Transfer remaining florets to an airtight container and refrigerate for up to 3 days.

5. Meanwhile, in a small bowl add avocado and, using a fork, mash until desired consistency. Stir in lemon juice to taste. Stir in cilantro, if using, and pepper flakes, if using. Serve as a dip with the broccoli and cauliflower

149

TIP

Cut florets smaller only after they are cooked, if desired. Cutting them into bite-size pieces for your baby before cooking will not get the desired results.

NUTRITION TIP

Avocado is a perfect food for little ones, as it's high in healthy fats. To offer slices as a finger food, roll avocado in ground flax seeds (flaxseed meal) or infant cereal so that it's less slippery.

CREAMED PEAS AND COD

MAKES 2 TO 3 SERVINGS

This old-fashioned dish has remained in families for generations and for good reason. It is so easy to make and the flavors are purely comforting.

Steam rack
Two 18- by 12-inch (45 by 30 cm) sheets parchment paper

6 oz (175 g) cod fillet

Virgin olive oil

2 fresh thyme sprigs

1 cup (250 g) frozen peas

Freshly ground black pepper

2 tbsp (30 mL) butter

2 tbsp (30 mL) all-purpose flour or cornstarch

½ cup (125 mL) milk

1. Add 1½ cups (375 mL) water to the inner pot and place the steam rack in the pot. Place cod on prepared piece of parchment paper and brush top with oil. Place thyme sprigs on top. Arrange peas around cod. Season with pepper. Fold parchment paper into tent-style packets (see page 62).

2. Close and lock lid and turn steam release handle to Sealing. Set Instant Pot to pressure cook on Low for 3 minutes.

3. When the cooking time is done, press Cancel and turn the steam release handle to Venting. When the float valve drops down, remove the lid. The fish should be opaque and should flake easily when tested with a fork. (If more cooking time is needed, continue pressure cooking on Low for 1 minute.)

4. Open packets, draining any excess liquid from the packet. Cut or flake cod into bite-size pieces that are easy to grasp. Set aside. Discard liquid in the pot and return pot to cooker.

5. Set your Instant Pot to sauté on Less. Add butter and cook until butter is melted. Add flour and cook, whisking continuously, 1 minute or until combined. Slowly stir in the milk and cook, stirring, until milk begins to bubble. Gently stir in the cod and peas and cook just until warmed through. Cancel cooking.

6. Spoon into individual serving bowls. Test temperature before serving.

SERVING SUGGESTION
Serve over saltine crackers or toast.

TIP

The mixture can be covered tightly and refrigerated up to 3 days. Reheat before serving. We do not recommend freezing this recipe.

NUTRITION TIP

Frozen peas are a great veggie to keep stored in your freezer. They are an easy finger food and you can use them to cool down hot dishes like stews and soups!

150

TUNA MACARONI AND CHEESE

MAKES 4 SERVINGS

Classic macaroni and cheese remains a family favorite, from kids to adults. Here, the tuna adds a unique taste and texture and ups the nutrient values.

2 cups (500 mL) dried elbow macaroni

Salt

2 cups (500 mL) Low-Sodium Vegetable Stock (variation, page 211) or ready-to-use reduced-sodium vegetable broth

1 can (12 oz/370 mL) evaporated milk

2½ cups (625 mL) shredded Cheddar cheese

2 cans (5 oz/150 g) light tuna in water, drained

Freshly ground black pepper

1. In the inner pot, combine macaroni, ¼ tsp (1 mL) salt and stock. Close and lock the lid and turn the steam release handle to Sealing. Set your Instant Pot to pressure cook on Low for 3 minutes.

2. When the cooking time is done, press Cancel and turn the steam release handle to Venting. When the float valve drops down, remove the lid. The pasta should be al dente. (If more cooking time is necessary, close and lock the lid and let stand for 1 minute.)

3. Stir in milk. Set your Instant Pot to sauté on Less. Cook, stirring, for 2 to 3 minutes or until sauce has thickened and pasta is done to your liking. Press Cancel. Add cheese, ½ cup (125 mL) at a time, stirring until melted and combined before adding more. Add tuna, stirring, 2 minutes or until heated through. Season to taste with pepper. Test temperature before serving.

Variations

You can omit the tuna for a vegetarian version of this dish.

In step 1, stir in 1 tsp (5 mL) dry mustard with the stock.

....

TIPS

Two cups (500 mL) elbow macaroni is about 8 oz (250 g).

When using the Quick Release method to release pressure, keep your hands and face away from the hole on top of the steam release handle so you don't get scalded by the escaping steam.

NUTRITION TIP

As you may remember from pregnancy, certain fish are higher in mercury than others. Canned light tuna has lower mercury (with no limits on intake) than canned white or albacore tuna. Health Canada has no recommended limit on intake for light tuna, and it's a good source of protein and omega-3 fats.

SWEET AND TANGY MEATBALLS

MAKES 36 MEATBALLS

It is always a good idea to keep a bag of frozen meatballs in the freezer for a quick meal. This fun recipe is just one of the many reasons why.

Steamer basket

1 package (3 lbs/1.5 kg) frozen fully cooked beef meatballs

2¼ cups (550 mL) barbecue sauce

2 cups (500 mL) grape jelly

¼ cup (60 mL) apple cider vinegar

1. Add 1 cup (250 mL) water to the inner pot. Stack meatballs in the steamer basket, alternating the spacing, and place in the pot. Close and lock the lid and turn the steam release handle to Sealing. Set your Instant Pot to pressure cook on High for 5 minutes.

2. When the timer beeps, press Cancel and turn the steam release handle to Venting. When the float valve drops down, remove the lid. Check to make sure the meatballs are heated through. (If more cooking is needed, continue cooking for 2 minutes.) Carefully remove the steamer basket. Discard water.

3. Add barbecue sauce, jelly and vinegar to the pot, stirring well. Press Sauté and cook, stirring often, for 5 to 7 minutes or until sauce is smooth. Add meatballs and cook, stirring to coat, for 2 minutes.

4. Using a slotted spoon, transfer meatballs to a serving platter. Spoon sauce into small bowls for dipping. Test temperature before serving

TIPS

See page 215 for an All-Around Barbecue Sauce recipe.

Peach or apricot jelly is a good substitute for the grape jelly.

While meatballs are often served on toothpicks or small bamboo skewers, it is not something we recommend for small children.

Older siblings or parents may want to add 3 of these meatballs to a toasted hoagie roll and drizzle with sauce.

NUTRITION TIP

Serve these meatballs on a bed of rice with vegetable side dish for a meal. They would also make a great appetizer for a family get together or kid's birthday party!

TIP

Use any of your favorite barbecue sauces, but do not choose a sweeter variety, because the grape jelly adds plenty of sweetness.

SPICY RED LENTIL AND CARROT SOUP

MAKES 6 CUPS (1.5 L)

Conjuring up stories of the Arabian nights, this soup is just as mystical and intriguing with its bright color and fragrant spices. This soup is satisfying to many ages.

Immersion blender (see tip, page 63)

2 tbsp (30 mL) vegetable oil

1 large onion, chopped

1½ tbsp (22 mL) ras el hanout (see tips)

2 large carrots, chopped

1½ cups (375 mL) dried red lentils, rinsed

4 cups (1 L) Low-Sodium Vegetable Stock (page 211) or Low-Sodium Chicken Stock (page 210) or ready-to-use reduced-sodium vegetable or chicken broth

Freshly ground black pepper

Salt (optional)

1. Set your Instant Pot to sauté on Normal. When the display says Hot, add oil and heat until shimmering. Add onion and cook, stirring often, for 5 minutes or until softened. Stir in ras el hanout and cook, stirring, for 30 seconds. Stir in carrots, lentils and stock. Press Cancel.

2. Close and lock the lid and turn the steam release handle to Sealing. Set your Instant Pot to pressure cook on High for 10 minutes.

3. When the cooking time is done, press Cancel and turn the steam release handle to Venting. When the float valve drops down, remove the lid. The lentils and carrots should be tender. (If more cooking time is needed, continue pressure cooking on High for 1 minute.)

4. Using the immersion blender, purée soup until smooth. Season to taste with pepper. Older eaters may want to season with salt, but do not add salt for babies. Transfer soup to sippy cups for toddlers and test test temperature before serving (see tip).

TIPS

Ras el hanout is a traditional Moroccan spice blend that combines many different spices. It can be found in the spice section of the grocery store. You can use it on dishes made with poultry, pork, beef or lamb. Choose a blend without added salt.

Do not use green or brown lentils, as the results will not be the same.

NUTRITION TIP

If your toddler isn't yet scooping with a spoon and has difficulty eating soup, here's a tip: serve it in an open cup to drink! Or offer a bread stick to dip into the soup.

GREEK-INSPIRED QUINOA, CUCUMBER AND TOMATOES

MAKES 6 SERVINGS

This bright, fresh salad is a great way to share lunch with your little one. You will both be energized to carry on the remainder of the day.

1½ tbsp (22 mL) vegetable oil

1 cup (250 mL) quinoa, rinsed

½ cup (125 mL) dried green lentils, rinsed

2¼ cups (550 mL) water

8 oz grape (250 g) tomatoes, quartered

1 seedless cucumber, cut into ½-inch (1 cm) chunks (see tip)

½ cup (125 mL) Greek vinaigrette

Fresh minced mint

Freshly ground black pepper

1. Set your Instant Pot to sauté on Normal. When the display says Hot, add oil and heat until shimmering. Add quinoa and cook, stirring, for 2 to 3 minutes or until lightly toasted. Press Cancel. Add lentils and water, stirring well.

2. Close and lock the lid and turn the steam release handle to Sealing. Set your Instant Pot to pressure cook on High for 10 minutes.

3. When the cooking time is done, press Cancel and turn the steam release handle to Venting. When the float valve drops down, remove the lid. The quinoa and lentils should be tender, with a bit of texture. (If more cooking time is needed, close and lock the lid and let stand for 2 minutes.)

4. Transfer quinoa mixture to a fine-mesh sieve and rinse with cold water until chilled. Let drain for 10 minutes.

5. Meanwhile, add tomatoes and cucumbers to a colander set in a sink. Let drain in sink.

6. In a large bowl, combine quinoa mixture, tomatoes, cucumber and vinaigrette. Sprinkle with mint. Season to taste with pepper. Serve immediately or, for optimum flavor, cover and refrigerate overnight.

TIP

The salad can be refrigerated in an airtight container for up to 2 days.

NUTRITION TIP

I love to make a salad like this one on a Sunday and have it available for lunches during the busy week. If you're sending your kiddo off to daycare (or yourself off to work!) you can pre-portion the salad in ready-to-grab containers.

OLD-FASHIONED CHICKEN NOODLE SOUP

MAKES 8 SERVINGS

With this recipe, you can make enough chicken soup to keep your little ones warm and happy all winter. Freeze it in serving-size portions, so you can whip it out when you want a quick comforting meal. You can easily cut this recipe in half too.

2 tbsp (30 mL) butter

1 onion, chopped

2 carrots, peeled and chopped

2 stalks celery, chopped

Whole celery leaves (cut from the stalks)

1½ tbsp (22 mL) fresh chopped parsley

1 tbsp (15 mL) fresh chopped oregano

4 cups (1 L) Low-Sodium Chicken Stock (page 210) or ready-to-use reduced-sodium chicken broth

4 cups (1 L) water

4 to 5 bone-in, skin-on chicken thighs (about 2 lbs/1 kg total)

2 cups (500 mL) wide egg noodles

1. Set your Instant Pot to sauté on Normal. Add the butter and heat until melted. Add onions, carrots and celery; cook, stirring, 5 minutes or until the onion is softened. Press Cancel.

2. Add the celery leaves, parsley, oregano, stock and water, stirring well. Add the chicken thighs.

3. Close and lock the lid and turn the steam release handle to Sealing. Set your Instant Pot to pressure cook on High for 7 minutes.

4. When the cooking time is done, press Cancel. Let stand 10 minutes and then turn the steam release handle to Venting. When the float valve drops down, remove the lid. An instant-read thermometer inserted horizontally into the thickest part of the thighs should register 165°F (74°C) (If more cooking time is needed, close and lock the lid and cook for 2 minutes.)

5. Using tongs, transfer chicken thighs to a work surface. Using 2 forks, shred the chicken. Discard the bones and skin. Remove and discard the celery leaves.

6. Set your Instant Pot to sauté on Normal. Add the noodles to the pot and follow the package instructions for cooking time. When the cooking time is done, press Cancel. Stir in the shredded chicken. Ladle soup into serving bowls. Cut any vegetables and chicken into smaller pieces, if necessary. Test temperature before serving.

NUTRITION TIP

Chicken noodle soup is the classic easy-to-digest food when you're feeling under the weather. It will also help your little one stay hydrated.

JUST MY SIZE PUMPKIN PIE

MAKES 8 SERVINGS

Watch with delight as each family member gets their very own pumpkin pie. These scrumptious pumpkin pies are so easy to make when you don't have to fuss with a crust. You also free up your oven for other fixings for a holiday meal.

Eight 4-oz (125 mL) ramekins

Steam rack

Tall steam rack (see tip)

2 large eggs

1 tbsp (15 mL) cornstarch

2½ tsp (12 mL) pumpkin pie spice

Pinch salt

½ tsp (2 mL) vanilla extract

1 can (14 oz or 300 mL) sweetened condensed milk

1 can (15 oz/426 mL) pumpkin purée (not pie filling)

1. In a large bowl, whisk eggs. Whisk in cornstarch, pie spice, salt, vanilla and milk until well combined. Stir in pumpkin until thoroughly combined. Pour into ramekins, dividing evenly.

2. Add 1½ cups (375 mL) hot water to the inner pot and place the steam rack in the pot. Arrange 4 ramekins on the rack. Place the tall steam rack over the ramekins and place the remaining ramekins on top.

3. Close and lock the lid and turn the steam release handle to Sealing. Set your Instant Pot to pressure cook on High for 9 minutes.

4. When the cooking time is done, press Cancel and let stand, covered, for 10 minutes, then turn the steam release handle to Venting. When the float valve drops down, remove the lid. A tester inserted in the center of a ramekin should come out clean. (If more cooking time is needed, continue pressure cooking on High for 2 minutes, then quickly release the pressure.)

5. Carefully remove ramekins from the pot and let cool to room temperature.

SERVING SUGGESTION

Serve with graham crackers or shortbread cookies and a dollop of whipped cream.

TIPS

Remove the lid carefully in step 4 to avoid dripping any moisture from the lid onto the pies.

The pies can be cooled, covered tightly and refrigerated for up to 3 days.

If you don't have a tall steam rack, you can stack the ramekins on the rack in alternating layers (like stacking bricks). The pies on the bottom layer may not be as smooth on top, but they will be just as delicious.

Family Meals

BROCCOLI, ROASTED PEPPER AND GARLIC EGG BITES

MAKES 7 EGG BITES

Start everyone's day off right with these protein- and vegetable-powered bites. You can always make them ahead of time and reheat when you are ready.

Blender

Silicone egg bites mold with 7 cups, sprayed with nonstick cooking spray

Steam rack

3 large eggs

2 tbsp (30 mL) egg whites

1 cup (250 mL) shredded Swiss cheese

½ cup (125 mL) cottage cheese

¼ cup (60 mL) heavy or whipping (35%) cream

2 tsp (10 mL) minced garlic

Pinch salt

⅓ cup (75 mL) chopped frozen broccoli florets, thawed

3 tbsp (45 mL) drained (from a jar) roasted red peppers

1. In blender, combine eggs, egg whites, Swiss cheese, cottage cheese, cream, garlic, salt, broccoli and peppers; blend until combined with small bits of cheese, broccoli and peppers visible.

2. Pour into prepared egg bites mold, dividing evenly between cups.

3. Add 1 cup (250 mL) water to the inner pot. Place the egg bites mold on the steam rack and place in the pot.

4. Close and lock the lid and turn the steam release handle to Sealing. Set your Instant Pot to pressure cook on High for 8 minutes.

5. When the cooking time is done, press Cancel and let stand, covered, for 5 minutes, then turn the steam release handle to Venting. When the float valve drops down, remove the lid. A tester inserted in the center should come out clean. (If more cooking time is needed, continue pressure cooking on High for 1 minute.)

6. To serve immediately, invert a plate on top of the mold, flip it over and gently squeeze the cups to release the egg bites. Transfer bites onto serving plates. For babies and toddlers, test temperature before serving. Return any remaining bites to the mold.

TIP

Instead of inverting egg bites onto a plate, let bites stand 3 minutes or until firmer, and then gently scoop out with a spoon to serve.

SPINACH, MUSHROOM AND BELL PEPPER CRUSTLESS QUICHE

MAKES 4 SERVINGS

A mouthwatering combination of vegetables adds inviting textures and flavors to this hearty quiche. Serve it for breakfast, lunch or dinner.

4-cup (1 L) round soufflé dish, bottom and sides buttered

Steamer basket

Steam rack

3 cups (750 mL) loosely packed baby spinach leaves

1 tbsp (15 mL) butter

8 oz (250 g) sliced button mushrooms

½ red bell pepper, chopped

6 eggs

1 cup (250 mL) shredded Swiss cheese

1 cup (250 mL) milk

½ tsp (2 mL) kosher salt

¼ tsp (1 mL) freshly ground black pepper

1. Add 1 cup (250 mL) water to the inner pot and place the steamer basket in the pot (see tip). Arrange spinach leaves in the basket.

2. Close and lock the lid and turn the steam release handle to Sealing. Set your Instant Pot to pressure cook on High for 1 minute.

3. When the cooking time is done, press Cancel and turn the steam release handle to Venting. When the float valve drops down, remove the lid. Drain spinach and squeeze dry. Set aside. Rinse cooking pot and wipe dry.

4. Set your Instant Pot to sauté on Normal. When the display says Hot, add butter and heat until melted. Add mushrooms and bell pepper and cook, stirring frequently, 5 minutes or until liquid from mushrooms has evaporated. Press Cancel.

5. In a large bowl, whisk eggs. Add in cheese, milk, salt, pepper, spinach, mushrooms and peppers, stirring. Pour mixture into prepared soufflé dish and cover loosely with foil.

6. Add 1 cup (250 mL) water to the inner pot and place the steam rack in the pot. Place the soufflé dish on the rack. Close and lock the lid and turn the steam release handle to Sealing. Set your Instant Pot to pressure cook on High for 10 minutes.

7. When the cooking time is done, press Cancel and let the cooker stand, covered, for 5 minutes. Release the remaining pressure and remove lid. Check to see whether a knife inserted in the center comes out clean. (If more cooking time is needed, continue pressure cooking on High for 2 minutes.)

8. Remove quiche from cooker and let stand 5 minutes. Cut into wedges and serve. For babies and toddlers, test temperature before serving.

FARMHOUSE BEEF STEW

MAKES 6 TO 8 SERVINGS

A classic beef stew is always welcomed. The chunky stew can be enjoyed by adults, cut into smaller pieces for toddlers or mashed into a soft medley for babies.

2 lbs (1 kg) cubed beef stew meat or boneless stewing beef, cut into 1½-inch (4 cm) cubes

Salt and freshly ground black pepper

3 tbsp (45 mL) vegetable oil (approx.)

1½ tsp (7 mL) onion powder

1½ tsp (7 mL) paprika

¾ tsp (3 mL) dried basil leaves

¾ tsp (3 mL) dried parsley

½ tsp (2 mL) dried oregano

2 cups (500 mL) Low-Sodium Beef Bone Broth (page 212) or ready-to-use reduced-sodium beef broth

3 carrots, cut into 1½-inch (4 cm) chunks

1 lb (500 g) small white potatoes, quartered

¼ cup (60 mL) cold water

3 tbsp (45 mL) all-purpose flour

1. Season beef lightly with salt and pepper. Set your Instant Pot to sauté on Normal. When the display says Hot, add 2 tbsp (30 mL) oil and heat until shimmering. Working in batches, add beef and cook, stirring, for 2 minutes or until browned on all sides, adding more oil as needed between batches. Using tongs, transfer beef to a plate as it browns.

2. Add onion powder, paprika, basil leaves, parsley, oregano and broth to the pot; cook, stirring and scraping up any brown bits from the bottom of the pot, for 2 minutes. Return beef and any accumulated juices to the pot and stir in carrots and potatoes. Press Cancel.

3. Close and lock the lid and turn the steam release handle to Sealing. Set your Instant Pot to pressure cook on High for 20 minutes.

4. When the cooking time is done, press Cancel and let stand, covered, for 10 minutes, then turn the steam release handle to Venting. When the float valve drops down, remove the lid. The beef and vegetables should be fork-tender. (If more cooking time is needed, continue pressure cooking on High for 5 minutes.)

5. Add cold water to a small bowl and whisk in flour until smooth.

6. Set your Instant Pot to sauté on Normal. Slowly pour flour mixture into the pot and cook, stirring often, for 5 minutes or until stew is thickened to your liking. Season to taste with salt and pepper.

Variation

Omit 1 tsp (5 mL) onion powder and add 1 onion, cut into thin wedges, with the carrots and potatoes in step 2.

NUTRITION TIP

Beef stew is great for babies, as it is full of soft veggies and iron-rich beef.

ROOT VEGETABLE AND CHICKEN STEW

MAKES 1¼ CUPS (300 ML)

There is nothing quite like a bowl of warm chicken stew, and we think your baby will agree.

Countertop blender

1 tbsp (15 mL) butter

2 carrots, peeled and thinly sliced

1 cup (250 mL) cubed parsnips

3 tbsp (45 mL) diced onion

½ cup (125 mL) chicken cubes

1 cup (250 mL) No-Salt-Added Chicken Stock (page 210) or ready-to-use no-salt-added chicken broth

2 tsp (10 mL) dried parsley

1 tsp (5 mL) ground thyme

1. Set your Instant Pot to sauté on Normal. Add the butter and heat until melted. Add carrots, parsnips and onion; cook, stirring often, 3 minutes or until carrots and onions are softened. Add chicken and cook, stirring, 2 minutes. Stir in stock, parsley and thyme. Press Cancel.

2. Close and lock the lid and turn the steam release handle to Sealing. Set your Instant Pot to pressure cook on High for 2 minutes.

3. When the cooking time is done, press Cancel and turn the steam release handle to Venting. When the float valve drops down, remove the lid. The chicken should no longer be pink in the middle and the vegetables should be tender (If more cooking time is needed, close and lock the lid and let stand 2 minutes.)

4. Spoon a small amount into serving bowl. Test temperature before serving. Transfer remainder to ice cube trays.

Variation

Stir in a pinch of turmeric in step 5 for an added boost of nutrients.

......

TIP

Stew can be refrigerated in airtight containers for up to 2 days and frozen in individual portions for up to 3 months.

NUTRITION TIP

While colorful veggies generally contain more nutrients, white vegetables count too! Parsnips are a source of fiber, potassium and vitamin C.

CHICKEN AND WHITE BEAN CHILI

MAKES 6 TO 8 SERVINGS

Here, traditional chicken chili gets a flavor boost from spicy, aromatic salsa verde. Using your Instant Pot you can make everything from scratch or use or tips for alternatives.

1½ cups (375 mL) dried cannellini (white kidney) beans

Water

3 cups (750 mL) diced leftover rotisserie chicken (store-bought or see recipe, page 184)

1 tsp (5 mL) ground cumin

1 bay leaf

3½ cups (875 mL) Chicken Stock (page 210) or ready-to-use chicken broth

2 cups (500 mL) salsa verde

Salt and freshly ground black pepper

Hot pepper flakes (optional)

1. Place beans in a large bowl, add 6 cups (1.5 L) cold water and let soak at room temperature for 8 hours or overnight. Drain and rinse beans.

2. In the inner pot, combine beans, chicken, cumin, bay leaf, stock and salsa. Season to taste with salt and pepper.

3. Close and lock the lid and turn the steam release handle to Sealing. Set your Instant Pot to pressure cook on High for 10 minutes.

4. When the cooking time is done, press Cancel and let stand, covered, until the float valve drops down. Remove the lid. The beans should be tender. (If more cooking time is needed, continue pressure cooking on High for 2 minutes, then quickly release the pressure.) Discard bay leaf.

5. If you prefer a thicker chili, use a potato masher to mash some of the beans and break up some of the chicken until the chili is your desired consistency. Season to taste with salt and pepper. If desired, sprinkle with hot pepper flakes.

SERVING SUGGESTIONS:
Serve garnished with diced avocado, shredded cheese, sour cream and crumbled tortilla chips.

164

TIPS

Replace the dried cannellini beans with 1 can (15 oz/435 g) cannellini beans drained. Omit step 1.

3 cups (750 mL) diced chicken is equal to about 11 oz (330 g) cooked boneless skinless chicken.

The chili can be stored in airtight containers in the refrigerator for up to 3 days or in the freezer for up to 3 months. Thaw in the refrigerator or defrost in the microwave. Reheat in a saucepan over medium heat, stirring occasionally, until warmed through. For freezer storage, measure chili into serving-size portions and label the containers.

MEATY LENTIL CHILI

MAKES 6 TO 8 SERVINGS

When you want a chili that carries powerhouse nutrients from brown lentils, ground beef spiciness from chipotle pepper and green chile pepper, give this version a try.

1 tbsp (15 mL) vegetable oil

1 lb (500 g) lean ground beef

½ cup (125 mL) chopped red onion

1½ cups (375 mL) dried brown lentils, rinsed and drained

2 tsp (10 mL) chipotle chile powder

1 can (28 oz/796 mL) diced tomatoes with mild green chile peppers, with juice

4 cups (1 L) Low-Sodium Vegetable Stock (variation, page 211) or ready-to-use reduced-sodium vegetable broth

1. Set your Instant Pot to sauté on Normal. When the display says Hot, add oil and heat until shimmering. Add the ground beef and onion and cook, stirring and breaking beef up with a spoon, for 5 minutes or until the beef is no longer pink and the onion is softened. Stir in lentils, chile powder, tomatoes with juice and stock. Press Cancel.

2. Close and lock the lid and turn the steam release handle to Sealing. Set your Instant Pot to pressure cook on High for 10 minutes.

3. When the cooking time is done, press Cancel and let stand, covered, for 10 minutes, then turn the steam release handle to Venting. When the float valve drops down, remove the lid. The lentils should be tender. (If more cooking time is needed, continue pressure cooking on High for 2 minutes, then quickly release the pressure.)

SERVING SUGGESTION

Serve garnished with shredded cheese, sour cream and chopped red onions.

Omit the beef for a vegetarian version.

Use diced tomatoes without green chiles for a less spicy version.

TIPS

If you cannot find diced tomatoes with mild green chilies, you can use tomatoes with green peppers or with garlic, or just plain diced tomatoes.

The chili can be stored in airtight containers in the refrigerator for up to 3 days or in the freezer for up to 3 months. Thaw in the refrigerator or defrost in the microwave. Reheat in a saucepan over medium heat, stirring occasionally, until warmed through.

NUTRITION TIP

The ground beef, tomatoes and lentils in this dish are great finger foods to pick out and place on your baby's tray, if they haven't yet mastered utensils.

HEARTY MIDWESTERN CHILI

MAKES 8 SERVINGS

There are so many different versions of chili and an equally diverse group of opinions on which type is the best. In addition to the beef, tomatoes and onions, this Midwestern version includes kidney beans.

1 tbsp (15 mL) vegetable oil

1 onion, finely chopped

2 lbs (1 kg) ground beef

2 tbsp (30 mL) chili powder

3 cans (each 14½ oz/411 mL) diced tomatoes, with juice

2 cans (each 14 to 19 oz/398 to 540 mL) red kidney beans, drained and rinsed

1 cup (250 mL) Low-Sodium Beef Bone Broth (page 212) or ready-to-use reduced-sodium beef broth

Salt and freshly ground black pepper

1. Set your Instant Pot to sauté on Normal. When the display says Hot, add oil and heat until shimmering. Add onion and cook, stirring, for 3 to 5 minutes or until translucent. Add beef and cook, breaking it up with a spoon, for 10 minutes or until no longer pink. Stir in chili powder, tomatoes with juice, beans and broth. Season to taste with salt and pepper. Press Cancel.

2. Close and lock the lid and turn the steam release handle to Sealing. Set your Instant Pot to pressure cook on High for 15 minutes.

3. When the cooking time is done, press Cancel and let stand, covered, for 15 minutes, then turn the steam release handle to Venting. When the float valve drops down, remove the lid. The flavors should be melded. (If more cooking time is needed, continue pressure cooking on High for 2 minutes, then quickly release the pressure.) Stir well and season to taste with salt and pepper.

SERVING SUGGESTION
Serve garnished with shredded cheese, sour cream, sliced green onions and/or chopped red onions.

TIP

You can adjust the chili powder to your taste preferences. If increasing the amount, start with 1 tsp (5 mL) at a time, or add more after pressure cooking.

NUTRITION TIP

If you like your chili spicy and your child doesn't, here's a trick: place your child's portion of chili in a colander and rinse under running water. Much of the spice will be washed off.

166

BUTTERFLY PASTA CARBONARA

MAKES 6 TO 8 SERVINGS

This variation of a traditional carbonara uses farfalle pasta instead of linguine. Not only does it look like tiny little butterflies, but it has more nooks and crannies for the decadent sauce to cling to, making every bite a bit of splendor.

1½ tbsp (22 mL) virgin olive oil

5 oz (150 g) slab pancetta or side bacon, cut into ¼-inch (0.5 cm) cubes

1 lb (500 g) dried farfalle pasta

Salt

7 cups (1.75 L) water

5 large eggs, at room temperature

1 cup (250 mL) freshly grated Parmesan cheese

Freshly ground black pepper

1. Set your Instant Pot to sauté on Normal. When the display says Hot, add oil and heat until shimmering. Add pancetta and cook, stirring, for 3 to 5 minutes or until fat is rendered but not yet crispy on the edges. Press Cancel. Using a slotted spoon, transfer pancetta to a plate. Discard all but 1 tbsp (15 mL) fat from the pot.

2. Add pasta, ¼ tsp (1 mL) salt and water to the pot. Close and lock the lid and turn the steam release handle to Sealing. Set your Instant Pot to pressure cook on High and adjust the time to half the time recommended on the pasta package minus 1 minute. (If the cooking time is a range, use half of the higher number minus 1 minute.)

3. When the cooking time is done, press Cancel and turn the steam release handle to Venting. When the float valve drops down, remove the lid. The pasta should be slightly more tender than al dente. (If more cooking time is needed, continue pressure cooking on High for 1 minute.) Drain pasta, reserving 1 cup (250 mL) pasta water.

4. Meanwhile, separate 2 of the eggs and save the whites for another use (see tip). In a medium bowl, whisk together 3 eggs, 2 egg yolks and Parmesan. Season with salt and pepper.

5. Return pasta and pancetta to the pot. Set your Instant Pot to sauté on Less. Cook, stirring gently, for 2 minutes or until warmed through. Press Cancel. Quickly stir in egg mixture until creamy, adding reserved pasta water, 2 tbsp (30 mL) at a time, if needed for creaminess. Season to taste with pepper.

NUTRITION TIPS

The eggs in this recipe are only lightly cooked. For optimal food safety, use pasteurized in-shell eggs if they are available in your area.

Have you noticed the different colors of egg yolks? Depending on the chicken's diet, the egg yolk can be very light yellow (wheat produces this color) to very dark yellow (grasses and corn produce a darker yolk). Both are nutritious!

DEEP DISH LASAGNA

MAKES 4 TO 6 SERVINGS

When you are craving lasagna and your whole crew is hungry right now, this recipe is a quick and easy solution that is simply sensational.

6-inch (15 cm) springform pan (about 3 inches/7.5 cm deep), sprayed with nonstick cooking spray (see tip)

Steam rack

2 tsp (10 mL) vegetable oil

¾ lb (375 g) ground Italian sausage

½ onion, chopped

1 jar (24 oz/682 mL) pasta sauce

1 large egg

2½ cups (625 mL) shredded Italian cheese blend, divided

1 cup (250 mL) ricotta cheese

6 oz (175 g) oven-ready (no-boil) lasagna noodles

1. Set your Instant Pot to sauté on Normal. When the display says Hot, add oil and heat until shimmering. Add the sausage and onion; cook, stirring, for 5 minutes or sausage is no longer pink and onion is softened. Press Cancel. Drain fat from mixture.

2. In a mixing bowl, combine sausage mixture and 2½ cups (625 mL) pasta sauce. Add ½ inch (1 cm) sauce to prepared baking pan. Set aside. Stir ¼ cup (60 mL) water into remaining pasta sauce.

3. In a large bowl, whisk egg. Stir in 1¾ cups (425 mL) Italian cheese blend and ricotta.

4. Layer one-quarter of the noodles on top of sauce in pan, breaking noodles as needed to evenly cover sauce. Top with one-third of the cheese mixture, then one-quarter of the sauce. Continue with two more layers each of noodles, cheese mixture and sauce, gently pressing down on the noodles between each layer. Finish with a layer of noodles and a layer of sauce. (The pan will be very full.)

5. Add 1½ cups (375 mL) water to the pot. Place the baking pan on the rack and transfer to the pot.

6. Close and lock the lid and turn the steam release handle to Sealing. Set your Instant Pot to pressure cook on High for 14 minutes.

7. When the cooking time is done, press Cancel and turn the steam release handle to Venting. When the float valve drops down, remove the lid. Sprinkle with the remaining Italian cheese blend. Close and lock the lid and let stand for 10 minutes or until cheese is melted.

8. Using the handles of the rack, carefully remove rack and pan. Let lasagna stand for 10 minutes. Cut into wedges.

NUTRITION TIP

Lasagna is a family favorite. All of the ingredients are soft and easy for your baby to eat. Add a steamed vegetable as a side dish to balance out the meal.

BEETS WITH DIJON VINAIGRETTE AND MOZZARELLA

MAKES 2 TO 4 SERVINGS

Steaming whole beets under pressure keeps them moist and reduces bleeding and spattering. A classic Dijon vinaigrette highlights their flavor even more, and the mozzarella cheese adds a salty twist.

Steamer basket

8 small red beets (about 2 lbs/1 kg total)

Ice water

2½ tbsp (37 mL) white wine vinegar

1¼ tsp (6 mL) Dijon mustard Salt

⅓ cup (75 mL) extra virgin olive oil

Freshly ground black pepper

¼ cup (60 mL) finely shredded mozzarella

Chopped walnuts (optional)

1. Cut greens from beets, leaving 1 inch (2.5 cm) stem on. Do not cut root end. Scrub beets well.

2. Add 1 cup (250 mL) hot water to the inner pot and place the steamer basket in the pot. Arrange beets in the basket.

3. Close and lock the lid and turn the steam release handle to Sealing. Set your Instant Pot to pressure cook on High for 18 minutes.

4. When the cooking time is done, press Cancel and turn the steam release handle to Venting. When the float valve drops down, remove the lid. The beets should be fork-tender. (If more cooking time is needed, continue pressure cooking on High for 2 minutes.)

5. Transfer beets to a bowl of ice water and let cool. Cut off stems and root ends; discard. Peel beets and discard skins. Cut each beet into 6 wedges and transfer to a serving plate.

6. In a small bowl, whisk together vinegar, mustard and ¼ tsp (1 mL) salt. Gradually whisk in oil. Season to taste with salt and pepper.

7. Drizzle beets with vinaigrette and toss gently to coat. Sprinkle beets with mozzarella. Serve garnished with walnuts, if desired.

Variations

TARRAGON VINAIGRETTE: Replace the Dijon mustard with 1 tbsp (15 mL) minced fresh tarragon.

GARLIC VINAIGRETTE: Replace the Dijon mustard with 2 tsp (10 mL) minced garlic.

TIPS

When handling beets, wear disposable kitchen gloves and place them in the bottom of a clean sink while cutting or peeling to reduce splashing and staining surfaces.

Save the beet greens for another meal, on their own or as a great addition to a stir-fry.

GINGER AND ORANGE BRAISED CARROTS

MAKES 6 SERVINGS

Ginger and orange juice add a bit of spice and citrus notes to buttery, tender carrots. The bright colors of this side dish are always inviting.

1½ lbs (750 g) carrots, cut diagonally into ½-inch (1 cm) thick slices

4 tsp (20 mL) grated gingerroot

¾ (175 mL) cup water

½ cup (125 mL) orange juice, divided

3 tbsp (45 mL) butter, softened, divided

Chopped fresh parsley (optional)

1. In the inner pot, combine carrots, ginger, water, ¼ cup (60 mL) orange juice and 1 tbsp (15 mL) butter.

2. Close and lock the lid and turn the steam release handle to Sealing. Set your Instant Pot to pressure cook on High for 2 minutes.

3. When the cooking time is done, press Cancel and turn the steam release handle to Venting. When the float valve drops down, remove the lid. Drain carrots.

4. Set your Instant Pot to sauté on More. When the display says hot, add the remaining butter and heat until melted. Stir in carrots and the remaining orange juice; cook, stirring gently occasionally, for 3 minutes or until liquid has evaporated and carrots are fork-tender.

5. Transfer carrots to a serving bowl and season to taste with salt and pepper. If desired, sprinkle with parsley.

TIPS

A 1-inch (2.5 cm) square piece of ginger will yield about 4 tsp (20 mL) grated.

Jarred or frozen grated ginger works fine in this recipe, too.

For a slightly spicier, herbal tone, substitute ½ tsp (2 mL) ground cardamom for the ginger.

This recipe can easily be doubled for a large gathering.

NUTRITION TIP

Just ½ cup (125 mL) of carrots contains 214% of your daily vitamin A intake. Vitamin A is a fat-soluble vitamin, so the addition of butter to this side dish will maximize absorption!

GREEN BEANS AND PIMIENTOS

MAKES 6 SERVINGS

Here, sweet, succulent pimientos add delightful taste and color to simple pressure-cooked beans. You have a new way to eat these wonderful vegetables.

2 lbs (1 kg) frozen green beans

1 jar (4 oz/114 mL) pimientos, drained

1 tsp (5 mL) garlic powder

Salt

1 tbsp (15 mL) extra virgin olive oil

1. Arrange beans in the inner pot. Add pimientos, garlic powder and 1 cup (250 mL) water. Season with salt.

2. Close and lock the lid and turn the steam release handle to Sealing. Set your Instant Pot to pressure cook on High for 3 minutes.

3. When the cooking time is done, press Cancel and turn the steam release handle to Venting. When the float valve drops down, remove the lid. The beans should be tender-crisp. (If more cooking time is needed, continue pressure cooking on High for 0 minutes.)

4. Stir beans, drain and transfer to a serving bowl. Drizzle with oil. Serve immediately.

173

TIPS

Substitute fresh green beans, trimmed, for the frozen beans. Decrease the cooking time to 2 minutes.

Mix green and yellow beans for an even more colorful dish.

NUTRITION TIP

Beans are a good source of dietary fiber. Fiber helps keep you feeling full, controls blood sugars and promotes gut health. To calculate your child's fiber intake, add 5 grams of fiber to their age. Adult women should get 25 g of fiber per day and men need 38 g.

HOMESTYLE BUTTERY MASHED POTATOES

MAKES 4 SERVINGS

This creamy, homestyle version of mashed potatoes has a mouthwatering dose of butter, garlic, chicken stock and cream. No watching over a pot of boiling water!

Steamer basket

4 russet potatoes (about 1½ lbs 750 g total), peeled and cut into 1½-inch (4 cm) pieces

5 tbsp (75 mL) butter, softened, divided

3 cloves garlic, minced

¼ cup (60 mL) Low-Sodium Chicken Stock (page 210) or ready-to-use reduced-sodium chicken broth

¼ cup (60 mL) heavy or whipping (35%) cream (approx.)

Salt and freshly ground black pepper

1. Add 1 cup (250 mL) hot water to the inner pot and place the steamer basket in the pot (see tip). Place potatoes in the basket.

2. Close and lock the lid and turn the steam release handle to Sealing. Set your Instant Pot to pressure cook on High for 8 minutes.

3. When cooking time is done, press Cancel and turn steam release handle to Venting. When float valve drops down, remove lid. The potatoes should be fork-tender. (If more cooking time is needed, continue pressure cooking on High for 1 minute.) Remove steamer basket and set aside. Discard water.

4. Set your Instant Pot to sauté on Normal. When the display says Hot, add 2 tbsp (30 mL) butter and heat until melted. Add garlic and cook, stirring, for 1 minute or until fragrant. Add potatoes and the remaining butter; start mashing potatoes. When butter is absorbed, add stock, mashing until combined. Press Cancel.

5. Gradually add cream, mashing, until potatoes are your desired consistency. (Use only as much cream as is needed to reach that consistency.) Season to taste with salt and pepper. Transfer to a serving bowl. Serve immediately.

TIPS

You can substitute small yellow-fleshed potatoes, as long as they weigh about 1½ lbs (750 g) total. Reduce the pressure cooking time to 5 minutes. You don't need to peel the potatoes before mashing them.

Mash potatoes just until they are your desired consistency and everything is combined. Do not overmash, as the potatoes will become starchy.

SPICY POACHED COD

MAKES 3 TO 4 SERVINGS

Chili powder, oregano and cumin add a bit of spice to milk cod. The fresh lime juice adds cooling citrusy notes to complement the spices.

Steam rack

2 pieces parchment paper, cut to fit fillets

1 cup (250 mL) Low-Sodium Chicken Stock (page 210) or ready-to-use reduced-sodium chicken broth

14 oz (425 g) skinless cod fillet, cut into 2 equal portions

Virgin olive oil

½ tsp (2 mL) chili powder

½ tsp (2 mL) dried oregano

¼ tsp (1 mL) salt

Juice of ½ lime

⅛ tsp (0.5 mL) ground cumin

1. Add stock to the inner pot and place the steam rack in the pot. Brush cod on both sides with oil and place 1 piece, skin side down, on each prepared piece of parchment paper, tucking the thin end of the fish under to create an even thickness. Arrange both pieces on steam rack, without overlapping. Sprinkle cod with chili powder, oregano and salt.

2. Close and lock the lid and turn the steam release handle to Sealing. Set your Instant Pot to pressure cook on Low for 3 minutes.

3. When the cooking time is done, press Cancel and turn the steam release handle to Venting. When the float valve drops down, remove the lid. The fish should be opaque and should flake easily when tested with a fork. (If more cooking time is needed, continue pressure cooking on Low for 1 minute.)

4. Transfer fish to a serving plate, squeeze lime juice over top and serve sprinkled with cumin. Cut cod into portions suitable for each person.

SERVING SUGGESTION:
Serve with a side of rice or steamed vegetables.

TIP

Using your fingers, carefully check cod for tiny pin bones. Remove any bones with tweezers or needle-nose pliers.

NUTRITION TIP

The American Heart Association recommends eating fish two times per week. If that is challenging for you, talk to your doctor or dietitian about a fish oil supplement for the whole family.

176

FISH AND PINEAPPLE TACOS

MAKES 4 TO 6 SERVINGS

Pineapple and hot pepper flakes work beautifully with the mild tilapia in this Baja Peninsula inspired dish.

1 tbsp (15 mL) vegetable oil (approx.)

Eight 6-inch (15 cm) corn tortillas

Salt

1 can (20 oz/568 mL) pineapple chunks, with juice

½ tsp (2 mL) hot pepper flakes (see tip)

¾ cup (175 mL) water

1½ lbs (750 g) skinless tilapia fillets, cut into large pieces

1 cup (250 mL) deli-packed coleslaw

1 avocado, cut into chunks

1. Set your Instant Pot to sauté on Normal. When the display says Hot, add 1 tsp (5 mL) oil, turning pot to coat bottom, and heat until shimmering. Add 1 tortilla and cook, turning once, for 2 minutes or until lightly browned. Transfer to a plate lined with paper towel. Season with salt. Transfer drained tortilla to a foil sheet. Repeat with the remaining tortillas, adding more oil as necessary between tortillas and stacking drained tortillas on the foil. Wrap tortillas in foil to keep warm. Press Cancel.

2. Set aside 2 tbsp (30 mL) pineapple juice. Add pineapple and the remaining juice to the pot. Stir in hot pepper flakes (see tip) and water. Add tilapia on top, overlapping as necessary; do not stir.

3. Close and lock the lid and turn the steam release handle to Sealing. Set your Instant Pot to pressure cook on Low for 3 minutes.

4. When the cooking time is done, press Cancel and turn the steam release handle to Venting. When the float valve drops down, remove the lid. The fish should be opaque and should flake easily when tested with a fork. (If more cooking time is needed, continue pressure cooking on Low for 1 minute.)

5. Meanwhile, stir reserved pineapple juice into coleslaw.

6. Layer 2 tortillas, mostly overlapping, on each serving plate. Using a slotted spoon, spoon fish and pineapple onto tortillas. Top with coleslaw. Serve garnished with avocado.

177

TIP

If you prefer not to add the hot pepper flakes in step 2, you can sprinkle them on the fish before serving or stir into the coleslaw for those who desire the spiciness.

NUTRITION TIP

Having theme nights for family dinner like "Taco Tuesday" takes some of the guess-work out of meal planning. And it's fun for the whole family!

LEMON PEPPER FLOUNDER

MAKES 3 TO 4 SERVINGS

Light, delicate flounder is infused with steaming leeks from the bottom and tart lemon from the top. Refreshing cucumber completes this one-pot meal.

Two 18- by 12-inch (45 by 30 cm) sheets parchment paper

Steam rack

2 leeks, thinly sliced and separated into rings

Virgin olive oil

Salt and freshly ground black pepper

3 skinless flounder fillets (each about 5 oz/150 g)

15 thin slices cucumber

9 thin slices lemon

1. Arrange leek rings in a line down the middle of each sheet of parchment paper. Drizzle with oil and season with salt and pepper. Place fish on top, drizzle with oil and season with salt and pepper. Arrange cucumber on top of fish and season with salt. Arrange lemon slices on top of cucumber. Fold parchment paper into tent-style packets (see page 62) and seal edges tightly.

2. Add 1 cup (250 mL) hot water to the inner pot and place the steam rack in the pot. Arrange packets on the rack, with room between them.

3. Close and lock the lid and turn the steam release handle to Sealing. Set your Instant Pot to pressure cook on Low for 6 minutes.

4. When the cooking time is done, press Cancel and turn the steam release handle to Venting. When the float valve drops down, remove the lid. Carefully open a packet. The fish should be opaque and should flake easily when tested with a fork. (If more cooking time is needed, reseal packet and continue pressure cooking on Low for 1 minute.)

5. Transfer packets to serving plates and cut open with scissors. Cut flounder and cucumber into bite-size pieces for toddlers (do not serve with lemon slices). Serve.

TIPS

Using your fingers, carefully check the fish fillet for tiny pin bones. Remove any bones with tweezers or needle-nose pliers.

Try with haddock, sole, snapper or any thin lean light-meat fish with a delicate flavor.

NUTRITION TIP

Flounder is low in mercury, a toxin that builds up in fish and can build up in humans as well. High mercury fish tend to be larger fish, as mercury bio-accumulates in fish at the top of the food chain. Avoid tilefish, swordfish and shark for this reason.

POACHED TOMATO BASIL HALIBUT

MAKES 2 SERVINGS

This Mediterranean-inspired dish pulls together the fresh regional flavors from tomatoes, basil and olive. It is a perfect size for single-parent-toddler nights.

4-cup (1 L) round heatproof dish, sprayed with nonstick cooking spray

Steam rack

3 tomatoes, thickly sliced, divided

10 oz (300 g) skinless halibut fillet, cut in half

3 cloves garlic, minced

1 tbsp (15 mL) virgin olive oil

Salt and freshly ground black pepper

3 tbsp (45 mL) fresh basil chiffonade (see tip)

1 tbsp (15 mL) sliced drained kalamata olives

1. Arrange half the tomatoes in prepared dish, overlapping as necessary. Carefully place fish in a single layer on top.

2. In a small bowl, combine garlic and oil. Brush top of fish with garlic oil. Season with salt and pepper. Top with basil. Arrange the remaining tomatoes on top.

3. Add $1\frac{1}{2}$ cups (375 mL) hot water to the inner pot and place the steam rack in the pot. Place the dish on the rack.

4. Close and lock the lid and turn the steam release handle to Sealing. Set your Instant Pot to pressure cook on Low for 6 minutes.

5. When the cooking time is done, press Cancel and turn the steam release handle to Venting. When the float valve drops down, remove the lid. The fish should be opaque and should flake easily when tested with a fork. (If more cooking time is needed, close and lock the lid for 1 minute.)

6. Using a spatula, carefully transfer fish with tomatoes to serving plates. Serve garnished with olives.

TIPS

You can substitute tilapia, grouper, flounder, cod or sole for the halibut; decrease the pressure cooking time to 3 minutes.

Do not double the size of this dish, as the results will not be the same.

To chiffonade basil, remove the stems and stack 10 or more leaves. Roll the leaves up lengthwise into a fairly tight spiral, then cut crosswise into thin strips. Fluff the strips.

NUTRITION TIP

Fresh herbs such as basil are so easy to grow yourself. Or buy some in the store — fresh is almost always more flavorful than dried!

SALMON WITH SWEET MUSTARD SAUCE

MAKES 3 SERVINGS

Salmon gets a uniquely flavored treatment of caramelized sugar paired with mustard and Worcestershire.

6-cup (1.5 L) round heatproof dish
Steam rack

4 tsp (20 mL) packed brown sugar

1 tbsp (15 mL) butter

1 tbsp (15 mL) virgin olive oil

1 tbsp (15 mL) Dijon mustard

1 tbsp (15 mL) Worcestershire sauce

14 oz (425 mL) skin-on salmon fillet, cut into 3 serving-size pieces

1. In the heatproof dish, combine brown sugar and butter.

2. Add 1 cup (250 mL) hot water to the inner pot and place the steam rack in the pot. Place a sling on the rack and place the dish in the sling. Set your Instant Pot to sauté on More. Stir mixture until sugar is melted and combined. Press Cancel.

3. Stir oil, mustard and soy sauce into sugar mixture, mixing well. Add salmon, turning to coat in sauce and arranging skin side down.

4. Close and lock the lid and turn the steam release handle to Sealing. Set your Instant Pot to pressure cook on Low for 5 minutes.

5. When the cooking time is done, press Cancel and turn the steam release handle to Venting. When the float valve drops down, remove the lid. The fish should be opaque and should flake easily when tested with a fork. (If more cooking time is needed, continue pressure cooking on Low for 1 minute.)

6. Using the sling, remove dish from the pot. Transfer salmon to serving plates and drizzle sauce over top. Serve immediately.

TIPS

Using your fingers, carefully check the salmon fillet for tiny pin bones. Remove any bones with tweezers or needle-nose pliers.

You can purchase one of the many silicone slings available for the Instant Pot.

NUTRITION TIP

If you have leftover salmon, it's great the next day on top of a salad. Or mix it with some mayonnaise and make a salmon salad sandwich.

HERBED SALMON WITH ASPARAGUS

MAKES 2 ADULT AND 1 BABY SERVINGS

This gourmet one-pot meal is simple and pleasantly satisfying.

Steam rack

3 pieces of parchment paper, cut to fit salmon pieces

1 cup (250 mL) Low-Sodium Chicken Stock (page 210) or ready-to-use reduced-sodium chicken broth

12 oz (375 g) skin-on salmon fillet

Virgin olive oil

Herbes de Provence

8 oz (250 g) asparagus spears, tough ends trimmed and spears halved

Coarse salt and freshly ground black pepper

3 tbsp (45 mL) butter

1 tbsp (15 mL) freshly squeezed lemon juice

1. Add stock to the inner pot and place the steam rack in the pot. Cut salmon into two 5 oz (150 g) and one 2 oz (60 g) serving. Check for and remove tiny pin bones. Place 1 piece of salmon, skin side down, on each prepared piece of parchment paper and brush top with oil. Sprinkle with herbes de Provence. Arrange both pieces on steam rack, without overlapping. Arrange asparagus on top of salmon. Drizzle with a little oil and season with salt and pepper, omitting salt for baby's portion.

2. Close and lock the lid and turn the steam release handle to Sealing. Set your Instant Pot to pressure cook on Low for 5 minutes.

3. When the cooking time is done, press Cancel and turn the steam release handle to Venting. When the float valve drops down, remove the lid. The fish should be opaque and should flake easily when tested with a fork. (If more cooking time is needed, continue pressure cooking on Low for 1 minute.)

4. Transfer larger salmon pieces to serving plates and arrange asparagus on top of and around salmon. For baby's serving, cut salmon into bite-size pieces that are easy to grasp. Cover with foil to keep warm.

5. Set your Instant Pot to sauté on More. Cook, stirring often, for 3 minutes or until liquid is reduced to $1/4$ cup (60 mL). Add butter and lemon juice; cook, stirring, until butter is melted. Drizzle sauce over fish and asparagus. Test temperature before serving.

NUTRITION TIP

Salmon is one of the best sources of omega-3. Aim to serve fish twice per week, to get enough of this fat, which is important for your baby's brain and eye development.

TILAPIA WITH CORN AND PEAS

MAKES 2 TO 3 SERVINGS

Preparing a meal in a paper packet — known as cooking *en papillote* — is a technique often used in fancier restaurants, but it works magically at home in your pressure cooker. Here, the subtle taste of tilapia is matched by the sweetness of corn and pea pods.

Two 18- by 12-inch (45 by 30 cm) sheets parchment paper

Steam rack

1 lemon

¾ cup (175 mL) frozen sweet corn kernels

4 oz (125 g) sugar snap peas

2 skinless tilapia fillets (each about 5 oz/150 g)

1 tbsp (15 mL) virgin olive oil

1½ tsp (7 mL) seafood seasoning (such as Old Bay)

Salt and freshly ground black pepper

1. Grate lemon zest and measure 2 tsp (10 mL) zest. Juice enough of the lemon to measure 2 tbsp (30 mL) juice. Cut remaining lemon into wedges and set aside.

2. Arrange corn and peas in the center of each sheet of parchment paper, in a mound the size and shape of your tilapia fillet, dividing equally. Sprinkle with lemon zest. Place fish on top and drizzle with lemon juice and olive oil. Sprinkle with seafood seasoning. Season with salt and pepper. Fold parchment paper into tent-style packets (see page 62) and seal edges tightly.

3. Add 1½ cups (375 mL) hot water to the inner pot and place the steam rack in the pot. Arrange packets on the rack, with room between them.

4. Close and lock the lid and turn the steam release handle to Sealing. Set your Instant Pot to pressure cook on Low for 3 minutes.

5. When the cooking time is done, press Cancel and turn the steam release handle to Venting. When the float valve drops down, remove the lid. Carefully open a packet. The fish should be opaque and should flake easily when tested with a fork. (If more cooking time is needed, reseal packet and continue pressure cooking on Low for 1 minute.)

6. Transfer packets to serving plates and cut open with scissors. Serve immediately, with reserved lemon wedges to squeeze over top, if desired.

TIPS

You can substitute any thin (½-inch/1 cm thick or less) flaky white fish for the tilapia.

If your Instant Pot doesn't have a Low pressure setting, cook on High for 1 minute.

TENDER BARBECUE CHICKEN

MAKES 3 SERVINGS

You can get the same juicy, tender chicken slathered in your favorite barbecue sauce as slow roasting or grilling without the extra time. This dish makes for an easy, delectable weeknight dinner. You can shred the leftover chicken and make a drool-worthy barbecue sandwich.

4 bone-in skin-on chicken thighs

1 tsp (5 mL) paprika

Salt

1 tbsp (15 mL) vegetable oil

½ red onion, finely chopped

1 clove garlic, minced

1 cup (250 mL) barbecue sauce (store-bought or see recipe, page 215)

2 tbsp (30 mL) water

1. Sprinkle chicken with paprika and season with salt. Set your Instant Pot to sauté on Normal. When the display says Hot, add oil and heat until shimmering. Add chicken and cook, turning once, for 5 minutes or until browned on both sides. Using tongs, transfer chicken to a plate.

2. Add onion to the fat remaining in the pot and cook, stirring often, for 4 minutes or until softened. Add garlic and cook, stirring, for 1 minute or until fragrant. Press Cancel.

3. Stir in barbecue sauce and water. Return chicken and any accumulated juices to the pot, turning chicken to coat with sauce and finishing with the skin side up.

4. Close and lock the lid and turn the steam release handle to Sealing. Set your Instant Pot to pressure cook on High for 5 minutes.

5. When the cooking time is done, press Cancel and turn the steam release handle to Venting. When the float valve drops down, remove the lid. The juices should run clear when the chicken is pierced. (If more cooking time is needed, continue pressure cooking on High for 1 minute, then quickly release the pressure.)

6. Transfer chicken to a serving platter and spoon sauce over top.

183

TIP

If the sauce is not the desired consistency at the end of step 5, transfer chicken to the platter, then set your Instant Pot to sauté on Normal. Simmer the sauce, stirring often, until it is thickened to your liking.

NUTRITION TIP

Chicken thighs are often preferred to chicken breasts for young eaters. They are more tender and moist. And that's okay — being higher in fat and iron than white meat, dark meat is nutritious for your little ones.

TENDER ROTISSERIE-STYLE WHOLE CHICKEN

MAKES ABOUT 4 SERVINGS OR 3 CUPS (750 ML) SHREDDED CHICKEN

This is one of the recipes that shows off the diversity of recipes you can make simply with one core recipe in the Instant Pot. This delicately seasoned, moist, tender chicken can be served as is or shredded and used in a variety of recipes. Or you can do a little bit of each.

Steam rack

1 whole chicken trussed with wings and legs tied together (see tip), patted dry (about 3 lbs/1.5 kg)

1½ tbsp (22 mL) poultry seasoning (see tip)

2 tsp (10 mL) paprika

1½ tsp (7 mL) salt

2 tbsp (30 mL) butter

1½ tbsp (22 mL) vegetable oil (approx.)

¾ cup (175 mL) Chicken Stock (page 210) or ready-to-use chicken broth

1 bay leaf (optional)

1. Season chicken all over with poultry seasoning, paprika and salt. Set your Instant Pot to sauté on Normal. When the display says Hot, add butter and oil; heat until butter is melted. Add chicken and cook for about 8 minutes, turning often and adding more oil as necessary, until browned on all sides. Using tongs, transfer chicken to a plate.

2. Pour in stock and cook, scraping up any browned bits from the bottom of the pot, for about 1 minute. Add bay leaf (if using). Press Cancel.

3. Place the steam rack in the pot. Transfer chicken to the rack, breast side up. Add any accumulated juices from the chicken.

4. Close and lock the lid and turn the steam release handle to Sealing. Set your Instant Pot to pressure cook on High for 18 minutes.

5. When the cooking time is done, press Cancel and turn the steam release handle to Venting. When the float valve drops down, remove the lid. An instant-read thermometer inserted in the thickest part of the breast should register at least 165°F (74°C). (If more cooking time is needed, continue pressure cooking on High for 2 minutes.)

6. Transfer chicken to a cutting board, cover with foil and let rest for 10 minutes or until ready to carve or shred. Strain cooking liquid and make gravy (see tip), or let cool, cover and refrigerate for up to 3 days to use as stock (see tip).

TIPS

While it is not necessary to truss the chicken, it makes for easier handling and a better presentation if you are serving it whole.

To make gravy, transfer the cooking liquid to a glass measuring cup, and spoon off as much fat as possible. In a small bowl, stir together 1 tbsp (15 mL) all-purpose flour and 2 tbsp (30 mL) cold water to make a slurry. Stir slurry into cooking liquid until well combined. Set your Instant Pot to sauté on Less. When the display says Hot, add gravy and cook, stirring, for about 2 minutes or until thickened to your liking. If using the leftover cooking liquid as stock, cover and refrigerate for up to 3 days. Skim fat from stock before using. You will have $2/3$ to 1 cup (150 to 250 mL) stock.

In place of poultry seasoning, you can use $1\frac{1}{2}$ tsp (7 mL) each dried sage, thyme and rosemary.

If your chicken came with giblets, you can add them to the pot in step 4.

NUTRITION TIP

If you have leftover chicken, it's easy to use up in a chicken sandwich, stir-fry or pasta dish. And the leftover bones are perfect for your homemade Instant Pot No-Salt-Added Chicken Stock! (See page 210.)

Making your own chicken stock to use in recipes like this ensures you can control the sodium added. And homemade stock also contains some minerals and protein (like collagen) from the chicken bones.

TRUSSING A CHICKEN

To truss, measure the diameter of your inner pot and purchase a chicken that will fit in it. If your chicken didn't come trussed, here's how to truss it: Cut a long piece of kitchen string (about 3 feet/90 cm). Place the chicken on a work surface, with the legs pointing away from you. Slide the middle of the string underneath the tail and back. Bring both ends up and over the legs, then crisscross the string between the legs and wrap it around the foot end. Pull the string tight until the legs are up and tight to the body. Pull the string down to the work surface and over the top of the wings. Flip the chicken over, pulling the string over the top. Wind the string three times around itself and, with the string under the neck, pull it very tight. Tie a knot in the string and cut off excess. Turn the chicken over, tuck the wing tips down behind the body and push the breast tip into the cavity. Your chicken should now be nice and compact.

LEMON CHICKEN AND PEAS

MAKES 3 SERVINGS

Cooking chicken in the Instant Pot keeps it moist and infuses the flavors of the herbs and spices. This one-pot dish is so easy to make on busy weeknights and the cleanup is easy too.

Steamer basket

4 cloves garlic, minced

½ tsp (2 mL) salt

⅛ tsp (0.5 mL) freshly ground black pepper

Grated zest and juice of 1 lemon

2 tbsp (30 mL) virgin olive oil (approx.), divided

4 bone-in skin-on chicken thighs (about 1½ lbs/750 g total)

1 cup (250 mL) Chicken Stock (page 210) or ready-to-use chicken broth

10 oz (300 g) frozen peas

1. In a large sealable plastic bag, combine garlic, salt, pepper, lemon zest, lemon juice and 1 tbsp (15 mL) oil. Add chicken to bag, seal and turn bag to coat chicken in marinade. Refrigerate for at least 1 hour or overnight.

2. Remove chicken from marinade, scraping any garlic and zest stuck on chicken back into the bag; reserve marinade.

3. Set your Instant Pot to sauté on Normal. When the display says Hot, add the remaining oil to the pot and heat until shimmering. Add chicken and cook, turning once, for 5 minutes or until browned on both sides. Press Cancel.

4. Add marinade to stock, stirring to combine. Pour over chicken.

5. Arrange peas in steamer basket and place on top of chicken.

6. Close and lock the lid and turn the steam release handle to Sealing. Set your Instant Pot to pressure cook on High for 4 minutes.

7. When the cooking time is done, press Cancel and turn the steam release handle to Venting. When the float valve drops down, remove the lid. Remove the steamer basket and set aside.

8. Close and lock the lid and turn the steam release handle to Sealing. Set your Instant Pot to pressure cook on High for 1 minute.

9. When the cooking time is done, press Cancel and turn the steam release handle to Venting. When the float valve drops down, remove the lid. The juices should run clear when the chicken is pierced. (If more cooking time is needed, continue pressure cooking on High for 1 minute.)

10. Transfer chicken to serving plates and drizzle with some of the liquid from the pot, discarding the remainder. Serve peas alongside chicken.

SERVING SUGGESTION
Serve with Easy Rice Pilaf (page 213).

CHICKEN CACCIATORE

MAKES 4 SERVINGS

This take on the traditional cacciatore has the same robust flavors but is ready to eat in much less time. Italian seasoning and hot pepper flakes take boring chicken breasts and turn them into a spicy and intriguing dish.

4 bone-in skin-on chicken breasts (about 1½ lbs/750 g total)

Salt and freshly ground black pepper

2 tbsp (30 mL) virgin olive oil (approx.)

¾ cup (175 mL) Low-Sodium Chicken Stock (variation, page 210) or ready-to-use reduced-sodium chicken

1 tbsp (15 mL) dried Italian seasoning

1 tsp (5 mL) hot pepper flakes

1 can (14 oz/398 mL) diced tomatoes with garlic and onion, with juice

1. Season chicken with salt and pepper. Set your Instant Pot to sauté on Normal. When the display says Hot, add 1 tbsp (15 mL) oil and heat until shimmering. Working in batches, add chicken, skin side down, and cook for 3 minutes or until skin is browned, adding more oil as needed between batches. Using tongs, transfer chicken to a plate as it is browned.

2. Add stock to the pot and cook, scraping up any browned bits from the bottom of the pot, for 1 minute. Press Cancel. Stir in Italian seasoning, hot pepper flakes and tomatoes with juice. Return chicken and any accumulated juices to the pot, arranging chicken skin side up.

3. Close and lock the lid and turn the steam release handle to Sealing. Set your Instant Pot to pressure cook on High for 12 minutes.

4. When the cooking time is done, press Cancel and turn the steam release handle to Venting. When the float valve drops down, remove the lid. An instant-read thermometer inserted in the thickest part of a breast should register 165°F (74°C) and the chicken should no longer be pink inside. (If more cooking time is needed, continue pressure cooking on High for 2 minutes.)

5. Using tongs, transfer chicken to serving plates. For younger children, cut chicken into bite-size pieces. Spoon sauce over top. Test temperature before serving to toddlers or babies.

TIPS

Do not use boneless skinless chicken breasts, as you will not get the intended results.

Meal planning can save money by cutting back on or omitting unnecessary grocery trips, food waste and takeout meals! It also saves you time during the week and avoids the stress of not knowing what's for dinner.

CHICKEN PAELLA

MAKES 6 SERVINGS

Paella can be prepared in many different styles. This is a Valencia-style paella, originating in the Valencia region of Italy. This streamlined version reduces the traditionally long cooking time but still offers impeccable taste.

2 tbsp (30 mL) virgin olive oil (approx.)

12 oz (375 g) smoked cured linguiça or chorizo sausage, cut into chunks

1 lb (500 g) boneless skinless chicken thighs, cut into 1-inch (2.5 cm) pieces

2¼ cups (550 mL) long-grain white rice

1 tbsp (15 mL) dried onion flakes

1 tsp (5 mL) garlic powder

1 tsp (5 mL) ground turmeric

1//2 tsp (2 mL) salt

Pinch saffron threads

2 cups (500 mL) No-Salt-Added Chicken Stock (page 210) or ready-to-use no-salt-added chicken broth

2 cups (500 mL) water

½ jar (16 oz/473 mL) sliced roasted red peppers, drained

1 cup (250 mL) frozen green peas

1. Set your Instant Pot to sauté on Normal. When the display says Hot, add oil and heat until shimmering. Add sausage and cook, stirring often, for 5 minutes or until slightly crispy. Using a slotted spoon, transfer sausage to a large bowl.

2. Working in batches, add chicken to the pot and cook, stirring, for 1 minute or until it turns white on all sides. Using a slotted spoon, add chicken to sausage as it is browned.

3. Add rice to the pot and cook, stirring, for 1 minute. Stir in stock and water; bring to a boil, scraping up any brown bits from the bottom of the pot. Return chicken, sausage and any accumulated juices to the pot. Stir in onion flakes, garlic powder, turmeric, salt, saffron, roasted peppers and peas. Press Cancel.

4. Close and lock the lid and turn the steam release handle to Sealing. Set your Instant Pot to pressure cook on High for 4 minutes.

5. When the cooking time is done, press Cancel and let stand, covered, for 10 minutes, then turn the steam release handle to Venting. When the float valve drops down, remove the lid. The juices should run clear when the chicken is pierced and the rice should be tender. Gently stir paella. Spoon onto individual serving plates. Remove skins from the sausage and test temperature before serving to younger children.

NUTRITION TIP

Always slice your child's hot dog or sausage lengthwise until they are age 4. These are one of the top choking hazards for your children, as the perfectly round shape can block their air tube.

TURKEY MEATBALL BITES

MAKES 7 BITES

These delightful little bites are lean, flavorful and a treat as appetizers or main dishes. They can be served with a variety of sauces, made into a meatball sandwich, or stirred into a marinara sauce sauce and ladled over noodles.

Silicone egg bites mold with 7 cups, sprayed with nonstick cooking spray

Steam rack

1 lb (500 g) ground turkey

¼ cup (125 mL) plain bread crumbs

1 egg

1 tbsp (15 mL) Dijon mustard

2 tsp (10 mL) dried onion flakes

1 tsp (5 mL) ground paprika

1 tsp (5 mL) garlic powder

1 tsp (5 mL) dried basil leaves

½ tsp (2 mL) freshly ground black pepper

¼ tsp (1 mL) salt

1. In a large bowl, combine turkey, bread crumbs, egg, mustard, onion flakes, paprika, garlic powder, basil, pepper and salt. Using your hands, form mixture into 7 evenly sized balls.

2. Place balls into prepared egg bites mold.

3. Add 1 cup (250 mL) water to the inner pot. Place the egg bites mold on the rack and place in the pot.

4. Close and lock the lid and turn the steam release handle to Sealing. Set your Instant Pot to pressure cook on High for 25 minutes.

5. When the cooking time is done, press Cancel and let stand, covered, for 5 minutes, then turn the steam release handle to Venting. When the float valve drops down, remove the lid. The turkey balls should no longer be pink in the middle. (If more cooking time is needed, continue pressure cooking on High for 5 minutes.)

6. Using tongs or a fork, transfer turkey bites to a paper towel–lined plate.

7. Transfer bites onto serving plates. Serve with your choice of sauce. For babies and toddlers, test temperature before serving.

Variations

Replace the ground turkey with ground chicken, lean beef or pork. If using beef or pork, in step 6 add an additional sheet of paper towel to the plate.

Toast sliced hoagie rolls. Arrange meatballs on roll and drizzle with your favorite sauce.

NUTRITION TIP

While you can use any ground meat in this recipe, turkey is an economical choice for nutrient-dense meat. And it doesn't just have to be served for Thanksgiving!

MOLASSES PULLED PORK SANDWICHES

MAKES 8 SERVINGS

Molasses gives these mouthwatering pulled pork sandwiches a wonderful depth of flavor and sweetness. Leftover pulled pork can be used to make tacos or poutine or served up with a little barbecue sauce in a second round of sandwiches.

3½ lb (1.75 kg) boneless pork shoulder blade roast

2 tsp (10 mL) freshly ground black pepper

2 tsp (10 mL) onion powder

1½ tsp (7 mL) salt

2 tbsp (30 mL) vegetable oil (approx.)

3 cloves garlic, minced

1¼ cups (300 mL) Chicken Stock (page 210) or ready-to-use chicken broth

2 tbsp (30 mL) molasses

1 tbsp (15 mL) yellow mustard

2 tsp (10 mL) apple cider vinegar

8 sandwich buns, split

1. Cut roast into 2 pieces that will fit easily inside the pot. Pat pork dry. Rub pork all over with pepper, onion powder and salt.

2. Set your Instant Pot to sauté on Normal. When the display says Hot, add 1 tbsp (15 mL) oil and heat until shimmering. Working with one piece at a time, add pork and cook, turning, for 8 minutes or until browned on all sides, adding more oil as needed between batches. Using tongs, transfer pork to a plate as it is browned.

3. Add garlic and cook, stirring, for 1 minute or until fragrant. Press Cancel. Stir in stock, molasses, mustard and vinegar. Return pork and accumulated juices to pot, turning to coat.

4. Close and lock the lid and turn the steam release handle to Sealing. Set your Instant Pot to pressure cook on High for 60 minutes.

5. When the cooking time is done, press Cancel and let stand, covered, until the float valve drops down. Remove the lid. The pork should be fork-tender. (If more cooking time is needed, continue pressure cooking on High for 5 minutes, then quickly release the pressure.)

6. Transfer pork to a cutting board and, using two forks, shred pork. Discard any excess fat. Reserve cooking liquid.

7. Serve shredded pork on toasted sandwich buns.

TIP

To store, pour reserved reserved cooking liquid over the pork to cover.

NUTRITION TIP

Not only does molasses help provide a sweet and savory flavor to the pulled pork, but it's also one of the most nutritious sweeteners, as it's high in iron!

PORK, APPLES AND ROSEMARY MEDLEY

MAKES 4 TO 6 SERVINGS

Fit for company or a relaxing Sunday dinner, this pork roast is tender juicy and marries well with the flavors of apple and rosemary.

1½ lb (750 g) boneless pork single loin roast (less than 8 inches/20 cm long), untied

Salt and freshly ground black pepper

2 tbsp (30 mL) virgin olive oil

2 small tart green apples (such as Granny Smith), peeled and chopped

1 onion, chopped

2 cloves garlic, peeled (optional)

2 sprigs fresh rosemary

1 cup (250 mL) Low-Sodium Chicken Stock (page 210) or ready-to-use reduced-sodium chicken broth

2 tbsp (30 mL) all-purpose flour

¼ cup (60 mL) water

1. Season roast with ¼ tsp (1 mL) salt and pepper to taste. Set your Instant Pot to sauté on Normal. When the display says Hot, add oil and heat until shimmering. Add roast and cook, turning, for about 7 minutes or until browned on all sides. Press Cancel. Stir in apples, onion, garlic (if using) and rosemary to coat in oil, then stir in stock.

2. Close and lock the lid and turn the steam release handle to Sealing. Set your Instant Pot to pressure cook on High for 12 minutes.

3. When the cooking time is done, press Cancel and let stand, covered, for 5 minutes, then turn the steam release handle to Venting. When the float valve drops down, remove the lid. An instant-read thermometer inserted in the thickest part of the roast should register at least 150°F (66°C) for medium. (If more cooking time is needed, continue pressure cooking on High for 2 minutes, then quickly release the pressure.)

4. Using tongs, transfer roast to a cutting board and tent with foil to keep warm.

5. Place flour in a small bowl and whisk in water to make a slurry.

6. Set your Instant Pot to sauté on Normal. Pour in slurry, whisking to combine. Cook, whisking, for 2 to 3 minutes or until thickened. Discard rosemary stems. Season to taste with salt and pepper.

7. Cut pork across the grain into ½-inch (1 cm) thick slices. Transfer pork slices to a serving platter and serve with gravy.

NUTRITION TIP

Pork is a cost-effective and healthy meat, packed with protein and zinc. The Instant Pot is the perfect way to cook pork so that it's nice and tender for your baby to eat.

TIPS

You can use any apples with a tart flavor, such as Cortland, Empire or Honeycrisp.

Make sure to purchase a pork loin roast and not a pork tenderloin, which would not provide the intended results.

A slurry is a blend of flour and water that is used to thicken liquids during cooking. The risk of clumping flour is eliminated by blending the flour into the water before adding to the rest of the ingredients.

COCONUT CURRY BEEF

MAKES 4 SERVINGS

Thai red curry paste adds interesting flavor notes to the beef chunks in this recipe without making it over-the-top spicy. Serve it with rice or vegetables.

1½ lbs (750 g) beef brisket, cut into 1½-inch (4 cm) cubes

Salt

3 tbsp (45 mL) coconut oil or vegetable oil (approx.)

1 onion, finely chopped

2 tbsp (30 mL) Thai red curry paste

¾ cup (175 mL) strained tomato purée (passata)

1 can (14 oz/400 mL) coconut milk

2 green onions, sliced diagonally (optional)

1. Season beef with salt. Set your Instant Pot to sauté on Normal. When the display says Hot, add 2 tbsp (30 mL) oil and heat until shimmering. Working in batches, add beef and cook, stirring, for 3 to 5 minutes or until browned on all sides, adding more oil as needed between batches. Using a slotted spoon, transfer beef to a plate as it is browned.

2. Add onion to the fat remaining in the pot and cook, stirring often, for 3 minutes or until translucent. Add curry paste and cook, stirring, for 1 minute or until fragrant. Stir in tomato purée, scraping up any browned bits from the bottom of the pot. Press Cancel. Return beef and any accumulated juices to the pot, stirring well.

3. Close and lock the lid and turn the steam release handle to Sealing. Set your Instant Pot to pressure cook on High for 35 minutes.

4. When the cooking time is done, press Cancel and turn the steam release handle to Venting. When the float valve drops down, remove the lid. The beef should be fork-tender. (If more cooking time is needed, continue pressure cooking on High for 3 minutes.)

5. Set your Instant Pot to sauté on Normal. Add coconut milk and cook, stirring, for 5 minutes or until sauce is thickened to your liking. Season to taste with salt. Serve garnished with green onions, if using.

SERVING SUGGESTIONS

Serve over Easy White Rice (variation, page 213) or Jasmine rice.

NUTRITION TIP

Curry paste is an easy way to add a delicious combination of premixed spices. Exposing your toddler to lots of different flavors and tastes may help prevent picky eating later on!

CREAMY BEEF STROGANOFF

MAKES 6 ADULT SERVINGS

A classic combination of beef, mushrooms and sour cream makes a rich, hearty gravy begging to be ladled over noodles or blended with the noodles into a purée for your little one. This timeless dish is perfect for the whole family.

1½ lbs (750 g) boneless beef chuck roast, cut into 1½-inch (4 cm) pieces

Salt and freshly ground black pepper

3 tbsp (45 mL) virgin olive oil (approx.)

¼ cup (60 mL) butter

1 large onion, cut in half, sliced and rings separated

1 lb (500 g) mushrooms, sliced

1¼ cups (300 mL) Low-Sodium Beef Bone Broth (page 212) or ready-to-use reduced-sodium beef broth

12 oz (375 g) broad egg noodles

1 cup (250 mL) sour cream

1. Season beef with salt and pepper. Set your Instant Pot to sauté on Normal. When the display says Hot, add 2 tbsp (30 mL) oil and heat until shimmering. Working in batches, add beef and cook, stirring, for 3 to 5 minutes or until browned on all sides, adding more oil as needed between batches. Using a slotted spoon, transfer beef to a plate as it is browned.

2. Add butter to the pot and heat until melted. Add onion and mushrooms; cook, stirring, for about 15 minutes or until onion and mushrooms are softened and liquid is evaporated. Stir in broth. Press Cancel. Return beef and any accumulated juices to the pot, stirring well.

3. Close and lock the lid and turn the steam release handle to Sealing. Set your Instant Pot to pressure cook on High for 20 minutes.

4. Meanwhile, in a large pot of boiling salted water, cook egg noodles according to package directions. Drain and set aside.

5. When the cooking time is done, press Cancel and turn the steam release handle to Venting. When the float valve drops down, remove the lid. The beef should be fork-tender. (If more cooking time is needed, continue pressure cooking on High for 3 minutes.)

6. If you prefer a thicker sauce, set your Instant Pot to sauté on Normal. Cook, stirring, for about 5 minutes or until sauce is the desired consistency. Stir sour cream into sauce. Set your Instant Pot to keep warm. For toddlers and babies, see tips.

7. Season beef mixture in pot to taste with salt and pepper. Serve over noodles.

NUTRITION TIP

The noodles, mushrooms and beef cooked in the Instant Pot are all nice and tender and easy enough for those little pincer-fingers to grasp!

BBQ BABY BACK RIBS

MAKES 4 TO 6 SERVINGS

Looking for off-the-bone tender ribs? The whole family, from toddlers to grandparents, will love these juicy, meaty ribs.

2 slabs baby back pork ribs (4 to 6 lbs/2 to 3 kg total)

2 tbsp (30 mL) Montreal steak seasoning

2 cups (500 mL) barbecue sauce, divided

1 cup (250 mL) water

1 onion, chopped

¾ cup (175 mL) apple or peach preserves

1. Cut ribs into 3- to 4-bone sections and season with steak seasoning.

2. In the inner pot, combine ½ cup (125 mL) barbecue sauce and water, stirring well. Stir in onion. Arrange ribs, standing on cut ends of bones, on top.

3. Close and lock the lid and turn the steam release handle to Sealing. Set your Instant Pot to pressure cook on High for 35 minutes.

4. When the cooking time is done, press Cancel and let stand, covered, for 10 minutes, then turn the steam release handle to Venting. When the float valve drops down, remove the lid. The ribs should be fork-tender. (If more cooking time is needed, continue pressure cooking on High for 5 minutes, then quickly release the pressure.)

5. In a medium bowl, combine apple preserves and the remaining barbecue sauce. Brush ribs with sauce.

6. Close and lock the lid and turn the steam release handle to Venting. Set your Instant Pot to slow cook on Less for 30 minutes.

7. When the cooking time is done, press Cancel. Transfer ribs to a serving platter and serve immediately. For babies and toddlers, test temperature before serving.

Variations

Replace the preserves with ½ cup (125 mL) hoisin sauce, 2 tbsp (30 mL) Worcestershire sauce and 1 tbsp (15 mL) soy or tamari sauce.

For a darker glaze and stickier ribs, preheat the broiler with the rack 6 inches (15 cm) from the heat. After step 4, transfer ribs to a baking sheet lined with foil. Follow step 5, then, in place of step 6, broil ribs for 5 minutes. Serve immediately. (We do not recommend this last variation for younger children, as the internal temperature may be too hot.)

NUTRITION TIP

Ribs are a fun food for the whole family, including your toddler! They are a great choice of meat because rib meat is tender and the bones make them easy to grasp. And they make a fun photo op!

BETTER THAN TAKEOUT BEEF AND BROCCOLI

MAKES 6 SERVINGS

This is so easy to make in your Instant Pot that you may never go out again for this takeout favorite. You can make it with your own quality ingredients, either from fresh or frozen, and also control the sodium levels to fit your preferences. Serve with a side of cooked rice or noodles.

1½ lb (750 g) beef sirloin roast, cut into thin strips

Salt and freshly ground black pepper

1 tbsp (15 mL) virgin olive oil

1 onion, finely chopped

4 cloves garlic, minced

⅓ cup (75 mL) packed brown sugar

2 tsp (10 mL) minced gingerroot

¾ cup (175 mL) Low-Sodium Beef Bone Broth (page 212) or ready-to-use low-sodium beef broth

⅓ cup (75 mL) soy sauce or liquid amino acids

2 tbsp (30 mL) sesame oil

1 lb (500 g) broccoli florets

1. Season beef with salt and pepper. Set your Instant Pot to sauté on Normal. Add the olive oil and heat until shimmering. Working in batches, add beef and cook, turning occasionally, for 3 to 5 minutes or until browned on all sides. Transfer beef to a plate.

2. Add onion to the pot and cook, stirring, for 2 to 3 minutes or until softened. Add garlic and cook, stirring, for 1 minute or until fragrant. Add brown sugar, ginger, broth, soy sauce and sesame oil, stirring until sugar is dissolved. Press Cancel. Return beef to the pot, along with any accumulated juices.

3. Close and lock the lid and turn the steam release handle to Sealing. Set your Instant Pot to pressure cook on High for 12 minutes.

4. When the cooking time is done, press Cancel and turn the steam release handle to Venting. When the float valve drops down, remove the lid.

5. Stir in broccoli florets. Close and lock the lid and turn the steam release handle to Sealing. Set your Instant Pot to pressure cook on Low for 2 minutes.

6. When the cooking time is done, press Cancel and turn the steam release handle to Venting. When the float valve drops down, remove the lid. Test the broccoli to see if it is done to your liking. (If more cooking is needed, cover pot and let stand for 1 minute.)

TIP

You can use frozen broccoli florets, but add 1 minute to the cooking time in step 5.

DOWN HOME BEEF POT ROAST

MAKES 6 SERVINGS

This classic Sunday dinner is so reminiscent of family meals that it brings back all those good memories. Start your own tradition with this mouthwateringly tender beef roast that is ready in far less time than Grandma used to make.

3 lb (1.5 kg) boneless beef chuck roast (less than 8 inches/20 cm in diameter), cut into 2 pieces

Freshly ground black pepper

2 tsp (10 mL) onion powder

2 tsp (10 mL) garlic powder

1 tsp (5 mL) salt

1 tbsp (15 mL) vegetable oil (approx.)

1½ cups (375 mL) Low-Sodium Beef Bone Broth (page 212) or ready-to-use reduced-sodium beef broth

1 tbsp (15 mL) Worcestershire sauce

1 large onion, cut into wedges

1½ lbs (750 kg) small yellow potatoes

4 carrots, peeled and cut into 1-inch (2.5 cm) chunks

1. Season roast with pepper. Sprinkle onion powder, garlic powder and salt all over the roast. Set your Instant Pot to sauté on Normal. When the display says Hot, add oil and heat until shimmering. Working in batches, add beef and cook, turning once, for 5 minutes or until browned on all sides, adding more oil as needed between batches. Transfer roast to a plate.

2. Stir in beef stock and Worcestershire, scraping up any browned bits from the bottom. Press Cancel. Place roast in the inner pot and arrange onions around roast.

3. Close and lock the lid and turn the steam release handle to Sealing. Set your Instant Pot to pressure cook on High for 45 minutes.

4. When the cooking time is done, press Cancel and let stand, covered, for 10 minutes, then turn the steam release handle to Venting. When the float valve drops down, remove the lid. The roast should be fork-tender. (If more cooking time is needed, continue pressure cooking on High for 5 minutes, then quickly release the pressure.)

5. Using a slotted spoon, remove onions, potatoes and carrots from pot and set aside. Using tongs, transfer roast to a cutting board, cover with foil and let stand for 5 minutes.

6. Slice roast across the grain and transfer slices to a serving platter. Skim off fat from cooking liquid and drizzle roast with some of the liquid. Arrange onions, potatoes and carrots around roast.

Variation

Replace Low-Sodium Beef Bone Broth with water. Season with additional salt in step 1, if desired.

MAPLE CINAMMON RICE PUDDING

MAKES 6 SERVINGS

This old-time favorite comfort food takes on many flavors. The addition of maple syrup and a hint of cinnamon just can't be beat.

2 tbsp (30 mL) unsalted butter, divided

1 cup (250 mL) Arborio or other short-grain white rice

$\frac{1}{8}$ tsp (0.5 mL) salt

2 cups (500 mL) water

$1\frac{1}{2}$ cups (375 mL) milk, divided

$\frac{1}{2}$ tsp (2 mL) vanilla extract

$\frac{1}{3}$ cup (75 mL) pure maple syrup

Ground cinnamon

1. Set your Instant Pot to sauté on Normal. When the display says Hot, add 1 tbsp (15 mL) butter and heat until melted. Add rice and cook, stirring, for 1 to 2 minutes or until rice is coated with butter and starting to crackle. Press Cancel. Stir in salt, water, 1 cup (250 mL) milk and vanilla.

2. Close and lock the lid and turn the steam release handle to Sealing. Set your Instant Pot to pressure cook on High for 7 minutes.

3. When the cooking time is done, press Cancel and let stand, covered, for 5 minutes, then turn the steam release handle to Venting. When the float valve drops down, remove the lid. The rice should be tender. (If more cooking time is needed, continue pressure cooking on High for 1 minute, then quickly release the pressure.)

4. Stir in the remaining milk, maple syrup and the remaining butter. Press Sauté until Less is highlighted and cook, stirring often, for 3 minutes or until pudding is slightly thickened. (Note: it will continue to thicken after it is removed from the heat.) Serve sprinkled with cinnamon.

Variations

MAPLE RICE PUDDING WITH DRIED FRUIT: Add $\frac{1}{3}$ cup (75 mL) raisins or dried cranberries with the maple syrup in step 4.

Substitute $\frac{1}{2}$ cup (125 mL) granulated sugar for the maple syrup.

Garnish with ground cardamom instead of cinnamon.

NUTRITION TIP

Pudding is a great dish to encourage utensil use from your toddler or preschooler! Start with a shallow-bowled spoon, which will be easier to eat from than a spoon with a deeper bowl.

BLUEBERRY FRENCH TOAST PUDDING

MAKES 4 SERVINGS

Mmm, French toast. Just the sound of it brings tears of joy. Cinnamon swirl bread is the magic ingredient, along with blueberries and pure maple syrup. The best part is, you can eat it for breakfast or serve it up as bread pudding for dessert.

4-cup (1 L) round soufflé dish, bottom and sides buttered

Steam rack

3 large eggs

¼ tsp (1 mL) salt

1½ cups (375 mL) milk

3 tbsp (45 mL) pure maple syrup

1 lb (500 g) cinnamon swirl bread, crusts trimmed off and bread cubed

½ cup (125 mL) dried blueberries

1. In a large bowl, whisk eggs. Stir in salt, milk and maple syrup. Fold in bread cubes and blueberries, gently pressing down on bread to cover with liquid. Let stand for 30 minutes or until bread has absorbed liquid.

2. Pour bread mixture into prepared soufflé dish. Add 1 cup (250 mL) hot water to the inner pot and place the steam rack in the pot. Place the soufflé dish on the rack and cover with foil.

3. Close and lock the lid and turn the steam release handle to Sealing. Set your Instant Pot to pressure cook on High for 30 minutes.

4. When the cooking time is done, press Cancel and turn the steam release handle to Venting. When the float valve drops down, remove the lid. A tester inserted in the center should come out clean. (If more cooking time is needed, continue pressure cooking on High for 5 minutes.)

5. Using the handles of the rack, carefully remove the rack and dish from the pot. Remove foil and let stand for 5 minutes. Cut into 4 wedges and serve immediately.

Variation

Try a cinnamon swirl bread made with raisins, apples or chocolate chips. You can keep or omit the dried blueberries when using one of these breads.

SERVING SUGGESTION
If serving this dish for dessert, add a scoop of ice cream or a dollop of whipped cream on top.

201

NUTRITION TIP

Maple syrup is a safe sweetener for babies under a year, unlike honey (which may contain botulism). And it does contain small amounts of nutrients and antioxidants. However, in the small portions you consume of maple syrup it doesn't add up to much.

DREAMY PEACH COBBLER WITH RAISINS

MAKES ABOUT 5 CUPS (1.25 L)

When peaches are at their juicy, lip-smacking best, it's time to make this delightfully tasty cobbler. Raisins add an extra bit of texture and nutrients.

6-cup (1.5 L) round soufflé dish, bottom and sides buttered

Steam rack

Silicone sling

5 peaches, peeled (see tip) and sliced (about 2½ cups/625 mL)

1½ cups (375 mL) all-purpose baking mix (such as Bisquick)

½ cup (125 mL) packed brown sugar, divided

¼ tsp (1 mL) ground nutmeg

⅓ cup (75 mL) raisins

1 cup (250 mL) milk

1. Arrange peaches, with any accumulated juices, in prepared soufflé dish.

2. In a medium bowl, whisk together baking mix, ⅓ cup (75 mL) brown sugar and nutmeg. Whisk in milk and raisins just until moistened and a few lumps remain. Pour evenly over peaches.

3. Add 1½ cups (375 mL) hot water to the inner pot and place the steam rack in the pot. Place the silicone sling on the rack and place the soufflé dish in the sling.

4. Close and lock the lid and turn the steam release handle to Sealing. Set your Instant Pot to pressure cook on High for 20 minutes.

5. When the cooking time is done, press Cancel and let stand, covered, for 10 minutes, then turn the steam release handle to Venting. When the float valve drops down, remove the lid and foil. A tester inserted in the center of the cobbler should come out clean. (If more cooking time is needed, continue pressure cooking on High for 2 minutes, then quickly release the pressure.)

6. Meanwhile, preheat broiler with rack about 7 inches (18 cm) from the heat.

7. Using the sling, remove dish from the pot. Sprinkle with the remaining brown sugar. Broil for about 5 minutes or until topping is browned. Let cool on rack.

8. Spoon a small amount into serving bowl. Test temperature before serving.

NUTRITION TIPS

Dried fruit can be a source of iron for your baby. To serve raisins safely, cook them until they're soft in a recipe like this cobbler.

Dessert can contain some nutrition too! The peaches provide vitamin C and fiber.

TIPS

To quickly peel peaches, fill the inner pot halfway with water. Set your Instant Pot to sauté on Normal. When the water is boiling, use tongs to dunk each peach in the water for 10 to 20 seconds or until the skin starts to split. Quickly plunge peach in a bowl of ice water. Use your fingers to peel the skin off the peaches. Reserve $1\frac{1}{2}$ cups (375 mL) water in the pot for step 3 and discard the remainder.

You can use $2\frac{1}{2}$ cups (625 mL) frozen sliced peaches, thawed, in place of fresh. Combine the peaches with 3 tbsp (45 mL) orange juice or water before adding them to the soufflé dish.

Instant Pot Staples

HOMEMADE YOGURT

MAKES 5 CUPS (1.25 L)

Yogurt is so easy to make in your Instant Pot, but you will need to allow at least 16 hours to pasteurize and incubate the milk and then to cool the yogurt until it is ready to use. Yogurt-making takes practice to get exactly the flavors and consistency you prefer, but it is so worth the effort.

5 sterilized canning jars (preferably 8 oz/250 mL), with two-piece lids or screw caps

Steam rack

Instant-read thermometer

4 cups (1 L) whole milk

Greek yogurt with live active cultures (see tips)

JAR METHOD

1. Divide milk evenly among jars, leaving room at the top for the yogurt and leaving jars uncovered. Add $1^1/_2$ cups (375 mL) hot water to the inner pot and place the steam rack in the pot. Place the jars on the rack. Close and lock the lid and turn the steam release handle to Sealing. Set your Instant Pot to pressure cook on High for 0 minutes.

2. Meanwhile, add 2 tbsp (30 mL) yogurt to a measuring cup with a pour spout.

3. When the cooking time is done, press Cancel and let stand, covered, until the float valve drops down, then remove the lid. An instant-read thermometer inserted into the milk in each jar should register at least 180°F (82°C). (If more cooking time is needed, continue pressure cooking on High for 0 minutes.)

4. Carefully transfer jars to a wire rack and let cool until an instant-read thermometer inserted in the center of

a jar registers between 110°F and 115°F (43°C and 46°C). Remove and discard any skin on the milk.

5. Spoon 1 tbsp (15 mL) milk from each jar into the yogurt, stirring well. Pour back into the jars, dividing evenly.

6. Return the uncovered jars to the rack. Close and lock the lid and turn the steam release handle to Venting or Sealing. Select Yogurt and set your Instant Pot to cook on Normal for 6 to 12 hours (see tip).

7. When the incubation time is done, press Cancel and remove the lid.

8. Remove jars from the pot, cover with flat lids and twist on screwbands until there is a little resistance. Refrigerate for at least 6 hours, until chilled, or for up to 10 days.

POT METHOD

1. Add milk to the inner pot. Close and lock the lid and turn the steam release handle to Venting or Sealing. Select Yogurt and adjust the temperature to More. The display will say Boil.

2. Meanwhile, add 2 tbsp (30 mL) yogurt to a measuring cup with a pour spout.

3. When the display says Yogt, press Cancel and remove the lid. Using a rubber spatula, stir milk, without scraping the bottom. An instant-read thermometer

inserted into the milk in several places should register at least 180°F (82°C). (If more cooking time is needed, set your Instant Pot to slow cook on Less for 5 minutes.)

4. Transfer pot to a wire rack and let cool, uncovered, until an instant-read thermometer registers between 110°F and 115°F (43°C and 46°C). Remove and discard any skin on the milk.

5. Spoon ¼ cup (60 mL) milk from the pot into the yogurt, stirring well. Pour back into the pot.

6. Return the inner pot to the Instant Pot. Close and lock the lid and turn the steam release handle to Venting or Sealing. Select Yogurt and set your Instant Pot to cook on Normal for 6 to 12 hours (see tip).

7. When the incubation time is done, press Cancel and remove the lid.

8. Spoon yogurt into jars, cover with flat lids and twist on screwbands until there is a little resistance. Refrigerate for at least 6 hours, until chilled, or for up to 10 days.

Variations

HOMEMADE GREEK YOGURT: After step 7, pour the yogurt into a fine-mesh kitchen towel set in a strainer over a bowl. Let drain in the refrigerator for 2 to 6 hours or until desired consistency. (The liquid left in the bowl is whey. Whey can be refrigerated for up to 7 days for use in smoothies and juices, to add protein, vitamins and minerals. Whey can also be used as a cooking liquid for rice, grains and pasta.) Spoon yogurt into jars, cover with flat lids and twist on screwbands until there is a little resistance.

FLAVORED YOGURT: After the yogurt has chilled, add vanilla extract and either liquid honey or pure maple syrup, starting with a small amount and adding more to taste; stir well.

JAM OR JELLY YOGURT: After the yogurt has chilled, add jam or jelly, starting with a small amount and adding more to taste; stir well.

BERRY YOGURT: After the yogurt has chilled, add fresh or thawed frozen berries, starting with a small amount and adding more to taste; stir well.

207

TIPS

Purchase high-quality yogurt with live active cultures to use as your starter. Or save some of your homemade yogurt, in a separate jar, to use as the starter for your next batch. Homemade yogurt can be refrigerated for up to 7 days.

Use only jars and lids or screw caps that are specifically made for canning.

Adjust the yogurt incubation time in step 6 according to your taste preferences. Longer times will yield a tangier yogurt. Do not reduce the time to less than 6 hours, as the yogurt will not set properly.

Place your Instant Pot where it will not be bumped or moved, to ensure that the yogurt sets properly.

Do not use a "cold-start method" to make yogurt. Harmful bacteria can still be present. Follow the steps listed above to sterilize and boil your milk.

PERFECTLY BOILED EGGS

MAKES 1 TO 6 EGGS

Power up any meal or snack with these easy to cook and peel eggs. You can soft-cook, medium-cook, hard-cook or even poach the eggs, however you like them.

Steam rack

1 to 6 large eggs, in the shell

1. Add 1 cup (250 mL) water to the inner pot and place the steam rack in the pot. Place egg(s) on the rack.

2. Close and lock the lid and turn the steam release handle to Sealing. Set your Instant Pot to pressure cook on Low for 6 minutes for hard-cooked. (See also variations).

3. When the cooking time is done, press Cancel. Let stand, covered, for 5 minutes and then turn the steam release handle to Venting. When the float valve drops down, remove the lid.

4. Remove inner pot, transfer pot to the sink and discard water. If eating warm, as soon as you can handle them carefully peel egg under cold running water and transfer to a plate. If using cold, add cold water and ice cubes to the pot. When cold, peel the egg and discard shell.

Variations

MEDIUM OR SOFT-COOKED EGGS: Pressure cook on Low for 4 minutes for medium and 3 minutes for soft. When the cooking time is done, press Cancel. Let stand, covered, for 5 minutes for medium or quickly release the handle for soft. When the float valve drops down, remove the lid. Remove inner pot, transfer pot to the sink and discard water. Carefully peel eggs under cold running water and transfer to a plate. Continue with step 4.

POACHED EGGS: Spray one to four 4-oz (125 mL) ramekin(s) with nonstick cooking spray. Crack an egg into each prepared ramekin, centering yolk as much as possible. Cover ramekin tightly with foil and place on rack, stacking ramekins as necessary, like stacking bricks. Pressure cook on Low for 3 minutes. When the cooking time is up, quickly release the pressure. Remove ramekin from pot and uncover. Serve egg in ramekin or slide out onto an English muffin, toast or a serving plate.

NUTRITION TIP

Eggs are a nutrition powerhouse and one of the best sources of hard-to-find choline in the diet.

NO-SALT-ADDED CHICKEN STOCK

MAKES ABOUT 8 CUPS (2 L)

Homemade chicken stock is noticeably richer and denser than store-bought broth. Making it in the Instant Pot significantly cuts down on the preparation time for traditional stock, and the exceptional flavors are well worth it. We especially like that you can omit or reduce the sodium for your younger ones. The variations give you the option to increase the salt levels as your needs change.

2 tbsp (30 mL) vegetable oil

3 stalks celery (green tops included), chopped

1 large onion, coarsely chopped

5 sprigs fresh parsley

2 bay leaves

8 cups (2 L) water

3 lbs (1.5 kg) chicken wings or other parts (see tip)

1. Set your Instant Pot to sauté on Normal. When the display says Hot, add the oil and heat until shimmering. Add celery and onion; cook, stirring often, for 5 to 7 minutes or until onion is browned and celery is softened. Press Cancel. Add the parsley, bay leaves, water and wings.

2. Close and lock the lid and turn the steam release handle to Sealing. Set your Instant Pot to pressure cook on High for 55 minutes.

3. When the cooking time is done, press Cancel and let stand, covered, until the float valve drops down, then remove the lid.

4. Strain stock through a fine-mesh strainer into a large container, pressing on solids to extract more liquid. Discard solids.

5. To use immediately, skim fat from stock and serve. If using later, set container in a sink of ice water until broth is cool, then cover and refrigerate for at least 8 hours or overnight. Skim congealed fat from top of stock.

Variations

LOW-SODIUM CHICKEN STOCK: Add 1/4 tsp (1 mL) salt in step 1.

TRADITIONAL CHICKEN STOCK: Add 1 tsp (5 mL) salt in step 1.

TIPS

You can use any chicken parts or bony scraps you have on hand, but parts such as wings, backs and feet will produce stocks that are much richer and thicker.

For deeper flavor, brown the chicken parts before use. Before step 1, press Sauté until Normal is highlighted. When the display says Hot, add 2 tbsp (30 mL) vegetable oil or schmaltz (rendered chicken fat) and heat until shimmering. Working in batches, add chicken parts to the pot and cook, turning often, until browned. Press Cancel and continue with step 1.

NO-SALT-ADDED VEGETABLE STOCK

MAKES ABOUT 8 CUPS (2 L)

Homemade vegetable stock is a great way to use leftover vegetable scraps and is a wonderful replacement for chicken stock in vegetarian and vegan recipes. We especially like that you can omit or reduce the sodium for your younger ones. The variations give you the option to increase the salt levels as your needs change.

2 large onions, chopped

2 carrots, diced

2 stalks celery, diced

$\frac{1}{2}$ oz (15 g) dried shiitake mushrooms

2 cloves garlic, smashed

5 sprigs fresh parsley or thyme

1 tbsp (15 mL) whole black peppercorns

8 cups (2 L) water

1. In the inner pot, combine onions, carrots, celery, mushrooms, garlic, parsley, peppercorns and water.

2. Close and lock the lid and turn the steam release handle to Sealing. Set your Instant Pot to pressure cook on High for 15 minutes.

3. When the cooking time is done, press Cancel and let stand, covered, until the float valve drops down, then remove the lid.

4. Strain stock through a fine-mesh strainer into a large container, pressing on solids to extract more liquid. Discard solids.

5. Let stand at room temperature until cool. Cover and refrigerate for 8 hours, until chilled, before using.

Variations

LOW-SODIUM VEGETABLE STOCK: Add 2 tsp (10 mL) coconut amino acids. Omit the mushrooms, if desired.

TRADITIONAL VEGETABLE STOCK: Add 1 tsp (5 mL) salt in step 1. Omit the mushrooms if desired.

TIPS

Use a combination of vegetables you have on hand, but keep the onions, carrots and garlic, as they form a good foundation. You can add leftover broccoli stems, chopped celery root, corn cobs or the dark green ends of leeks for added flavor and texture and to use up leftover ingredients.

The stock can be stored in airtight containers in the refrigerator for up to 3 days or in the freezer for up to 3 months.

LOW-SODIUM BEEF BONE BROTH

MAKES 8 CUPS (1 L)

Homemade beef bone broth bestows a deep, rich flavor upon many dishes, adding greater depth than store-bought broth. You can also drink it, for a satisfying, nutrient-rich paleo treat. Making bone broth in the Instant Pot significantly cuts down on the preparation time. Beef bone broth naturally has more sodium, so we do not recommend using this for babies' foods until after 1 year of age.

2 tbsp (30 mL) vegetable oil (approx.)

4 lbs (2 kg) beef shanks, oxtails or short ribs

2 leeks (middle green parts only), thickly sliced

½ oz (15 g) dried shiitake mushrooms

3 bay leaves

1 tbsp (15 mL) whole black peppercorns

8 cups (2 L) water

1 tsp (5 mL) apple cider vinegar or dry red wine (optional)

1. Set your Instant Pot to sauté on Normal. When the display says Hot, add 1 tbsp (15 mL) oil and heat until shimmering. Working in batches, add beef and cook, turning often, for 5 to 7 minutes or until browned on all sides, adding more oil as needed between batches. Using tongs, transfer beef to a plate as it is browned. Press Cancel.

2. Return all beef and any accumulated juices to the pot. Add leeks, mushrooms, bay leaves, peppercorns, water and vinegar (if using), stirring well.

3. Close and lock the lid and turn the steam release handle to Sealing. Set your Instant Pot to pressure cook on High for 90 minutes.

4. When the cooking time is done, press Cancel and let stand, covered, until the float valve drops down, then remove the lid.

5. Strain stock through a fine-mesh strainer into a large container, discarding bones and pressing on solids to extract more liquid. Discard solids.

6. To use immediately, skim fat from broth and serve. If using later, set container in a sink of ice water until broth is cool, then cover and refrigerate for at least 8 hours or overnight. Skim congealed fat from top of broth.

TIPS

Instead of browning the beef in the pressure cooker, you can roast it in the oven. Arrange beef on a foil-lined rimmed baking sheet and drizzle with oil. Bake at 400°F (200°C) for 1 hour, turning once. Add beef and any accumulated juices to the cooker and continue with step 2.

The broth can be stored in airtight containers in the refrigerator for up to 3 days or in the freezer for up to 6 months.

EASY RICE PILAF

MAKES 6 SERVINGS

A classic rice pilaf is the perfect side dish for a variety of main dishes, especially salmon or chicken. Not only does the Instant Pot make perfect rice every time, but you can follow the variation to make a perfect one-pot meal.

1 (15 mL) tbsp virgin olive oil

½ onion, finely chopped

1⅓ cups (325 mL) long-grain white rice, rinsed

1 cup (250 mL) No-Salt-Added Chicken Stock (page 210) or chicken broth

¾ cup (175 mL) water

4 tsp (20 mL) chopped fresh parsley

1. Set your Instant Pot to sauté on Normal. When the display says Hot, add oil and heat until shimmering. Add onion and cook, stirring often, for 5 minutes or until translucent. Add rice and cook, stirring, for 1 to 2 minutes or until translucent and lightly browned. Press Cancel. Stir in broth and water.

2. Close and lock the lid and turn the steam release handle to Sealing. Set your Instant Pot to pressure cook on High for 3 minutes.

3. When the cooking time is done, press Cancel and let stand, covered, for 10 minutes, then turn the steam release handle to Venting. When the float valve drops down, remove the lid. The rice should be tender. (If more cooking time is needed, close and lock the lid and let stand for 2 minutes.)

4. Fluff rice with a fork, then stir in parsley. Serve immediately.

Variations

EASY WHITE RICE: Reduce the oil to 1 tbsp (15 mL) and omit the onion and parsley.

POT-IN-POT: To cook a complete meal, after step 1, place a steam rack on top of the rice. Add a recipe, such as Herbed Salmon with Asparagus (page 181), on top of the steam rack. Continue with step 2.

CARROT AND NUT RICE PILAF: Add ½ cup (125 mL) shredded carrots with the onion in step 1. Stir in 2½ tbsp (37 mL) slivered almonds with the parsley in step 4.

TIP

Short-grain white rice also works in this recipe. In step 2, increase the cooking time to 8 minutes.

QUICK AND EASY QUINOA

MAKES 4 SERVINGS

Quinoa is a protein-powered grain that pairs well with nuts, vegetables, meats and other grains, or is delicious all on its own. This simple base recipe will launch many fabulous meatless mains and breakfasts, and makes the ideal side dish for fish or chicken.

2 tsp (10 mL) vegetable oil

1 cup (250 mL) quinoa, rinsed and well drained

1½ cups (375 mL) water

1. Set your Instant Pot to sauté on Normal. When the display says Hot, add oil and heat until shimmering. Add quinoa and cook, stirring, for 2 to 3 minutes or until lightly toasted and fragrant. Press Cancel. Add ¼ tsp (1 mL) salt and water, stirring well.

2. Close and lock the lid and turn the steam release handle to Sealing. Set your Instant Pot to pressure cook on High for 2 minutes.

3. When the cooking time is done, press Cancel and let stand, covered, for 10 minutes, then turn the steam release handle to Venting. When the float valve drops down, remove the lid. The quinoa should be tender. (If more cooking time is needed, continue pressure cooking on High for 0 minutes, then quickly release the pressure.)

4. Fluff quinoa with a fork and season to taste with salt. Serve immediately.

TIPS

This recipe can be doubled, as long as you don't fill the pot more than halfway.

While some packages say the quinoa is already rinsed, I like to rinse it again to remove any bitter taste.

To reheat 1 serving of leftovers, microwave, stirring once, for 1 minute or until warmed through. You may need to add water, in 1-tbsp (15 mL) increments, if the mixture becomes too dry.

NUTRITION TIP

Quinoa is often called a superfood. It is higher in protein, magnesium, iron, fiber and zinc than most other grains.

ALL-AROUND BARBECUE SAUCE

MAKES ABOUT 2 CUPS (500 L)

This tasty all-around barbecue sauce is perfect for pork or chicken. Use it as is or dress it up for a specific recipe. It's sure to become your go-to barbecue sauce.

1 tbsp (15 mL) vegetable oil

¾ cup (175 mL) packed light brown sugar

1 cup (250 mL) apple cider vinegar

4 tsp (20 mL) smoked paprika

2 tsp (10 mL) ground cumin

2 tsp (10 mL) salt

2 tsp (10 mL) freshly ground black pepper

1⅓ cups (325 mL) ketchup

1. Add oil to the inner pot and swirl to coat the bottom. Add brown sugar and vinegar, stirring to combine. Stir in paprika, cumin, salt, pepper and ketchup.

2. Close and lock the lid and turn the steam release handle to Sealing. Set your Instant Pot to pressure cook on High for 8 minutes.

3. When the cooking time is done, press Cancel and let stand, covered, for 10 minutes, then turn the steam release handle to Venting. When the float valve drops down, remove the lid. Stir sauce, transfer to storage containers and let cool.

TIPS

If using the sauce for grilling, brush it on near the end of the cooking times so it caramelizes but doesn't burn.

The cooled sauce can be refrigerated for up to 1 month or frozen for up to 6 months.

REFERENCES

Brown, A. (2018). No difference in self-reported frequency of choking between infants introduced to solid foods using a baby-led weaning or traditional spoon-feeding approach. *Journal of Human Nutrition and Dietetics, 4*, 496–504. doi:10.1111/jhn.12528

Centers for Disease Control and Prevention. (2017). Raw milk questions and answers. June 15. Retrieved from https://www.cdc.gov/foodsafety/rawmilk/raw-milk-questions-and-answers.html

Du Toit, G., Roberts, G., Sayre, P. H., Bahnson, H. T., Radulovic, S., Santos, A., … Lack, G. (2015). Randomized trial of peanut consumption in infants at risk for peanut allergy. *New England Journal of Medicine 372*(9), 803–13. doi:10.1056/NEJMoa1414850

Fangupo, L. J., Heath, A-L. M., Williams, S. M., Erickson Williams, L. W., Morison, B. J., Fleming, … Taylor, R. W. (2016). A baby-led approach to eating solids and risk of choking. *Pediatrics, 138*(4). doi:10.1542/peds.20016-0772

Government of Canada (2012). Nutrition for Healthy Term Infants: Recommendations from six to 24 months. A joint statement of Health Canada, Canadian Paediatric Society, Dietitians of Canada, and Breastfeeding Committee for Canada. (September). Retrieved from https://www.canada.ca/en/health-canada/services/canada-food-guide/resources/infant-feeding/nutrition-healthy-term-infants-recommendations-birth-six-months/6-24-months.html

Institute of Medicine, Food and Nutrition Board (2001). Dietary Reference Intakes for Vitamin A, Vitamin K, Arsenic, Boron, Chromium, Copper, Iodine, Iron, Manganese, Molybdenum, Nickel, Silicon, Vanadium, and Zinc: A Report of the Panel on Micronutrients. Washington, DC: National Academy Press. Retrieved from https://www.nap.edu/read/10026/chapter/1

Mangels, A.R., & Messina, V. (2001). Considerations in planning vegan diets: Infants. *Journal of the American Dietetic Association, 101*(6), 670–77. doi:10.1016/S0002-8223(01)00169-9

Szajewska, H., Shamir, R., Mearin, L., Ribes-Koninckx, C., Catassi, C., Domello, M., … Troncone, R. (2016). Gluten introduction and the risk of coeliac disease: A position paper by the European Society for Pediatric Gastroenterology, Hepatology, and Nutrition. *Journal of Pediatric Gastroenterology and Nutrition, 62*(3), 507–13.doi:10.1097/MPG.0000000000001105

Zlotki, S. H, Ste-Marie, M., Kopelman, H., Jones, A., & Adams, J. (1996). The prevalence of iron depletion and iron-deficiency anaemia in a randomly selected group of infants from four Canadian cities. *Nutrition Research, 16*(5), 729–33

Library and Archives Canada Cataloguing in Publication

Title: Baby food in an Instant Pot : 125 quick, simple and nutritious recipes for babies and toddlers / Jennifer House, MSc, RD & Marilyn Haugen.

Names: House, Jennifer, 1980- author. | Haugen, Marilyn, author.

Description: "Authorized by Instant Pot". | Includes index.

Identifiers: Canadiana 20200151967 | ISBN 9780778806356 (softcover)

Subjects: LCSH: Baby foods. | LCSH: Infants—Nutrition. | LCSH: Smart cookers. | LCGFT: Cookbooks.

Classification: LCC TX740.H697 2020 | DDC 641.5/6222—dc23

INDEX

C

224